Collins

Cambridge IGCSE™

Maths

REVISION GUIDE

Chris Pearce, Andrew Milne

About this Revision book

REVISE

These pages provide a recap of everything you need to know for each topic and include key points to focus on and **key terms** to be learned (full definitions are given in the Glossary). Extended content, for the Extended papers, is clearly marked with **E** .

You should read through all the information before taking the Quick Test at the end. This will test whether you can recall the key facts. Non-calculator questions are marked **NC** .

NC Quick Test

1. Write down the value of $\sqrt{196}$.
2. Work out $2^5 - 5^2$.
3. Work out $\sqrt[3]{8} + \sqrt[3]{27}$.
4. Work out $\sqrt[5]{32}$.
5. Work out $\sqrt{10^2 - 6^2}$.

PRACTISE

These topic-based exam-style questions appear at the end of a revision section and will test whether you have understood the topic. If you get any of the questions wrong, make sure you read the correct answer carefully.

For selected questions, Show Me features give you guidance on how to structure your answer.

> **Show me**
>
> The population density of Spain is ... ÷ .... = ...
>
> The population density of Slovenia is ....

MIXED QUESTIONS

These pages feature a mix of exam-style questions for all the different topics, just like you would get in an exam. They will make sure you can recall the relevant information to answer a question without being told which topic it relates to.

PRACTICE PAPERS

These pages provide a full set of exam-style practice papers: Paper 1 Non-calculator (Core)/Paper 2 Non-calculator (Extended), and Paper 3 Calculator (Core)/Paper 4 Calculator (Extended). Practise your exam technique in preparation for the Cambridge IGCSE™.

ebook

To access the ebook visit
collins.co.uk/ebooks
and follow the step-by-step instructions.

CONTENTS

	Revise	Practise
Section 1: Number		

	Revise	Practise
Types of number	p. 6 ☐	p. 32 ☐
Sets	p. 8 ☐	p. 32 ☐
Powers and roots	p. 10 ☐	p. 33 ☐
Fractions, decimals and percentages	p. 12 ☐	p. 34 ☐
Ordering and the four operations	p. 14 ☐	p. 34 ☐
Indices and standard form	p. 16 ☐	p. 35 ☐
Estimation and limits of accuracy	p. 18 ☐	p. 36 ☐
Ratio and proportion	p. 20 ☐	p. 36 ☐
Rates	p. 22 ☐	p. 37 ☐
Percentages	p. 24 ☐	p. 38 ☐
Using a calculator	p. 26 ☐	p. 39 ☐
Exponential growth and decay	p. 28 ☐	p. 40 ☐
Surds	p. 30 ☐	p. 41 ☐

Section 2: Algebra and graphs

	Revise	Practise
Introduction to algebra	p. 42 ☐	p. 68 ☐
Algebraic manipulation	p. 44 ☐	p. 69 ☐
Algebraic fractions	p. 46 ☐	p. 70 ☐
Further indices	p. 48 ☐	p. 70 ☐
Equations	p. 50 ☐	p. 71 ☐
Inequalities	p. 52 ☐	p. 72 ☐
Sequences	p. 54 ☐	p. 72 ☐
Proportion	p. 56 ☐	p. 74 ☐
Graphs in practical situations	p. 58 ☐	p. 75 ☐
Graphs of functions	p. 60 ☐	p. 76 ☐
Sketching graphs	p. 62 ☐	p. 77 ☐

Differentiation	p. 64		p. 78	
Functions	p. 66		p. 79	

Section 3: Coordinate geometry

Linear graphs 1	p. 80		p. 84	
Linear graphs 2	p. 82		p. 85	

Section 4: Geometry

Geometric terms and constructions	p. 86		p. 98	
Scale drawings	p. 88		p. 99	
Similarity	p. 90		p. 100	
Symmetry	p. 92		p. 102	
Angles	p. 94		p. 103	
Circle theorems	p. 96		p. 104	

Section 5: Mensuration

Units of measure	p. 106		p. 116	
Perimeter and area	p. 108		p. 117	
Circles, arcs and sectors	p. 110		p. 118	
Surface area and volume	p. 112		p. 119	
Compound shapes and solids	p. 114		p. 120	

Section 6: Trigonometry

Right-angled triangles	p. 122		p. 130	
Trigonometric functions	p. 124		p. 131	
Non-right angled triangles	p. 126		p. 131	
Trigonometry in three dimension	p. 128		p. 132	

Section 7: Transformations and vectors

Transformations   p. 134 ☐   p. 138 ☐

Vectors   p. 136 ☐   p. 139 ☐

Section 8: Probability

Introduction to probability   p. 140 ☐   p. 144 ☐

Probability of combined events   p. 142 ☐   p. 145 ☐

Section 9: Statistics

Statistical data   p. 148 ☐   p. 160 ☐

Averages   p. 150 ☐   p. 161 ☐

Charts and diagrams   p. 152 ☐   p. 162 ☐

Scatter diagrams   p. 154 ☐   p. 163 ☐

Cumulative frequency   p. 156 ☐   p. 164 ☐

Histograms   p. 158 ☐   p. 165 ☐

Mixed exam-style questions: Core   p. 167 ☐

Mixed exam-style questions: Extended   p. 179 ☐

Practice Paper 1: Non-calculator (Core)   p. 187 ☐

Practice Paper 2: Non-calculator (Extended)   p. 195 ☐

Practice Paper 3: Calculator (Core)   p. 204 ☐

Practice Paper 4: Calculator (Extended)   p. 213 ☐

List of formulas (Core)   p. 224

List of formulas (Extended)   p. 225

Answers   p. 226

Glossary/Index   p. 238

Types of number

Learning aims:

Syllabus links:
C1.1; E1.1

- Identify and use natural numbers, integers, prime numbers, square numbers, cube numbers
- Identify and use common factors and common multiples
- Identify and use rational numbers, irrational numbers and reciprocals

Natural numbers

Natural numbers are whole positive numbers used for counting: 1, 2, 3, 4, 5,…

Natural numbers have **multiples**.

The multiples of 7 are $7 \times 1, 7 \times 2, 7 \times 3$ and so on. That is 7, 14, 21, 28, 35,…

The multiples of 25 are 25, 50, 75, 100,…

Natural numbers have **factors**.

The factor pairs of 20 are $1 \times 20 = 20, 2 \times 10 = 20$ and $4 \times 5 = 20$.

So 20 has six factors: 1, 2, 4, 5, 10 and 20.

A **prime number** has exactly two factors, 1 and the number itself.

23 is a prime number because 1 and 23 and the only two numbers that multiply to make 23.

1 is not a prime number, because it only has one factor: itself.

A **square number** is a natural number multiplied by itself.

16 and 81 are square numbers because $4 \times 4 = 16$ and $9 \times 9 = 81$.

We write $16 = 4^2$ and $81 = 9^2$.

The square numbers are 1, 4, 9, 16, 25, 36, 49, 64, 81, 100, 121,…

In a similar way, you can find **cube numbers**.

$2 \times 2 \times 2 = 8$ and $5 \times 5 \times 5 = 125$; 8 and 125 are cube numbers.

We write $8 = 2^3$ and $125 = 5^3$.

The cube numbers are 1, 8, 27, 64, 125,…

> **Key Point**
>
> 6^2 means 6×6 and 6^3 means $6 \times 6 \times 6$

Common factors and common multiples

The factors of 28 are **1**, **2**, 4, **7**, 14, 28.

The factors of 42 are **1**, **2**, 3, 6, **7**, 14, 21, 42.

The common factors (factors of both 28 and 42) are: 1, 2 and 7.

The **highest common factor** of 28 and 42 is 7.

The multiples of 6 are 6, 12, 18, **24**, 30, 36, 42, **48**, 54,…

The multiples of 8 are 8, 16, **24**, 32, 40, **48**, 56, 64,…

The common multiples (multiples of both 6 and 8) are 24, 48, 72,…

The **lowest common multiple** of 6 and 8 is 24.

Prime factorisation

Every natural number that is not 1 or a prime number can be written as a product of prime numbers.

Example 1   Write 90 as a product of prime numbers.

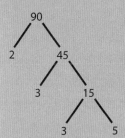

$90 = 2 \times 45$ (2 is prime)

$45 = 3 \times 15$ (3 is prime)

$15 = 3 \times 5$ (both are prime)

$90 = 2 \times 3 \times 3 \times 5 = 2 \times 3^2 \times 5$

Write the product of all the prime numbers.

Rational and irrational numbers

The **integers** are the natural numbers plus 0 and negative whole numbers.

…, −4, −3, −2, −1, 0, 1, 2, 3, 4,… are the integers

Rational numbers are integers and fractions.

For example, $6\frac{3}{4}$, -42, $\frac{7}{30}$, $25\frac{2}{3}$, $-\frac{3}{8}$

All fractions can be written as decimals.

For example, $6\frac{3}{4} = 6.75$ and $25\frac{2}{3} = 25.666\ldots$

On a calculator $\sqrt{2} = 1.41421356\ldots$. This number cannot be written as a fraction. (See Topic 3 for more about square roots.)

Numbers that cannot be written as fractions are called **irrational numbers**.

The **reciprocal** of number N is $\frac{1}{N}$

So the reciprocal of 8 is $\frac{1}{8}$ and the reciprocal of 1.5 is $\frac{1}{1.5} = \frac{2}{3}$

> **Key Point**
>
> The square root of any natural number that is not a square number is irrational.

> **Quick Test**
>
> 1. Here is a list of numbers: 31, 32, 33, 34, 35, 36, 37, 38
>   Write down:
>   a) a multiple of 5
>   b) a factor of 64
>   c) the prime numbers.
> 2. Write 150 as a product of prime numbers.
> 3. Here are two numbers: 18, 30
>   a) Find their highest common factor.
>   b) Find their lowest common multiple.

Sets

Syllabus links:
C1.2; E1.2

Learning aims:

*   Use set language and notation
*   Draw and use Venn diagrams

Notation

A **set** is a collection of objects. The members of a set are called **elements**.

Use curly brackets {} to indicate a set. $A = \{3, 4, 5, 6, 7, 8, 9\}$

You can list the elements of a set or describe them.
$A = \{\text{integer } x : 3 \leq x \leq 9\}$

$n(A)$ is the number of elements in the set A. $n(A) = 7$

A' is the **complement** of A, all the elements that are not in A.

If A and B are two sets:

*   the **intersection** $A \cap B$ are the elements in both sets A and B.
*   the **union** $A \cup B$ are the elements in A or B or both sets.

ξ is the **universal set**. It is all the possible elements you are looking at.

> **Key Point**
>
> Remember: ∪ means Union and ∩ means intersection

Example 1 $\xi = \{\text{natural number } x : 10 \leq x \leq 20\}$, $C = \{\text{even numbers}\}$,
$D = \{\text{multiples of 3}\}$

Find: **a)** $n(D)$ **b)** C' **c)** $C \cap D$ **d)** $C \cup D$

....

a) $n(D) = 3$ The multiples of 3 in ξ are 12, 15, 18. There are 3 elements.

b) $C' = \{11, 13, 15, 17, 19\}$ These are the odd numbers in the universal set ξ.

c) $C \cap D = \{12, 18\}$ These are the even multiples of 3 in ξ.

d) $C \cup D = \{12, 14, 15, 16, 18, 20\}$ These are the numbers in C or D. 12 and 18 are in both.

You can show sets on a **Venn diagram**.

Here is a Venn diagram for the sets in the worked example.

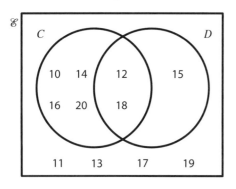

> **Key Point**
>
> Only write each element once when you list the union of sets.

$C \cap D$ is where the two circles cross.

The elements 11, 13, 15 and 19 are not in C or in D.

E Further notation

The symbol ∈ means "is an element of". The symbol ∉ means "is not an element of"

If $S = \{a,b,c,d,e,f,g,h,i\}$ then

- $d \in S$ means that d is an element of set S
- $m \notin S$ means that m is not an element of set S.

Set $X = \{c,d,e,h\}$. All the elements of set X are also elements of set S.

X is a **subset** of S. We write $X \subseteq S$.

Set $Y = \{a,b,c,l,m\}$. There are two elements in Y that are not in S, l and m.

Y is not a subset of S. We write $Y \not\subseteq S$.

We can show S, X and Y in a Venn diagram like this:

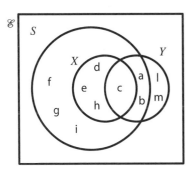

The circle for X is inside the circle for S because $X \subseteq Y$.

Example 2

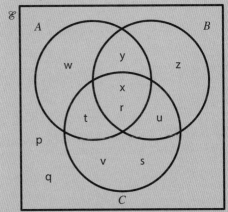

a) Find $n(A \cap B \cap C)$.

b) List the elements of $(A \cup B) \cap C'$.

....

a) 2 The elements in A, B and C are x and r.

b) $\{w,x,z\}$ $A \cup B = \{w,y,x,r,t,z,u\}$, $C' = \{p,q,w,y,z\}$ (You want the elements that appear in both these sets.)

The symbol ∅ means the **empty set**, a set with no elements.

If $V = \{a,e,i,o\}$ and $C = \{b,d,g,m,s,t\}$ then $V \cap C = \varnothing$.

> **Quick Test**

1. $A = \{30,33,36,38\}$ and $B = \{36,37,38,39,40\}$
   a) Show A and B in a Venn diagram. b) List the elements of $A \cup B$.
2. $\xi = \{\text{natural numbers}\}, E = \{\text{even numbers}\}, F = \{\text{multiples of 5}\}$
   a) Describe the elements of E'. b) Describe the elements of $E \cap F$.
   E 3. Look at the sets in question 1.
   a) Find $n(A \cap B)$. b) Is it true that $40 \in A$ and $40 \notin B$?
   E 4. $X = \{\text{multiples of 3}\}, Y = \{\text{multiples of 4}\}, Z = \{\text{multiples of 5}\}$
   Find the smallest positive integer in $(X \cup Y) \cap Z$.

Powers and roots

Syllabus links:
C1.3; E1.3

Learning aims:

- Calculate with squares and square roots
- Calculate with cubes and cube roots
- Calculate with other powers and roots of numbers

Squares and square roots

$7 \times 7 = 7^2 = 49$ is a square number. We say "the square of 7 is 49" or "7 squared is 49".

Here are the first 15 square numbers:

1^2	2^2	3^2	4^2	5^2	6^2	7^2	8^2	9^2	10^2	11^2	12^2	13^2	14^2	15^2
1	4	9	16	25	36	49	64	81	100	121	144	169	196	225

Memorise the first 15 square numbers.

Because $7^2 = 49$ we say that the **square root** of 49 is 7 and write $\sqrt{49}$.

Example 1   Find $\sqrt{5^2 + 12^2}$

$\sqrt{5^2 + 12^2} = \sqrt{25 + 144}$ First find the squares of 5 and 12.

$\qquad\qquad\quad = \sqrt{169} = 13$ You should know the square root of 169.

Cubes and cube roots

$2 \times 2 \times 2 = 8$ so 8 is a **cube number**. We say "2 cubed = 8" or "2 cubed is 8" and write $2^3 = 8$.

The fourth cube number is $4^3 = 4 \times 4 \times 4 = 64$

Here are the first five cube numbers:

1^3	2^3	3^3	4^3	5^3
1	8	27	64	125

Memorise the first five cube numbers.

Because $5^3 = 125$ we say that the **cube root** of 125 is 5 and write $\sqrt[3]{125} = 5$.

Example 2 Find $2^3 \times \sqrt{64} \div \sqrt[3]{64}$.

....

$2^3 \times \sqrt{64} \div \sqrt[3]{64} = 8 \times 8 \div 4$ Work out each **term** first. You should be able to recall them.

$= 64 \div 4 = 16$ Do the multiplication first, then divide by 4.

Other powers and roots

We can find powers of 4 or 5 and so on. We can also find the corresponding roots.

$3^4 = 3 \times 3 \times 3 \times 3 = 81$. You work out $3 \times 3 = 9$, then $9 \times 3 = 27$, then $27 \times 3 = 81$.

The fourth power of 3 is 81 and the fourth root of 81 is $\sqrt[4]{81} = 3$.

> **NC** **Quick Test**

1. Write down the value of $\sqrt{196}$.
2. Work out $2^5 - 5^2$.
3. Work out $\sqrt[3]{8} + \sqrt[3]{27}$.
4. Work out $\sqrt[5]{32}$.
5. Work out $\sqrt{10^2 - 6^2}$.

Fractions, decimals and percentages

Syllabus links:
C1.4; E1.4

Learning aims:

- Use proper fractions, improper fractions, mixed numbers, decimals and percentages
- Convert between fractions, decimals and percentages
- **E** Convert a recurring decimal to a fraction

Fractions

The fraction of this rectangle that is shaded is $\frac{8}{20}$.

Simplify fractions by dividing the numerator and the denominator by a common factor.

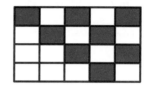

$$\overset{\div 4}{\frac{8}{20}} = \frac{2}{5}$$

8 and 20 have a common factor of 4: $\underset{\div 4}{\frac{8}{20}} = \frac{2}{5}$

$\frac{2}{5}$ is a **proper fraction** in its simplest form.

$\frac{14}{5}$ is an **improper fraction** because the numerator (14) is greater than the denominator (5).

A **mixed number** contains a whole number part and a fraction.

$$\frac{14}{5} = \frac{10}{5} + \frac{4}{5} = 2\frac{4}{5}$$

Example 1   Write $\frac{84}{72}$ as a mixed number in its simplest form.

....

$\frac{84}{72} = \frac{7}{6} = \frac{6}{6} + \frac{1}{6} = 1\frac{1}{6}$ Simplify by dividing the numerator and denominator by 12.

Decimals

Every fraction can be written as a decimal. Divide the numerator by the denominator.

Example 2   Write $12\frac{7}{8}$ as a decimal.

....

$7 \div 8 = 0.875$ $8\overline{)7.000}^{\,0.875}$ Put 0s after a decimal point and divide by 8.

$12\frac{7}{8} = 12.875$

To write a decimal as a fraction, write the decimal number over its place value and then simplify.

For example: $6.8 = 6\frac{8}{10} = 6\frac{4}{5}$ $1.35 = 1\frac{35}{100} = 1.35$

$0.375 = \frac{375}{1000} = \frac{3}{8}$

Sometimes a decimal is **recurring** and has a repeating pattern of digits. Use dots over the digits to show the repeating pattern.

For example, $\frac{1}{3} = 0.3333\ldots = 0.\dot{3}$ and $\frac{7}{11} = 0.636363\ldots = 0.\dot{6}\dot{3}$

E **Example 3**   Write $0.8\dot{1}$ as a fraction

Write $f = 0.818181\ldots$

Then $100f = 81.818181\ldots$ There are two recurring digits, so multiply by 100.

$100f - f = 81$ The digits after the decimal point cancel out.

$99f = 81$

$f = \dfrac{81}{99} = \dfrac{9}{11}$ 9 is a common factor so divide by 9.

Percentages

To write a percentage as a decimal, divide by 100.

$63\% = 0.63$ $8\% = 0.08$ $43.5\% = 0.435$

To write a decimal as a percentage, multiply by 100.

$0.41 = 41\%$ $0.03 = 3\%$ $0.124 = 12.4\%$

A percentage is equivalent to a fraction with a denominator of 100.

$75\% = \dfrac{75}{100} = \dfrac{3}{4}$ $205\% = \dfrac{205}{100} = 2\dfrac{5}{100} = 2\dfrac{1}{20}$

$17.5\% = \dfrac{17.5}{100} = \dfrac{175}{1000} = \dfrac{7}{40}$

To change a fraction to a percentage, find an equivalent fraction with a denominator of 100 or write it as a decimal first. You can use either method.

Example 4   Write each fraction as a percentage:

a) $\dfrac{13}{20}$

b) $\dfrac{7}{8}$

a) $\dfrac{13}{20} = \dfrac{65}{100}$ $20 \times 5 = 100$ so multiply numerator and denominator by 5.

$= 0.65 = 65\%$

b) $\dfrac{7}{8} = 0.875 = 87.5\%$

> **Key Point**
>
> If the denominator is a factor of 100 the method in **(a)** is simple. If the denominator is not a factor of 100, the method in **(b)** may be simpler.

> **NC** **Quick Test**

1. Write $\dfrac{100}{15}$ as a mixed number as simply as possible.
2. Write 8%:
   a) as a decimal
   b) as a fraction.
3. Write 0.125:
   a) as a percentage
   b) as a fraction.
E 4. Write $0.8\dot{3}$ as a fraction.

Ordering and the four operations

Syllabus links:
C1.5; E1.5; C1.6; E1.6

Learning aims:

- Order quantities by magnitude

- Use the symbols $=$, $\neq$, $>$, $<$, $\geq$ and $\leq$

- Do calculations with whole numbers, decimals or fractions

Calculation with integers

You can show the integers on a number line.

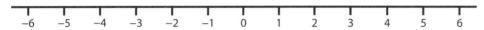

Numbers increase as you move right and decrease as you move left.	$-4 < -2, 3 > -5$
Adding a positive integer moves the value right on the number line. Adding a negative integer moves the value left on the number line.	$-2 + 5 = 3$ $1 + -8 = 1 - 8 = -7$
Subtracting a positive integer moves the value left on the number line. Subtracting a negative integer moves the value right on the number line.	$-1 - (+5) = -1 - 5 = -6$ $3 - (-4) = 3 + 4 = 7$
If you multiply or divide two integers with different signs, the answer is negative. If the signs are the same, the answer is positive.	$2 \times -5 = -10, -3 \times -4 = 12$ $18 \div -3 = -6,$ $-24 \div -2 = 12$

Calculations with fractions

To add or subtract two fractions, convert them to equivalent fractions with the same denominator.

Example 1   Work out $2\frac{1}{4} - \frac{2}{3}$

$2\frac{1}{4} - \frac{2}{3} = \frac{9}{4} - \frac{2}{3}$ Convert the mixed number to an improper fraction.

$= \frac{27}{12} - \frac{8}{12}$ 12 is the lowest common multiple of 4 and 3.

$= \frac{19}{12} = 1\frac{7}{12}$ Subtract the numerators. Write the answer as a mixed number.

To multiply two fractions, multiply the numerators and multiply the denominators.

To divide by a fraction, multiply by the reciprocal. The reciprocal of $\frac{a}{b}$ is $\frac{b}{a}$.

Example 2   Work out: a) $2\frac{1}{4} \times \frac{2}{3}$ b) $2\frac{1}{4} \div \frac{2}{3}$

a) $2\frac{1}{4} \times \frac{2}{3} = \frac{9}{4} \times \frac{2}{3}$ Convert the mixed number to an improper fraction.

$= \frac{18}{12} = \frac{3}{2} = 1\frac{1}{2}$ Multiply the numerators and denominators, then simplify.

b) $2\frac{1}{4} \div \frac{2}{3} = \frac{9}{4} \times \frac{3}{2} = \frac{27}{8} = 3\frac{3}{8}$ The reciprocal of $\frac{2}{3}$ is $\frac{3}{2}$.

Calculations with decimals

When you multiply or divide two decimals, take care with the decimal point.
Look at these examples:

$0.3 \times 6 = 1.8$ $0.3 \times 0.6 = 0.18$ $0.03 \times 0.6 = 0.018$

$18 \div 3 = 6$ $18 \div 0.3 = 60$ $18 \div 0.03 = 600$

Example 3   Work out:

a) 0.4×0.15

b) $3 \div 0.05$

....

a) $4 \times 15 = 60$ Multiply integers with the same digits.

So $0.4 \times 15 = 6$ $4 \div 10 = 0.4$ and $60 \div 10 = 6$

So $0.4 \times 1.5 = 0.6$ $15 \div 10 = 1.5$ and $6 \div 10 = 0.6$

and $0.4 \times 0.15 = 0.06$ $1.5 \div 10 = 0.15$ and $0.6 \div 10 = 0.06$

b) $3 \div 5 = 0.6$ Start with the integer 5.

So $3 \div 0.5 = 6$ $5 \div 10 = 0.5$ and multiply $0.6 \times 10 = 6$

and $3 \div 0.05 = 60$ $0.5 \div 10 = 0.05$ and multiply $6 \times 10 = 60$

Order of operations

If there are several operations, follow the BIDMAS rule.

Brackets, then **I**ndices (powers), then **M**ultiplications and **D**ivisions, then **A**dditions and **S**ubtractions.

$2 + -3 \times 4 = 2 + -12 = 10$ Do the multiplication first.

If you want to do the addition first, you must put in brackets:

$(2 + -3) \times 4 = -1 \times 4 = -4$

> **NC** **Quick Test**

1. Here are five temperatures in degrees Celsius: 3, −14, 8, −2, −7
   Put them in them correct positions here: ...< ... < ... < ... < ...
2. Find:
   a) $4 + -6 - -3$
   b) $(-4 \times -5) \div -2$
3. Work out:
   a) $\frac{3}{4} + \frac{5}{6}$
   b) $\frac{3}{4} \times \frac{5}{6}$
   c) $\frac{3}{4} \div \frac{5}{6}$
4. Work out:
   a) 0.4×0.2
   b) $20 \div 0.4$
5. Work out: $(0.5)^2 + (-3)^2$

Indices and standard form

Learning aims:

Syllabus links:
C1.7; E1.7; C1.8; E1.8

- Understand and use positive, zero and negative indices
- **E** Understand and use fractional indices
- Understand numbers in standard form
- **E** Do calculations with numbers written in standard form

Indices

A positive index tells you the number of times a number is multiplied together.

$$5^3 = 5 \times 5 \times 5 = 125$$
$$\text{and } 2^5 = 2 \times 2 \times 2 \times 2 \times 2 = 32$$

Any number (except 0) to the power 0 is 1.

$$5^0 = 1 \text{ and } 2^0 = 1$$

A negative index represents the reciprocal of the number with a positive index.

$$5^{-3} = \frac{1}{5^3} = \frac{1}{125} \text{ and } 2^{-5} = \frac{1}{2^5} = \frac{1}{32}$$

> **Key Point**
>
> If $a \neq 0$ and n is positive, then $a^0 = 1$ and $a^{-n} = \dfrac{1}{a^n}$

The rules of indices

To multiply two powers of the same number, add the indices.

$$4^2 \times 4^3 = 4^{2+3} = 4^5 \text{ and } 5^2 \times 5^{-3} = 5^{2+-3} = 5^{-1}$$

To divide two powers of the same number, subtract the indices.

$$2^8 \div 2^3 = 2^{8-3} = 2^5$$
$$\text{and } 3^{-2} \div 3^{-3} = 3^{-2--3} = 3^1 = 3$$

> **Key Point**
>
> $a^m \times a^n = a^{m+n}$
> $a^m \div a^n = a^{m-n}$

E Fractional indices

A fractional index shows that roots are involved.

$$32^{\frac{1}{5}} = \sqrt[5]{32} = 2 \text{ because } 2^5 = 32$$

A fractional index can mean a mixture of powers and roots.

$$32^{\frac{3}{5}} = (32^{\frac{1}{5}})^3 = 2^3 = 8$$

Fractional powers can be negative too.

The rules about multiplying and dividing powers apply to fractional indices.

$$4^{\frac{1}{2}} \times 4^{\frac{3}{2}} = 4^{\frac{1}{2}+\frac{3}{2}} = 4^2 = 16$$
$$5^{-\frac{3}{2}} \div 5^{\frac{1}{2}} = 5^{\frac{3}{2}+\frac{1}{2}} = 5^{-2} = \frac{1}{25}$$

> **Key Point**
>
> $a^{\frac{1}{n}} = \sqrt[n]{a}$
> and $a^{\frac{m}{n}} = (\sqrt[n]{a})^m$

Standard form

Here are some powers of 10: $10^6 = 1\,000\,000$, $10^5 = \dfrac{1}{10^5} = \dfrac{1}{100\,000} = 0.00001$

A number is in **standard form** when it is written as $A \times 10^n$ where $1 \leq A < 10$ and n is an integer.

Example 1   Write these numbers in standard form:

a)   265 000

b)   0.000 000 403

a) $265\,000 = 2.65 \times 100\,000$ Start with 265 and put a decimal point after the 2.

$\qquad\qquad = 2.65 \times 10^5$ The index is 5.

b) $0.000\,000\,403 = 4.03 \times 0.000\,000\,1$ Start with 403 and put a decimal point after the 4.
The index is −7.

$\qquad\qquad = 4.03 \times 10^{-7}$ Multiplying by 0.1 is the same as dividing by 10.

When a number is in standard form you can convert it to a normal number.

$8.42 \times 10^4 = 8.42 \times 10\,000 = 84\,200$

$2.19 \times 10^{-4} = 2.19 \times 0.0001 = 0.000\,219$

E Calculations with standard form

When you multiply or divide numbers in standard form, you can use the rules for calculations with indices.

Example 2 $A = 3.2 \times 10^5, B = 4 \times 10^9, C = 2.7 \times 10^6$

Work out the following. Write your answers in standard form.

a) $A \times B$

b) $A \div B$

c) $A + C$

a) $(3.2 \times 10^5) \times (4 \times 10^9)$ Multiply 3.2 and 4. Add the indices 5 and 9.

$\quad = 12.8 \times 10^{14}$ This is not in standard form because $12.8 > 10$.

$\quad = 1.28 \times 10^{15}$ This is in standard form. The index has increased by 1.

b) $(3.2 \times 10^5) \div (4 \times 10^9)$ Divide 3.2 by 4. The index is $5 - 9$.

$\quad = 0.8 \times 10^{-4}$ This is not in standard form because $0.8 < 1$.

$\quad = 8 \times 10^{-5}$ This is in standard form. The index has decreased by 1.

c) $(3.2 \times 10^5) + (2.7 \times 10^6)$ To add them the powers of 10 must be the same.

$\quad = (0.32 \times 10^6) + (2.7 \times 10^6)$ The first number has been changed.
The index now is 6.

$\quad = 3.02 \times 10^6$ $0.32 + 2.7 = 3.02$ The power of 10 does not change.

This answer is in standard form.

> **NC Quick Test**

1. Write $\dfrac{1}{3 \times 3 \times 3 \times 3}$ as a power of 3.
2. $5^n \div 5^2 = 5^6$. Find the value of n.
3. Write 52 million in standard form.
E 4. Find n when $n^{\frac{2}{3}} = 25$.
E 5. Write $(4 \times 10^7) \div (8 \times 10^{-5})$ in standard form.

Estimation and limits of accuracy

Syllabus links:
C1.9; E1.9; C1.10;
E1.10

Learning aims:

- Understand how to round numbers
- Make estimates for calculations
- Round answers to a reasonable degree of accuracy in a particular context
- Give bounds for data rounded to a specified accuracy
- **E** Find bounds for the results of calculations

Rounding values

Large numbers can be rounded. For example, 23 702 is 24 000 to the nearest thousand and 3 106 502 is 3 000 000 to the nearest million.

A calculator says that $400 \div 17 = 23.529411\ldots$

You can round to:

- decimal places (d.p.) $400 \div 17 = 23.5$ to 1 d.p. or 23.53 to 2 d.p. and so on.
- significant figures (s.f.) $400 \div 17 = 20$ to 1 s.f. or 24 to 2 s.f. and so on.

If the digit after the rounding value is 5 or more then round up, if it is 4 or less then round down.

Make sure you put in enough zeros to keep the number the right size.

Example 1   Round:

a)   40 529 to 2 s.f.

b)   0.003 241 9 to 3 s.f.]

....

a) $40\ 529 = 41\ 000$ (2 s.f.) $5 \geq 5$ so round 0 up to 1. Then add 0s.

b) $0.003\ 241\ 9 = 0.003\ 24$ (3 s.f.) $1 < 5$ so round down to 4. Do not add extra 0s

---

Estimating answers

It is useful to estimate an answer to check for errors when you use a calculator.

You can estimate by rounding all the numbers to 1 s.f. and then doing the resulting calculation.

Example 2   Estimate the value of $\dfrac{5.29 \times 9.63}{1.837}$.

....

$$\frac{5.29 \times 9.63}{1.837} \approx \frac{6 \times 10}{2} \qquad = 60 \div 2 = 30$$

When a calculation involves measurements you may need to round answers to a reasonable degree of accuracy.

Example 3 The sides of a cuboid are 43 cm, 32 cm and 27 cm to the nearest cm. Find the volume.

....

Volume = 43 × 32 × 27   Volume of a cuboid = length × width × height

= 37 152

= 37 000 cm^3 to 2 s.f.   The lengths are rounded to 2 s.f. so round the answer to 2 s.f.

Limits of accuracy

All measurements are made to a particular degree of accuracy. If a line is 63 cm to the nearest cm then it could be between 62.5 cm and 63.5 cm. We can write $62.5\text{cm} \leq$ actual length $< 63.5\text{cm}$. Any length in this interval will be rounded to 63 cm.

62.5 is the **lower bound** and 63.5 is the **upper bound** for the length of the line.

Example 4 Find upper and lower bounds for these measurements.

a) 3400 km to the nearest hundred km

b) 45.2 g to the nearest tenth of a gram.

....

a) upper bound = 3450   lower bound = 3350

b) upper bound = 45.25   lower bound = 45.15

E Bounds for calculations

When you do a calculation with measurements, you can use the bounds of the measurements to find bounds for the result of the calculation.

Example 5 Here are two measurements, correct to one decimal place:
$x = 4.7$ cm and $y = 6.2$ cm

Find upper and lower bound for:

a) $x + y$ b) $\dfrac{x}{y}$

....

$4.65 \leq x < 4.75$ and $6.15 \leq y < 6.25$ These are the bounds for x and y.

a) The lower bound for $x + y = 4.65 + 6.15 = 10.8$

The upper bound for $x + y = 4.75 + 6.25 = 11.0$

b) The lower bound for $x \div y = 4.65 \div 6.25 = 0.744$

The upper bound for $x \div y = 4.75 \div 6.15 = 0.7724$ to 4 d.p.

> **Key Point**
>
> Upper bound of $x - y =$ upper bound of x – lower bound of y.
> Upper bound of $x \div y$ = upper bound of $x \div$ lower bound of y.

> **Quick Test**

1. Round 24 621 to the nearest thousand.
2. Round 3.141 592 8 to 3 decimal places.
3. Round 0.050 823 1 to 3 significant figures.
4. **NC** Estimate 38.1×53.2 by rounding each number to 1 s.f.
5. **E** The area of a rectangle is 53 cm^2 to 2 s.f. The length is 9.6 cm to 1 d.p. Calculate the upper bound of the width.

Ratio and proportion

Syllabus links:
C1.11; E1.11

Learning aims:

- Simplify ratios
- Work out shares from a ratio
- Use proportional reasoning in context

Ratios

A **ratio** can be used to compare parts of a whole. It can also be used to divide a quantity into two or more parts.

Suppose one book has 40 pages and another book has 60 pages.

The ratio of the number of pages in each book is $40 : 60$; say this as "40 to 60".

The ratio $40 : 60$ can be simplified by dividing each number by a common factor.

The highest common factor of 40 and 60 is 20. Divide by 20; the ratio simplifies to $2 : 3$.

Example 1 Three people share $4500 in the ratio $1 : 3 : 5$.

Work out the three shares.

....

$1 + 3 + 5 = 9$	Imagine $4500 divided into 9 parts.
$4500 \div 9 = 500$	Each part is $500.

The shares are:

$1 \times 500 = \$500$	The first share is 1 part out of 9.
$3 \times 500 = \$1500$	The second share is 3 parts out of 9.
$5 \times 500 = \$2500$	The third share is 5 parts out of 9.

In the worked example the shares are fractions of 9; they are $\frac{1}{9}, \frac{3}{9} = \frac{1}{3}$ and $\frac{5}{9}$.

You can picture the shares like this:

You could be told one share and asked to work out the other shares or the total.

Example 2 Ade and Bella share some oranges in the ratio $5 : 2$. Ade has 35 oranges. How many does Bella have?

....

Ada has 5 parts and 35 oranges.

1 part $= 35 \div 5 = 7$ oranges.	Divide by 5 to find one part.
Bella has $7 \times 2 = 14$ oranges	Bella has 2 parts so multiply by 2.

Proportional reasoning

A recipe for a cake uses 2 eggs and 150 g of flour.

This is 75 g of flour for each egg.

For a larger cake with 3 eggs you need $3 \times 75\,g = 225\,g$ of flour.

The ratio of eggs is 2 : 3 and the ratio of flour is 150 : 225 = 2 : 3 which is the same.

The quantities are **proportional**.

Use proportional reasoning to answer value for money questions.

> **Key Point**
>
> "Justify you answer" means you must give a reason. Write down any calculation you do.

Example 3   A 500 g bag of rice costs $3.50   A 850 g bag of rice costs $5.61.

Which is better value for money? Justify your answer.

There are several ways to answer this question. You must give a reason for your answer. Here are two methods.

Method 1   Find the costs of equal masses.

If 500 g cost $3.50 $500\,g = 100\,g \times 5$

then 100 g cost $3.50 ÷ 5 = $0.70   Divide by 5 to find the cost of 100 g.

If 850 g cost $5.61 $850\,g = 100\,g \times 8.5$

then 100 g cost $5.61 ÷ 8.5 = $0.66   Divide by 8.5 to find the cost of 100 g. Use a calculator.

The 850 g bag is better value.   100 g costs less in the larger bag.

Method 2   Find the mass you can buy for the same amount of money.

If $3.50 buys 500 g   Find what $1 buys by dividing by 3.5

then $1 buys 500 ÷ 3.5 = 142.9 g   Use a calculator. The answer is rounded to 1 d.p.

If $5.61 buys 850 g   Find what $1 buys by dividing by 5.61

then $1 buys 850 ÷ 5.61 = 151.5 g   The answer is rounded to 1 d.p.

The 850 g bag is better value. $1 buys more rice in the larger bag.

Use the method you prefer.

> **Quick Test**
>
> **NC 1.** Simplify the ratio 125 : 75 as much as possible.
> **NC 2.** 45 kg of sand is divided into two piles in the ratio 1 : 8. Find the mass of the larger pile.
> **NC 3.** Ahmed, Boris and Cara share some counters in the ratio 2 : 2 : 3. Cara gets 18 counters. How many counters are there all together?
> **4.** 20 litres of petrol cost $46. Find the cost of 25 litres.

Rates

Learning aims:

Syllabus links:
C1.12; E1.12

- Calculate measures of rate, including rates of pay, exchange rates, fuel consumption, pressure and density
- Solve problems involving speed
- **E** Understand population density

Measures of rates

- Rates of pay can be in dollars/hour, dollars/month or dollars/year.
- Use an exchange rate to change from one currency to another.

Example 1 Carla earns $45 per hour.

a) How much does she earn if she works for 40 hours?

b) Here is an exchange rate: $1 = 83 rupees

Convert the amount Carla earns in 40 hours to rupees.

c) In another week Carla earns $1485. How many hours did she work?

....

a) $45 × 40 = $1800   rate of pay per hour × number of hours

b) 1800 × 83 = 149 400 rupees   multiply the number of dollars by 83

c) 1485 ÷ 45 = 33 hours   hours = money earned ÷ hourly rate

Compound measures

Compound measures are found from two other measures.

Example 2 A fuel pump fills a car at the rate of 1.6 litres/second.

a) How much fuel goes into the car in 20 seconds?

$$\text{Fuel consumption for a vehicle} = \frac{\text{distance travelled}}{\text{fuel used}}$$

A car travels 350 km and uses 21 litres of fuel.

b) Find the fuel consumption.

....

a) 1.6 × 20 = 32 litres   fuel = rate of flow × number of seconds

b) 350 ÷ 21 = 16.7 litre/s to 3 s.f.   distance in km ÷ fuel in litres =
                        consumption in km/litre

Pressure and density

$$\text{density} = \frac{\text{mass}}{\text{volume}} \qquad \text{pressure} = \frac{\text{force}}{\text{area}}$$

These formulae are similar. Calculations of density or pressure are done in the same way.

Example 3

a) A piece of copper has a volume of 13.5 cm³ and a mass of 122 g. Work out the density of copper.

b) A force of 50 N acts on an area of 0.04 m². Calculate the pressure.

....

a) density = 122 ÷ 13.5 = 9.0 g/cm³ to 2 s.f.   density = mass ÷ volume; units are grams per cubic centimetre

b) pressure – 50 ÷ 0.04 = 1250 N/m²   pressure = force ÷ area; units are newtons per square metre

Speed

The diagram helps you remember three formulas:

speed = $\dfrac{\text{distance}}{\text{time}}$ **distance** = speed × time   **time** = $\dfrac{\text{distance}}{\text{speed}}$

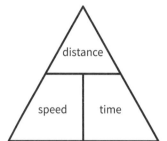

Example 4   A journey is 360 km.

a) What is the average speed if the journey takes 2.5 hours?

b) Work out the time when the average speed is 80 km/h.

....

a) average speed = 360 ÷ 2.5   Use the formula speed = $\dfrac{\text{distance}}{\text{time}}$
     = 144 km/h

b) time = 360 ÷ 80   Use the formula time = $\dfrac{\text{distance}}{\text{speed}}$
     = 4.5 hours

E Population density

The population density of a town or a country is the number of people for each square unit of land.

population density = $\dfrac{\text{population}}{\text{area}}$

Example 5   The population of Bangladesh is 163 million and the area is 148 000 km².

Calculate the population density.

....

163 million = 163 000 000   Write the population as a number.

Population density = 163 000 000 ÷ 148 000   Divide the population by the area in km².

= 1101 people/km²

> ### Quick Test

1. A man earns \$35 per hour. Find how many hours he works to earn \$980.
2. A woman walks 25.3 km in 5.5 hours. Work out her average speed.
3. Water flows from a tank at a rate of 4.5 litres/minute. Work out how much water leaves the tank in half an hour.
4. A piece of wood has a mass of 400 g and a volume of 420 cm³. Calculate the density of the wood.
5. **E** An island has a population of 25.2 million and an area of 36 000 km². Calculate the population density.

Percentages

Syllabus links:
C1.13; E1.13

Learning aims:

- Calculate a percentage of a quantity or a percentage increase or decrease
- Write one quantity as a percentage of another
- Calculate simple interest and compound interest
- **E** Reverse percentages

Calculating percentages

To calculate a percentage of a quantity, divide the percentage by 100 to write it as a fraction or as a decimal.

Example 1   Find:

a)   60% of $80

b)   57% of 143 m.

a) $60\% = \dfrac{60}{100} = \dfrac{3}{5}$ 60% is a simple fraction.

$\dfrac{3}{5} \times 80 = 3 \times 16 = \$48$ $\dfrac{1}{5} = 80 \div 5 = 16$ and $3 \times 16 = 48$

b) $57\% = 0.57$ 57% is not a simple fraction so use a decimal.

$0.57 \times 143 = 81.51$ m   Do this multiplication with a calculator.

To write one quantity as a percentage of another, write it as a fraction and multiply by 100.

Example 2

a)   Write 23 kg as a percentage of 64 kg.

a) $\dfrac{23}{64} = 23 \div 64 = 0.3593\ldots$ This is not a simple fraction so use a calculator.

$0.3593\ldots \times 100 = 35.9\%$ to 1 d.p.   Round the answer.

Percentage increases and decreases

You can calculate the result of a percentage increase or decrease with a single multiplication.

Example 3

a)   Increase $450 by 7%.

b)   Decrease 84 kg by 45%.

a) $\$450 = 100\%$ Start with 100%.

$100\% + 7\% = 107\% = 1.07$ Add 7% for an increase. Write the percentage as a decimal.

107% of $\$450 = 1.07 \times 450 = \$481.50$ Multiply by the decimal.

b) 84 kg $= 100\%$ Start with 100%.

$100\% - 45\% = 55\% = 0.55$ Subtract 45% for a decrease. Write it as a decimal.

55% of 84 kg $= 0.55 \times 84 = 46.2$ kg   Multiply by the decimal.

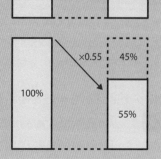

Simple interest and compound interest

When you invest money, you may be given interest.

Simple interest gives you interest each year on the amount you invested.

Compound interest gives you interest on the amount you invested *and* any previous interest.

Example 4 Tariq invests $2000. It earns 10% interest per year.

How much will Tariq have after 3 years if it is:

a) simple interest

b) compound interest.

....

a) 10% of 2000 = 200

$2000 + 3 \times 200 = \$2600$ The interest is the same each year.

b) $100\% + 10\% = 110\% = 1.1$ For an increase, add 10%

1 year: $2000 \times 1.1 = \$2200$ Multiply by 1.1.

2 years: $2200 \times 1.1 = \$2420$

3 years: $2420 \times 1.1 = \$2662$ You can also find the answer by calculating $2000 \times 1.1^3 = 2662$

E Repeated changes

When you have more than one percentage change you multiply separately for each change.

Example 5 The price of a chair is $640. The price is reduced by 20% and then it is reduced by a further 30%.

Find the price after these two reductions.

....

$100\% - 20\% = 80\% = 0.8$ Multiply by this for the first reduction.

$100\% - 30\% = 70\% = 0.7$ Multiply by this for the second reduction.

$640 \times 0.8 \times 0.7 = \$358.40$ This is *not* the same as a reduction of 50%.

E Reverse percentages

If you know the value of a quantity after a percentage increase or decrease, you do a reverse calculation to find the initial value.

The price of a bicycle increases by 14%. The price after the increase is $798.

Calculate the price before the increase.

....

Original price $\times 1.14 = 798$ This is the calculation for a 14% increase.

Original price $798 \div 1.14 = \$700$ Divide by 1.14 to solve the equation.

> **Key Point**
>
> To find the original quantity after a percentage change you will need to do a division.

> **Quick Test**
>
> 1. In a group of 385 people there are 217 women. What percentage of the group are women?
> 2. Find 3.8% of $5600.
> 3. The price of a table is $880. The price is reduced by 30% in a sale. Find the sale price.
> 4. Sam invests $9500 at 3% compound interest. Calculate the value after 5 years.
> **E 5.** The mass of a baby increases by 8% to 8.1 kg. Calculate the mass before the increase.

Using a calculator

Syllabus links:
C1.14; E1.14; C1.15; E1.15; C1.16; E1.16

Learning aims:

- Using a calculator efficiently
- Calculating with time and money
- Time and timetables

Using a calculator

When you use a calculator, you may need to include brackets to do the calculation correctly. Here are some examples:

a) Calculate $\dfrac{96.9 + 48.7}{13.2}$: enter $(96.9 + 48.7) \div 13.2$ Without brackets the answer will be incorrect.

b) Calculate $\dfrac{3.142}{1.89 \times 4.77}$:enter $3.142 \div (1.89 \times 4.77)$ The brackets are essential.

c) Calculate $\sqrt{107.3 - 45.8}$: enter $\sqrt{(107.3 - 45.8)}$

> **Key Point**
>
> When you use a calculator keep all the digits until the end. Only round the final answer.

Time

60 seconds = 1 minute, 60 minutes = 1 hour, 24 hours = 1 day, 7 days = 1 week, 365 days = 1 year

You can use the 12-hour clock or the 24-hour clock to indicate the time.

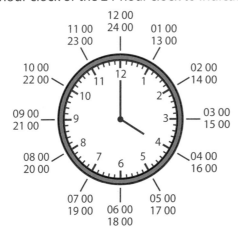

Example 1   Here is a coach timetable

Acton	08 40	09 50
Garford	09 25	10 40
Hurst	10 05	11 25

a)   How long does the 09 50 from Acton take to get to Hurst?

b)   The distance from Acton to Hurst is 45 km. Calculate the average speed of the 09 50 coach.

....

a)   The journey is from 09 50 to 11 25.   This is the last column of the timetable.

From 09 50 to 10 00 is 10 minutes.   Do not try to do this with a calculator. Do it In two parts. Go to the next whole hour first.

From 10 00 to 11 25 is 1 hour 25 minutes.

The total is 1 hour 35 minutes.   10 minutes + 1 hour 25 minutes

b)   1 hour 35 minutes = $1\frac{35}{60}$ hours   Write the minutes aa a fraction of 60 and convert to a decimal.

= 1.58333... hours   Do not round this number.

Average speed = distance ÷ time

= 45 ÷ 1.58333... = 28.421...   This is the full calculator answer.

= 28.4 km/h to 3 s.f.   Round the final answer sensibly.

Different parts of the world are in different time zones.

Example 2   The time in New York is 6 hours behind the time in Rome.

A flight from Rome to New York takes 9 hours and 50 minutes.

It leaves Rome at 08 35 on Sunday. When does it arrive in New York?

From 08 35 to 09 00 is 25 minutes.   Work out 08 35 + 9 hours 50 minutes. First find the time to 09 00.

There is another 9 hours 25 minutes of flying so the plane arrives at 09 00 + 9 hours 25 minutes = 18 25 Rome time.

New York is 6 hours behind Rome so the arrival time is 12 25 on Sunday.

Calculating with money

Currencies are written with two digits after the decimal point.

Exchange rates can be written with more than 2 digits after the decimal point.

Example 3

a)   5 identical books cost $86. Find the cost of each one.

b)   The exchange rate is $1 = 0.92379 euros. Convert the cost to euros.

a)   86 ÷ 5 = 17.2   There is just 1 d.p. in the answer.

The cost is $17.20   Add a zero for a currency.

b)   86 × 0.92379 = 79.44594   Use all the digits in the exchange rate

The cost is 79.45 euros   Round the final answer to 2 d.p.

Quick Test

1. Calculate $\frac{4.7 \times 5.1}{\sqrt{3.5^2 + 9.7^2}}$. Round your answer to 3 s.f.
2. A journey of 35 km has an average speed of 50 km/h. Find the journey time in minutes.
3. Find the time, in hours and minutes, from 18 30 on Sunday to 09 10 on Tuesday.
4. Juan exchanges $130 for 7202.89 pesos. Find the exchange rate in the form $1 = ... Round your answer to 4 d.p.
5. Calculate 83% of $627.45.

E Exponential growth and decay

Learning aims:

* **E** Do calculations involving exponential growth and decay

Exponential growth

Exponential growth occurs when a quantity increases by a constant percentage over equal time intervals. The way savings increase with compound interest is an example of exponential growth.

Example 1 1000 people are infected with a virus.

The number of infected people increases by 20% each week.

a) Make a table to show the number of infected people over the next 5 weeks.

b) If infection continues at the same rate, calculate the number of infected people after 10 weeks.

> **Key Point**
>
> Make sure you know how to use the power button on your calculator correctly.

a)

Week	Number of people Infected
0	1000
1	1200
2	1440
3	1728
4	2074
5	2488

$100\% + 20\% = 120\% = 1.2$

Multiply by 1.2 to increase by 20%.

$1000 \times 1.2 = 1200$

$1200 \times 1.2 = 1440$

$1440 \times 1.2 = 1728$

$1728 \times 1.2 = 2073.6$

$2073.6 \times 1.2 = 2488.32$

Round the numbers in the table but not in the calculation.

b) $1000 \times 1.2^{10} = 6192$ people   The answer is $6191.736\ldots$

Here is a graph of the exponential growth in the worked example.

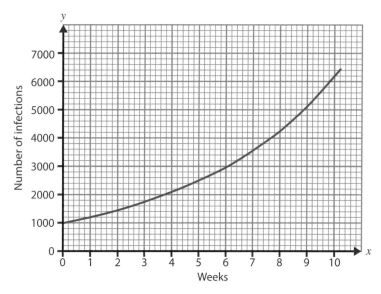

The graph of exponential growth always gets steeper as time passes.

Example 2 Ray invests $12 000 and earns compound interest. After 5 years it is worth $16 210.78. Calculate the rate of interest.

....

If the multiplier is m then $12\,000 \times m^5 = 16\,210.78$	m is 100% + rate of interest, written as a decimal.
$m^5 = 1.350833\ldots$	How the value is calculated.
$m = \sqrt[5]{1.350833\ldots} = 1.062$	Divide 16 210.78 by 12 000.
The rate of interest is 6.2%.	Find the fifth root on your calculator

Exponential decay

Exponential decay occurs when a quantity *decreases* by a constant percentage over equal time intervals. Radioactive decay is an example.

Example 3 The number of fish in a lake is decreasing by 12% each year.

This year there are 540 fish.

a) How many will there be in 2 years from now?

b) Show that in 6 years the population will be less than half what it is now.

....

a) 100% − 12% = 88% = 0.88	Multiply by 0.88 each year.
$540 \times 0.88^2 = 418$ fish	Multiply by 0.88^2 for 2 years. Round the answer.
b) $540 \times 0.88^6 = 251$	Multiply by 0.88^6 for 6 years.
Half of 540 = 270 > 251	Find half the population now.

This graph shows the number of fish in the worked example. A graph of exponential decay is steepest at the beginning and gets less steep as time passes.

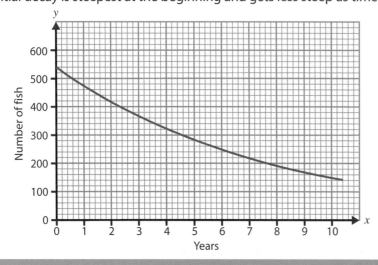

E Surds

Syllabus links:
E1.18

Learning aims:

- E Simplify expressions containing surds
- E Rationalise the denominator of a fraction containing surds

Surds

Square numbers have integer square roots. For example, $\sqrt{9} = 3$ and $\sqrt{121} = 11$.

Some square roots such as $\sqrt{12}$ or $\sqrt{99}$ are irrational. They are called **surds**.

Expressions such as $3 + \sqrt{8}$ or $5 + 2\sqrt{3}$ contain surds.

Surds can often be simplified.

For example, $\sqrt{12} = \sqrt{4 \times 3} = \sqrt{4} \times \sqrt{3} = 2\sqrt{3}$

and $\sqrt{99} = \sqrt{9 \times 11} = \sqrt{9} \times \sqrt{11} = 3\sqrt{11}$.

> **Key Point**
>
> If a and b are two numbers then $\sqrt{ab} = \sqrt{a} \times \sqrt{b}$

Example 1 Simplify each expression:

a) $\sqrt{48}$

b) $\sqrt{5} + \sqrt{20}$

....

a) $\sqrt{48} = \sqrt{16 \times 3}$ Choose 16 because it is a square number.

$\quad = \sqrt{16} \times \sqrt{3}$ $\sqrt{ab} = \sqrt{a} \times \sqrt{b}$

$\quad = 4\sqrt{3}$ $\sqrt{16} = 4$

b) $\sqrt{5} + \sqrt{20} = \sqrt{5} + \sqrt{5 \times 4}$ Choose 4 because it is a square number.

$\quad = \sqrt{5} + \sqrt{5} \times \sqrt{4}$ Split up the second square root.

$\quad = \sqrt{5} + 2\sqrt{5}$ $\sqrt{4} = 2$

$\quad = 3\sqrt{5}$ Add the two terms.

Simplifying expressions

Expressions with brackets can be simplified by multiplying out the brackets.

Example 2 Simplify each expression:

a) $\sqrt{2}(3 + \sqrt{8})$

b) $(4 + \sqrt{3})(2 - \sqrt{3})$

$\quad = 4(2 - \sqrt{3}) + \sqrt{3}(2 - \sqrt{3})$

....

a) $\sqrt{2}(3 + \sqrt{8}) = 3 \times \sqrt{2} + \sqrt{2} \times \sqrt{8}$ Multiply each term in the bracket by $\sqrt{2}$.

$\quad = 3\sqrt{2} + \sqrt{2 \times 8}$ The product of 2 square roots is the square root of the product.

$\quad = 3\sqrt{2} + \sqrt{16} = 4 + 3\sqrt{2}$ $\sqrt{16} = 4$

b) $(4 + \sqrt{3})(2 - \sqrt{3})$

First multiply the second bracket by 4 and then multiply it by $\sqrt{3}$.

$= 4(2 - \sqrt{3}) + \sqrt{3}(2 - \sqrt{3})$

$= 8 - 4\sqrt{3} + 2\sqrt{3} - 3$

The last term is 3 because $\sqrt{3} \times \sqrt{3} = 3$.

$= 5 - 2\sqrt{3}$

Combine pairs of terms.

Rationalising the denominator

When there is a surd in the denominator of a fraction, we can remove it by multiplying the numerator and the denominator by a suitable expression.

This is called **rationalising the denominator**. It will become a rational number.

Example 3   Rationalise the denominator of:

a) $\dfrac{6}{\sqrt{3}}$

b) $\dfrac{2}{3 + \sqrt{2}}$

....

a) $\dfrac{6}{\sqrt{3}} = \dfrac{6 \times \sqrt{3}}{\sqrt{3} \times \sqrt{3}}$

Multiply the numerator and denominator by $\sqrt{3}$.
The value of the fraction is not changed.

$= \dfrac{6\sqrt{3}}{3}$

$\sqrt{3} \times \sqrt{3} = 3$

$= 2\sqrt{3}$

$6 \div 3 = 2$

b) $\dfrac{2}{3 + \sqrt{2}} = \dfrac{2(3 - \sqrt{2})}{(3 + \sqrt{2})(3 - \sqrt{2})}$

Multiply the numerator and denominator by $3 - \sqrt{2}$.

Now $(3 + \sqrt{2})(3 - \sqrt{2})$

$= 9 - 3\sqrt{2} + 3\sqrt{2} - 2 = 7$

The $\sqrt{2}$ terms cancel and the answer is an integer.

So $\dfrac{2}{3 + \sqrt{2}} = \dfrac{2(3 - \sqrt{2})}{7} = \dfrac{2}{7}(3 - \sqrt{2})$ The denominator has been rationalised.

> **Key Point**
>
> If a and b are two positive integers then $(a + \sqrt{b})(a - \sqrt{b}) = a^2 - b$ which is an integer.

> **NC Quick Test**
>
> 1. Write $\sqrt{162}$ as a multiple of $\sqrt{2}$.
> 2. Simplify $\sqrt{63} - \sqrt{28}$.
> 3. Simplify $(-1 + \sqrt{2})(3 + \sqrt{2})$.
> 4. Rationalise the denominator of $\dfrac{5}{\sqrt{10}}$.
> 5. Rationalise the denominator of $\dfrac{12}{3 - \sqrt{5}}$.

NC Types of number

1 **a** The difference between two square numbers is 19. Find the square numbers. [2]

b 1 is both a square number and a cube number. Find another number that is both a square number and a cube number. [1]

2 Here is a list of numbers : 91, 93, 95, 97, 99

Find:

a a multiple of 13 **b** a factor of 297 **c** a prime number. [3]

3 Write down all the prime numbers between 30 and 40. [2]

4 **a** Write 264 as a product of prime numbers. [3]

b Find the largest odd number that is a factor of 264. [2]

5 **a** Find the lowest common multiple of 65 and 39. [2]

b Find the highest common factor of 65 and 39. [2]

6 Find the smallest natural number that is **not** a factor of 420. [2]

Sets

1 $\xi = \{$natural numbers $x: 1 \le x \le 12\}, A = \{3, 5, 7, 9, 11\}, B = \{$multiples of $3\}$

a Show these sets on a Venn diagram. [2]

b List the elements of $A \cap B$. [1]

c List the elements of A'. [1]

2 $X \cap Y = \{a, e\}$ $X' \cap Y = \{c, g, m, n\}$ $X \cap Y' = \{s\}$

a Show X and Y on a Venn diagram. [2]

b List the elements of $X \cup Y$. [1]

E 3 $A = \{9, 10, 11, 12, 13, 14\}$ $B = \{11, 12, 13, 14, 15, 16\}$ $C = \{8, 9, 11, 14, 16\}$

a Find $n(B \cup C)$. [1]

b Find the elements of $(A \cap B) \cup C$. [2]

c $n(C') = 18$. Find $n(\xi)$. [1]

E 4 $F = \{$factors of $30\}$

Put the correct signs in these expressions.

a $7 \dots F$ **b** $10 \dots F$ **c** $\{3, 5\} \dots F$ [3]

Powers and roots

1 Write down the value of:

a $\sqrt{121}$

b $\sqrt[3]{125}$ [2]

2 Show that $1^3 + 2^3 + 3^3$ is a square number [2]

> **Show me**
>
> $1^3 + 2^3 + 3^3 = \ldots + \ldots + \ldots = \ldots$
>
> But $\ldots = \ldots^2$ so the sum is a square number.

3 Find two different square numbers with a sum of 50. [2]

4 a Write 64 as a power of 8. [1]

b Write 64 as a power of 4. [1]

c Write 64 as a power of 2. [1]

5 Work out $6^2 \div \sqrt[3]{27}$. [2]

6 $3^5 = 243$

Use this fact to work out:

a 3^6 [2]

b 3^4 [2]

7 Work out $\sqrt{49} \times \sqrt[3]{125}$ [2]

8 Work out

a $5^2 + 5^3$ [2]

b $10^2 + 10^3$ [2]

NC Fractions, decimals and percentages

1

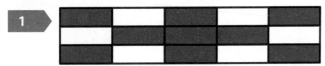

a What fraction of this shape is shaded? Write your answer in its simplest terms. [2]

b What percentage of this shape is not shaded? [2]

2 **a** Write $\frac{17}{20}$ as a percentage. [2]

b Write 2.5% as a decimal. [1]

3 Write $1\frac{5}{8}$ as a percentage. [2]

4 Here is an addition: 75% + 40% = 115%

Write each of the numbers as a fraction. [3]

5 Write each fraction as a decimal:

a $\frac{9}{4}$ [1]

b $\frac{4}{9}$ [2]

6 Show that $\frac{3}{5}$ is less than $\frac{2}{3}$. [2]

The phrase **show that** means that you must justify your answer. In this question you could write both fractions with the same denominator.

E **7** Write $1.5\dot{1}$ as a mixed number. [3]

E **8** Write $0.6444\dots$ as a fraction. [3]

NC Ordering and the four operations

1 At midnight the temperature is −9 °C.

It is twelve degrees colder than it was at midday.

Find the temperature at midday. [1]

2 Here are three fractions: $\frac{3}{4}, \frac{7}{10}, \frac{13}{20}$.

Write them in the correct positions here: ... < ... < ... [2]

3 Work out:

a $5 + 6 \times 3$ [1]

b $5 - (-7)$ [1]

c $20 \div -2 + -3$ [1]

4 Find:

a $0.3 + 0.12$ [1]

b 0.3×0.12 [2]

5 Find:

a $\dfrac{11}{12} - \dfrac{2}{3}$ [2]

b $1\dfrac{3}{4} + 1\dfrac{2}{3}$ [1]

6 **a** Write down the reciprocal of $2\dfrac{1}{2}$. [1]

Reciprocal is a key word. Make sure you remember what it means.

b Work out $4\dfrac{1}{2} \div 2\dfrac{1}{2}$. [2]

7 Work out $1\dfrac{1}{4} \times 2\dfrac{3}{5}$. Write the answer as a mixed number in its simplest terms. [3]

8 N is a number and $N \times \dfrac{3}{4} = 1\dfrac{1}{5}$. Find N. Write your answer as a mixed number. [3]

9 Work out $(0.6)^2 - (0.4)^2$. [2]

10 Work out:

a $0.8 \div 20$ [2]

b $20 \div 0.8$ [2]

11 Find three-quarters of two-thirds. [2]

NC Indices and standard form

1 **a** Write 3.62×10^{-5} as an ordinary number. [1]

b Write 721 000 000 in standard from. [1]

2 **a** Write the reciprocal of 27 as a power of 3. [2]

b Work out $9^{11} \div 9^9$. [2]

c Write $5^3 \times 5^{-4}$ as a decimal. [2]

3 **a** Write $\left(7^3\right)^{-5}$ as a power of 7. [1]

b Write 16^3 as a power of 2. [2]

4 **a** Find $\left(3 \times 10^{-4}\right) \times \left(4.2 \times 10^{-5}\right)$. Write your answer in standard form. [2]

b Find $\left(3 \times 10^{-4}\right) - \left(4.2 \times 10^{-5}\right)$. Write your answer in standard form. [2]

5 **a** Find the value of $4^{\frac{5}{2}}$.

b $25^3 \div 5^n = 5^{-3}$. Find the value of n. [2]

c Write $2\sqrt[3]{32}$ as a power of 2. [2]

Estimation and limits of accuracy

1 Round 26 098 to the nearest thousand. [1]

2 $\dfrac{1000}{17} = 58.823\,529\ldots$

a Round this decimal to 3 decimal places. [1]

> Make sure you know the difference between d.p. and s.f.

b Round this decimal to 3 significant figures. [1]

3 Round the decimal 0.008 130 08 to 2 significant figures. [1]

E 4 a Round 32.175 to 1 s.f. [1]

b Estimate the value of $\dfrac{8.31 \times 11.6}{3.95}$. [2]

5 The length of a line is 15.7 cm to the nearest millimetre.

Write down the upper bound for the length of the line. [1]

6 Estimate $\dfrac{(6.28)^2}{3.17 \times 3.98}$ by rounding each number to 1 s.f. [2]

7 The mass of an animal is 120 kg to the nearest kilogram.

Write down the lower bound of the mass. [1]

E 8 The sides of this rectangle are written to the nearest millimetre.

83 mm

64 mm

Calculate an upper bound for:

a the perimeter of the rectangle. [2]

b the area of the rectangle. [2]

E 9 The mass of a piece of metal is 93 g to the nearest gram.

The volume is 12.2 cm³ correct to 1 decimal place.

Find the lower bound of the density of the metal in g/cm³. Round your answer to 3 d.p.

(density = mass ÷ volume) [3]

Ratio and proportion

NC 1 Simplify the ratio 18 : 24 : 30 as much as possible. [1]

NC 2 Two brothers have $12.50 and $100.

Write the ratio of these two amounts as simply as possible. [1]

3 The ages of two people now are 15 and 20.

a Write down the ratio of their ages. Write your answer as simply as possible. [1]

b Find the ratio of their ages 5 years from now. [2]

c Find the ratio of their ages 10 years ago. [2]

4 Della and Francine share some money in the ratio 4 : 5.

Francine gets $100.

How much money is there all together? [2]

5

45 mm

18 mm A

30 mm B

a Find the ratio of the length to the width of rectangle A. [1]

b The ratio of the length to the width is the same for both rectangles.

Work out the length of rectangle B. [2]

6 30 litres of petrol cost $96.

a Work out the cost of 17 litres of petrol. [2]

b How many litres can you buy for $64? [2]

7 A recipe for 4 people uses 250 g of potatoes.

What mass of potatoes do you need for 10 people? [2]

8 A 1 kg bag of flour costs $8.50.

A 600 g bag of flour costs $5.00.

Which bag is better value? Justify your answer. [3]

The phrase **Justify you answer** means you must give a reason for your answer. You cannot just say the first (or second) bag is better value.

Rates

1 Kwan exchanges $220 into Baht. The exchange rate is $1 = 35.054 Baht.

How much does Kwan receive? [1]

2 A car travels 115 km at an average speed of 46 km/h and uses 5.2 litres of fuel.

a Find how long the journey takes. [1]

b Find the fuel consumption in km/litre. [1]

3 A stone has a mass of 6.5 kg and a volume of 1170 cm^3.

Find the density in g/cm^3. Round your answer to 3 s.f.

density = mass ÷ volume [2]

4 Material for curtains costs $18 per metre.

a Calculate the cost of 12.4 metres. [1]

b A customer buys some material. It costs $117. Work out the length they bought. [2]

5 Ahmed earns $3120 per month.

a Work out how much he earns in a year. [1]

b Work out how long it takes him to earn $25 000. [2]

6 The price of a phone is 179 euros.

The exchange rate is $1 = 0.913 euros

Find the price of the phone in dollars. [2]

7 An exchange rate is $1 = 4.87 Reals.

a Change $250 to Reals. [1]

b Change 250 Reals to dollars. [1]

8 The density of gold is $19.3 \, \text{g/cm}^3$.

a Work out the mass of $40 \, \text{cm}^3$ gold. [1]

b Work out the volume of 1 kg of gold. [2]

c The price of gold is $64.80/g. Calculate the price of $1 \, \text{cm}^3$. [2]

E **9** Look at this table.

Country	Area (km²)	Population (million)
Spain	506 000	46.7
Slovenia	20 700	2.1

Show that the population density of Spain is less than the population density of Slovenia. [2]

> **Show me**

The population density of Spain is . . . ÷ . . . . = ...

The population density of Slovenia is . . . .

Percentages

1 Jamil has $84 and spends $37. What percentage of his money does he have left? [2]

2 **a** Lara buys a picture for $150 and sells it for $210. Find her percentage profit. [2]

b Lara buys a second picture for $370.

She wants to sell it for the same percentage profit. Calculate the selling price. [2]

3 Peer invests $5200 at 3.5% simple interest.

Find the value of his investment after 5 years. [2]

4 A drink consists of 120 ml of orange juice, 70 ml of mango juice and 35 ml of apple juice.

a Find the percentage of apple juice in the drink. [2]

b Another drink has the same percentage of apple juice. The volume of the drink is 360 ml.

Find the volume of apple juice in this drink. [2]

5 Alan earns $728.20. Deductions for tax are $157.30.

Calculate the percentage of his earnings that is deducted in tax. [1]

6 **a** Lucy invests $4000 at 3.25% simple interest. Find the value after 4 years. [2]

b Cara invests $4000 at 3.25% compound interest. Find the value after 4 years. [2]

7 The price of a car is increased from $24 560 to $25 150. Calculate the percentage increase. [2]

8 Elen invests $6500 at n % compound interest. After 6 years it is worth $8368.

Show that $n = 4.3$ [2]

Show me

$100\% + 4.3\% = \ldots\% =$

$6500 \times \ldots^6 = \ldots = \pounds 8368$ to the nearest dollar.

---

9 The price of a coat is $350.

The price is increased by 10% and then later it is reduced by 15%.

Find the new price. [2]

10 Sam gets a 6.5% pay rise. His new salary is $5538 per month.

Calculate his monthly salary before the pay rise. [2]

Using a calculator

1 **a** A flight from Amsterdam to Dubai leaves at 20 30 on Friday and takes 6 hours 45 minutes.

Dubai is 3 hours ahead of Amsterdam.

Work out the arrival time in Dubai. [2]

b The cost of the flight is 1425 euros. 1 euro = 4.0149 dirhams.

Find the cost of the flight in dirhams. [1]

c The distance from Amsterdam to Dubai is 5163 km. Find the average speed. [2]

2 **a** Calculate $\dfrac{20^2 + 19^2}{21^2 - 17^2}$. Round your answer to 3 s.f. [2]

You may need to use brackets when you do the calculation

b Calculate $\dfrac{17.3 + \sqrt{145}}{4.06 + \sqrt[3]{31.5}}$. Round your answer to 3 s.f. [2]

3 **a** Work out the number of minutes in 7 days. [1]

b Write 1000 seconds in minutes and seconds. [2]

4 A clock gains 12 minutes every 24 hours.

One day it was correct at 11 00. How many days will it be until it is correct again? [2]

5 The time is 3.15 am.

a Write the 24-hour clock time 13.5 hours later. [1]

b Write the 24-hour clock time 5.25 days earlier. [2]

6 Here is a train timetable

Melbury	13 15	15 25
Tatton	13 58	16 12
Sidburn	14 29	16 47
Milham	15 02	17 28

a Sofia arrives at Tatton station at 15 49. How long must she wait for a train to Sidburn? [1]

b The second train from Melbury to Milham takes longer than the first train.

How many minutes longer? [2]

E Exponential growth and decay

1 The population of a country is increasing by 1.5% per year.

In 2020 the population was 3.65 million.

Calculate the population in 2027. [2]

2 A motor bike was bought for $14 500.

The value decreases by 11% per year.

a Find the value after 4 years. [2]

b How many years until the value is less than $7500? [2]

3 **a** Araf earns $52 600 a year.

He expects a pay rise of 7.5% every year.

Calculate his salary in five years' time. [2]

b Araf's apartment is worth $245 000

The value is increasing exponentially at a rate of 3.5% per year.

Find the value in 10 years' time. [2]

4 Matt invests $20 000 at $r\%$ compound interest.

After 8 years it is worth $32 239.63

Work out the value of r. [3]

5 Prices are increasing exponentially. Prices double over four years.

Find the annual percentage rise. **[3]**

6 The population of a city is falling exponentially.

Over a period of 10 years it falls from 1.359 million to 1.254 million.

Calculate the annual percentage reduction. **[3]**

NC E Surds

1 Write $\sqrt{363}$ as a multiple of $\sqrt{3}$. **[2]**

2 Simplify $\sqrt{32} - \sqrt{2}$. **[2]**

3 Simplify $\sqrt{125} + \sqrt{45}$. **[2]**

4 Simplify:

a $5\sqrt{18} \times 2\sqrt{2}$ **[2]**

b $5\sqrt{18} \div 2\sqrt{2}$ **[2]**

5 Simplify $(\sqrt{3} - 1)(\sqrt{3} + 2)$. **[2]**

6 Simplify $(2 + \sqrt{5})^2$. **[2]**

7 Simplify:

a $(1 + \sqrt{2})^2$ **[2]**

b $(1 + \sqrt{2})^3$ **[2]**

8 Rationalise the denominator of $\dfrac{10 - \sqrt{5}}{\sqrt{5}}$. **[2]**

Rationalise is a key word here. You must remember what it means.

9 Rationalise the denominator of $\dfrac{1 + \sqrt{2}}{2 + \sqrt{2}}$. **[3]**

10 Rationalise the denominator of $\dfrac{2\sqrt{5} - 1}{\sqrt{5} - 2}$. **[3]**

Introduction to algebra

Syllabus links:
C2.1; E2.1

Learning aims:

- Using letters to represent numbers
- Expressions and formulas

Using letters

In algebra, letters such as $a, b, c, \ldots$ are used to represent numbers.

Addition and subtraction are written like numbers: $a + b$, $x - y$, etc.

The multiplication sign is omitted. Write $a \times 4$ as $4a$; write $c \times d$ as cd.

Division is often written as a fraction. $m \div 5 = \dfrac{m}{5}$; $(a + b) \div c = \dfrac{a + b}{c}$

$a + b$, $x - y$, and so on are called **expressions**. Letters in an expression are called **variables**.

Example 1

a) Find the value of $2(x + 4)(x - 1)$ when $x = 2.5$

b) Find the value of $\dfrac{a^2 + 4}{b - 2}$ when $a = -3$ and $b = 7$.

....

a) $2(x + 4)(x - 1) = 2 \times 6.5 \times 1.5$ Evaluate the brackets before you multiply.

    $= 19.5$

b) $\dfrac{a^2 + 4}{b - 2} = \dfrac{(-3)^2 + 4}{7 - 2}$ Evaluate the numerator and denominator first.

    $= \dfrac{13}{5} = 2.6$ $(-3)^2 = 9$

Formulas

A **formula** expresses a variable in terms of one or more other variables.

For example, a formula to convert h hours and m minutes into s seconds is

$s = 360h + 60m$ or $s = 60(60h + m)$

Example 2   Here is a formula: $v = \sqrt{u^2 + 2as}$

a) Find the value of v when $u = 5$, $a = 3$ and $s = 4$.

b) Find the value of v when $u = 20$, $a = -7$ and $s = 24$.

....

a) $v = \sqrt{u^2 + 2as} = \sqrt{25 + 2 \times 3 \times 4}$ Substitute the three values into the formula.

    $= \sqrt{25 + 24}$

    $= \sqrt{49} = 7$ Evaluate the expression under the square root sign first.

b) $v = \sqrt{u^2 + 2as} = \sqrt{400 + 2 \times (-7) \times 24}$ Be careful with the negative number.

    $= \sqrt{400 - 324}$

    $= \sqrt{64} = 8$

Formulas are often used to calculate areas and volumes.

Example 3

The diagram shows a square picture in a frame.

Each side of the picture is s cm The frame is w cm wide.

A formula for the area (A cm^2) is $A = 4w(s + w)$

Find the area of the frame if each side of the picture is 15 cm and the frame is 3 cm wide.

··

$w = 3$ and $s = 15$ These are the two variables.

$A = 4 \times 3(15 + 3)$ Substitute the values and do the calculation.

$= 12 \times 18 = 216$

The area of the frame is 216 cm^2.   Put in the units for the area.

> **Quick Test**

1. Find the value of $\frac{1}{2}\sqrt{28 - 3a}$ when $a = 4$.
2. Find the value of $x^2 - y^2$ when $x = 10$ and $y = -9$.
3. Here is a formula: $y = mx + c$
   Find the value of y when $m = -2$, $x = -3$ and $c = 5$.
4. Look at this formula: $s = ut + 5t^2$
   Find the value of s when $u = 6$ and $t = 3$.
5. Here is a formula: $T = 10(a + 3)(a - 6)$
   Find the value of T when $a = 1.5$.

Algebraic manipulation

Syllabus links:
C2.2; E2.2

Learning aims:

- Simplifying expressions
- Expanding brackets
- Simple factorisation
- **E** More complex factorisation
- **E** Competing the square for quadratic expressions

Simplifying expressions

You simplify algebraic expressions by combining **like terms**.

Example 1   Simplify each expression:

a) $4x^2 - 3x + 5 - 3x^2 - 7x + 8$

b) $4ab + a^2 - 6ab + 5b^2 + 3a^2$

....

a) $4x^2 - 3x + 5 - 3x^2 - 7x + 8$ $\qquad$ $4x^2$ and $3x^2$ are like terms;
$\qquad\qquad\qquad\qquad\qquad\qquad\qquad\qquad$ $4x^2 - 3x^2 = x^2$

$\quad = x^2 - 10x + 13$ $\qquad\qquad\qquad$ $3x$ and $7x$ are like terms;
$\qquad\qquad\qquad\qquad\qquad\qquad\qquad\qquad$ $-3x - 7x = -10x$

$\quad$ 5 and 8 are like terms; $5 + 8 = 13$

b) $4ab + a^2 - 6ab + 5b^2 + 3a^2$ $\qquad$ $4ab$ and $6ab$ are like terms;
$\qquad\qquad\qquad\qquad\qquad\qquad\qquad\qquad$ $4ab - 6ab = -2ab$

$\quad = -2ab + 4a^2 - 5b^2$ $\qquad\qquad$ a^2 and $3a^2$ are like terms;
$\qquad\qquad\qquad\qquad\qquad\qquad\qquad\qquad$ $a^2 + 3a^2 = 4a^2$
$\qquad\qquad\qquad\qquad\qquad\qquad\qquad\qquad$ $5b^2$ is not like any of the other terms.

To **expand** a bracket, multiply everything in the bracket by the term outside the bracket.

$2a(3a - 5) = 6a^2 - 10a$ $\quad$ $2a \times 3a = 6a^2$ and $2a \times -5 = -10a$

To expand the product of two brackets, multiply each term in the first bracket by each term in the second bracket.

$(2a + 3)(3a - 5) = 2a(3a - 5) + 3(3a - 5)$

$= 6a^2 - 10a + 9a - 15$

$= 6a^2 - a - 15$ $\quad$ $10a$ and $9a$ are like terms so write them as a single term.

Factorising is the reverse of expanding. Put the highest common factor outside the bracket.

Look at this expression: $16ab - 12b^2$

b is a common factor; 4 is the largest number that is a common factor.

$16ab - 12b^2 = 4b(4a - 3b)$ $\qquad$ $4b \times 4a = 16ab$; $4b \times -3b = -12b^2$

E Factorising quadratic expressions

An expression like $x^2 - 3x - 10$ is called a **quadratic expression**.

Sometimes you can factorise a quadratic expression as the product of two brackets.

For example, $x^2 - 3x - 10 = (x - 5)(x + 2)$

Example 2 Factorise:

a) $x^2 - 9x + 20$

b) $2x^2 + 5x + 3$

· ·

a) $x^2 - 9x + 20 = (x \pm \ldots)(x \pm \ldots)$ Find two numbers with a product of 20 and a sum of –9.

$= (x - 4)(x - 5)$ They are –4 and –5.

b) $2x^2 + 5x + 3 = (2x \pm \ldots)(x \pm \ldots)$ For a product of 3 the numbers must be 1 and 3 or –1 and –3.

$= (2x + 3)(x + 1)$ Try different possibilities to find the answer.

E The difference of two squares

$x^2 - y^2 = (x + y)(x - y)$. This is the difference of two squares.

Example 3 Factorise $16a^2 - 9b^2$.

· ·

$16a^2 - 9b^2$ $16a^2 = (4a)^2$ and $9b^2 = (3b)^2$ so this is the difference of two squares.

$= (4a + 3b)(4a - 3b)$

E More complex factorising

Sometimes factorising takes several steps to get to the simplest possible form.

Example 4 Factorise $8x^3 - 8x^2 + 2x$.

· ·

$8x^3 - 8x^2 + 2x$

$= 2x(4x^2 - 4x + 1)$ $2x$ is a common factor; put it outside a bracket.

$= 2x(2x - 1)(2x - 1)$

$= 2x(2x - 1)^2$

The expression $x^2 - 6x + 13$ can be written in **completed square form**.

$x^2 - 6x + 13 = (x - 3)^2 + 4$ 3 is half of 6 and $(x - 3)^2 = x^2 - 6x + 9$ so add 4 to get 13.

> **Quick Test**

1. Simplify $2ab + a - 4ab - 3 + 5a$.
2. Expand $5x(3x - 2y)$.
3. Factorise as much as possible $12abc + 8a^2b^2$.

   E **4.** Factorise as much as possible $27a^2 - 3b^2$.

   E **5.** Expand $3x(x - 2)^2$.

E Algebraic fractions

Syllabus links: E2.3

Learning aims:

- E Add, subtract, multiply or divide algebraic fractions
- E Factorise and simplify algebraic fractions

Addition and subtraction of algebraic fractions

To add or subtract fractions they need to have the same denominator.

> **Example 1** Simplify:
>
> a) $\dfrac{x}{3} + \dfrac{2x-1}{5}$
>
> b) $\dfrac{4}{x-2} - \dfrac{2}{x-1}$
>
> ....
>
> a) $\dfrac{x}{3} + \dfrac{2x-1}{5} = \dfrac{5x}{15} + \dfrac{3(2x-1)}{15}$ The LCM of 3 and 5 is 15. Make that the denominator.
> Multiply out the bracket.
>
> $= \dfrac{5x + 6x - 3}{15}$
>
> $= \dfrac{11x - 3}{15}$ or $\dfrac{1}{15}(11x - 3)$ Collect like terms.
>
> b) $\dfrac{4}{x-2} - \dfrac{2}{x-1} = \dfrac{4(x-1) - 2(x-2)}{(x-2)(x-1)}$ Write as a single fraction.
>
> $= \dfrac{4x - 4 - 2x + 4}{(x-2)(x-1)}$ Multiply out the brackets in the numerator.
>
> $= \dfrac{2x}{(x-2)(x-1)}$ Collect like terms.

Multiplying and dividing algebraic fractions

To multiply two fractions, multiply the numerators and multiply the denominators.

For example, $\dfrac{2a}{3} \times \dfrac{5a}{6} = \dfrac{2a \times 5a}{3 \times 6} = \dfrac{10a^2}{18} = \dfrac{5a^2}{9}$

To divide by a fraction, multiply by its reciprocal.

For example, $\dfrac{2x}{3} \div \dfrac{x+2}{4} = \dfrac{2x}{3} \times \dfrac{4}{x+2} = \dfrac{8x}{3(x+2)}$

> **Key Point**
>
> The reciprocal of $\dfrac{a}{b}$ is $\dfrac{b}{a}$.

Example 2 Work out:

a) $\dfrac{4}{x} - \dfrac{2x}{3}$

b) $\dfrac{4}{x} \times \dfrac{2x}{3}$

c) $\dfrac{4}{x} \div \dfrac{2x}{3}$

a) $\dfrac{4}{x} - \dfrac{2x}{3} = \dfrac{4 \times 3 - 2x \times x}{x \times 3}$ Write as a single fraction.

$= \dfrac{12 - 2x^2}{3x}$ This is the simplest form.

b) $\dfrac{4}{x} \times \dfrac{2x}{3} = \dfrac{4 \times 2x}{x \times 3}$ Find the product of the numerators and of the denominators.

$= \dfrac{8x}{3x} = \dfrac{8}{3}$ The x is a common factor and it can be cancelled.

c) $\dfrac{4}{x} \div \dfrac{2x}{3} = \dfrac{4}{x} \times \dfrac{3}{2x}$ The reciprocal of $\dfrac{2x}{3}$ is $\dfrac{3}{2x}$.

$= \dfrac{12}{2x^2} = \dfrac{6}{x^2}$ 2 is a common factor.

Simplifying algebraic fractions

Algebraic fractions can sometimes be simplified by factorising the numerator and the denominator.

Example 3 Simplify $\dfrac{a^2 - a - 2}{a^2 - 4}$.

$a^2 - a - 2 = (a - 2)(a + 1)$ Factorise the numerator.

$a^2 - 4 = (a + 2)(a - 2)$ The denominator is the difference of two squares.

So $\dfrac{a^2 - a - 2}{a^2 - 4} = \dfrac{(a - 2)(a + 1)}{(a + 2)(a - 2)}$

$= \dfrac{a + 1}{a + 2}$ Cancel the common factor $a - 2$.

> **Quick Test**

1. Write $\dfrac{2(x + 1)}{3} - \dfrac{x - 2}{2}$ as a single fraction.

2. Work out $\dfrac{6x^2}{x + 1} \div \dfrac{3x}{2x + 2}$.

3. Write $\dfrac{a - 1}{a + 3} + \dfrac{a}{a + 2}$ as a single fraction.

4. Simplify $\dfrac{2a^2 + 6a}{a^2 + 6a + 9}$.

Further indices

Syllabus links:
C2.4; E2.4

Learning aims:

- Understand and integer indices
- **E** Understand and use fractional indices
- Use the rules of indices for multiplication, division and powers

Integer indices

If n is a positive integer, then

$$a^n = \underbrace{a \times a \times \text{......} \times a}_{n \text{ terms}} \qquad a^{-n} = \frac{1}{a^n} \qquad a^0 = 1$$

> **Key Point**
>
> If a is any number (except 0), then $a^0 = 1$.

Example 1 Write in index form:

a) $c \times c \times c \times c \times c$

b) $\dfrac{1}{d \times d \times d \times d}$

....

a) $c \times c \times c \times c \times c = c^5$ The product of 5 cs.

b) $\dfrac{1}{d \times d \times d \times d} = d^{-4}$ $d \times d \times d \times d = d^4$

E Fractional indices

If m and n are positive integers, then $a^{\frac{m}{n}} = \left(\sqrt[n]{a}\right)^m$ or $\sqrt[n]{a^m}$.

Example 2 Find $81^{\frac{3}{4}} \times 8^{-\frac{2}{3}}$.

....

$81^{\frac{3}{4}} = \left(\sqrt[4]{81}\right)^3 = 3^3 = 27$ $3^4 = 81$ so $\sqrt[4]{81} = 3$

$8^{\frac{2}{3}} = \left(\sqrt[3]{8}\right)^2 = 2^2 = 4$

So $8^{-\frac{2}{3}} = \dfrac{1}{4}$ $8^{-\frac{2}{3}}$ is the reciprocal of $8^{\frac{2}{3}}$.

and $81^{\frac{3}{4}} \times 8^{-\frac{2}{3}} \ 27 \times \dfrac{1}{4} = \dfrac{27}{4}$ or $6\dfrac{3}{4}$

Multiplying and dividing powers

There are several rules for multiplication and division of indices:

- to multiply two powers of the same number, add the indices: $a^m \times a^n = a^{m+n}$
- to divide one power by another, subtract the indices: $a^m \div a^n = a^{m-n}$
- to find a power of a power, multiply the indices: $(a^m)^n = a^{mn}$
- the power of a product is the product of separate powers: $(ab)^n = a^n b^n$.

Example 3   Simplify:

a) $\dfrac{a^{10} \times a^5}{a^7 \times a}$

b) $(2b)^4 \times (3b)^{-2}$

c) $(5c^2)^{-3}$

....

a) $\dfrac{a^{10} \times a^5}{a^7 \times a} = \dfrac{a^{15}}{a^8}$ Multiply the numerator and denominator first.

   $= a^7$ $15 - 8 = 7$

b) $(2b)^4 = 16b^4$ $2b \times 2b \times 2b \times 2b = 2^4 b^4$

   $(3b)^{-2} = 3^{-2} \times b^{-2} = \dfrac{1}{9}b^{-2}$

   So $(2b)^4 \times (3b)^{-2} = 16b^4 \times \dfrac{1}{9}b^{-2}$ $3^{-2} = \dfrac{1}{3^2} = \dfrac{1}{9}$

   $= \dfrac{16}{9}b^2$ $b^4 \times b^{-2} = b^{4-2} = b^2$

c) $(5c^2)^{-3} = 5^{-3} \times (c^2)^{-3}$ Separate the 5 and the c^2.

   $= \dfrac{1}{125}c^{-6}$ $5^3 = 125$ and $2 \times -3 = -6$.

E The rules for multiplication and division of powers apply to fractional indices.

Example 4   Simplify $(4x)^{\frac{3}{2}} \div (27x)^{\frac{2}{3}}$.

....

$(4x)^{\frac{3}{2}} \div (27x)^{\frac{2}{3}} = \left(4^{\frac{3}{2}} \times x^{\frac{3}{2}}\right) \div \left(27^{\frac{2}{3}} \times x^{\frac{2}{3}}\right)$ Treat the numbers and the powers of x separately.

$= 8x^{\frac{3}{2}} \div 9x^{\frac{2}{3}}$

$= \dfrac{8}{9}x^{\frac{5}{6}}$ $\dfrac{3}{2} - \dfrac{2}{3} = \dfrac{9}{6} - \dfrac{4}{6} = \dfrac{5}{6}$

> **Quick Test**

1. Find the value of n if $3^n = \dfrac{1}{9}$.
2. Simplify $(7x^4)^2$.
3. Simplify $18a^3 \div 6a^5$.
4. Find $3a^2b^2 \times 4a^3b^{-2}$.
E 5. Simplify $(4a)^{\frac{5}{2}} \div (3a)^2$.

Equations

Syllabus links:
C2.5; E2.5

Learning aims:

- Solve linear equations in one unknown and simultaneous linear equations in two unknowns
- Manipulate formulas
- **E** Solve quadratic equations
- **E** Solve non-linear simultaneous equations

Solving linear equations

To solve an equation, do the same thing to the expressions on each side of the equals sign (=) until you have the unknown on its own.

> **Example 1** Solve the equation $4(x - 2) = 25 - x$.
>
> $4(x + 2) = 25 - x$ First expand the bracket.
>
> $4x + 8 = 25 - x$
>
> $5x + 8 = 25$ Add x to both sides.
>
> $5x = 17$ Subtract 8 from both sides.
>
> $x = 3.4$ Divide both sides by 5.

Simultaneous equations

Two simultaneous equations will have two unknowns. Eliminate one unknown first to find the other unknown. Then substitute to find the other. There are several ways to do this.

> **Example 2** Solve these simultaneous equations: $2x + 3y = 34$ and $3x - y = 7$
>
> $2x + 3y = 34$ (1)
>
> $3x - y = 7$ (2)   Multiply (1) by 3. Now (2) and (3) have the same y coefficient.
>
> $9x - 3y = 21$ (3)   Add (1) and (3) to eliminate y.
>
> $11x = 55$
>
> $x = 5$ Find x.
>
> $15 - y = 8$ Substitute in (2) to find y.
>
> $y = 15 - 8 = 7$

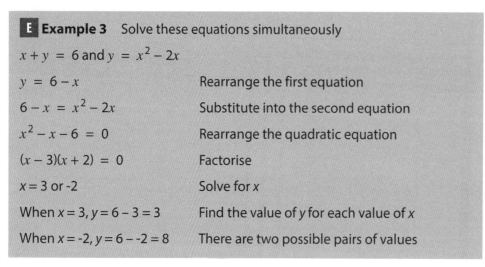

> **E** **Example 3** Solve these equations simultaneously
>
> $x + y = 6$ and $y = x^2 - 2x$
>
> $y = 6 - x$ Rearrange the first equation
>
> $6 - x = x^2 - 2x$ Substitute into the second equation
>
> $x^2 - x - 6 = 0$ Rearrange the quadratic equation
>
> $(x - 3)(x + 2) = 0$ Factorise
>
> $x = 3$ or -2 Solve for x
>
> When $x = 3$, $y = 6 - 3 = 3$ Find the value of y for each value of x
>
> When $x = -2$, $y = 6 - -2 = 8$ There are two possible pairs of values

Rearranging formulas

The subject of a formula is the variable on its own on one side of the equals sign. To change the subject of a formula, rearrange the formula to get that variable on its own.

Example 4   Make m the subject of the formula $e = \frac{1}{2}mv^2$

$e = \frac{1}{2}mv^2$ Multiply both sides by 2.

$2e = mv^2$

$\frac{2e}{v^2} = m$ or $m = \frac{2e}{v^2}$ Divide both sides by v^2.

E Quadratic equations

A quadratic equation can be written in the form $ax^2 + bx + c = 0$ where a, b and c are numbers.

To solve a quadratic equation, factorise, use the quadratic formula, or complete the square.

Example 5

a)   Solve the equation $x^2 + x = 30$ by factorising.

b)   Solve the equation $2x^2 - 3x - 6 = 0$ by using the formula

$x = \dfrac{-b \pm \sqrt{b^2 - 4ac}}{2a}$.

c)   Find the exact solution of $x^2 - 4x + 1 = 0$.

---

a) $x^2 + x - 30 = 0$ Rewrite in this form.

$(x + 6)(x - 5) = 0$ Find the factors.

Either $x + 6 = 0$ and $x = -6$

or $x - 5 = 0$ and $x = 5$ There are two possible solutions.

b) $a = 2, b = -3$ and $c = -6$ The coefficients in the formula.

$x = \dfrac{3 \pm \sqrt{(-3)^2 - 4 \times 2 \times (-6)}}{2 \times 2}$ Substitute into the formula.

$x = \dfrac{3 \pm \sqrt{57}}{4} = 2.64$ or -1.14 to 3 s.f.   Calculate the two possible solutions.

c) $x^2 - 4x + 1 = 0$

$(x - 2)^2 - 4 + 1 = 0$

$(x - 2)^2 = 3$ $x - 2 = \pm\sqrt{3}$ so $x = 2 \pm \sqrt{3}$

> **Quick Test**

1. Solve the equation $\dfrac{2x + 1}{4} = 5$.

2. Make b the subject of the formula $p = 2(a + b)$.

3. Solve the simultaneous equations $x + y = 8$ and $2x - y = 10$.

E **NC** **4.** Solve the equation $x^2 = 3x + 18$.

Inequalities

Syllabus links:
C2.6; E2.6

Learning aims:

- Represent inequalities on a number line
- **E** Solve linear inequalities
- **E** Inequalities with two variables

Inequalities on a number line

You can show inequalities on a number line.

$x > -2$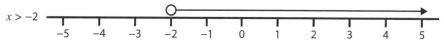

The open circle shows that –2 is not included.

$x \leq 3$

The closed circle shows that 3 is included.

$-2 < x \leq 3$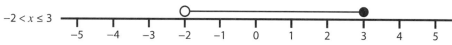

Here $x > -2$ and $x \leq 3$.

The values of x are between –2 and 3. 3 is included but –2 is not.

If x is an integer, the possible values are –1, 0, 1, 2 and 3.

> **Key Point**
>
> < means "less than"
> ≤ means "less than or equal to"
> > means "greater than"
> ≥ means "greater than or equal to"

> **Key Point**
>
> $-2 < x$ is the same as $x > -2$.

E Solving inequalities

You solve an inequality in the same way that you solve an equation.

Example 1   Solve each inequality:

a) $5(x - 12) \leq 24$

b) $14 - 3x > 6$

c) $5 < 2x - 3 < 13$

....

a)	$5(x - 12) \leq 24$	Divide both sides by 5.
	$x - 12 \leq 4.8$	Add 12 to both sides.
	$x \leq 16.8$	The answer is an inequality with x as the subject.
b)	$14 - 3x > 6$	Add $3x$ to both sides.
	$14 > 6 + 3x$	Subtract 6 from both sides.
	$8 > 3x$	Divide both sides by 3.
	$2\frac{2}{3} > x$ or $x < 2\frac{2}{3}$	Make x the subject.
c)	$5 < 2x - 3 < 13$	Add 3 to all expressions.
	$8 < 2x < 16$	Divide all three terms by 2.
	$4 < x < 8$	

E Inequalities with two variables

When x and y are coordinates, show the inequalities on a graph.

$x \geq 2$
is the
unshaded
region

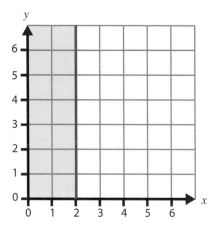

The solid line on $x = 2$
shows that it is included

$y > 1$
is the
unshaded
region

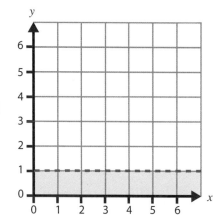

The broken line on $y = 1$
shows that it is not included

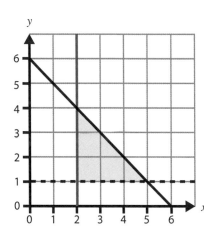

The diagonal line is $x + y = 6$

The shaded triangle is described by
three inequalities:

$x \geq 2$ and $y > 1$ and $x + y \leq 6$

The diagonal line is $x + y = 6$.

The shaded triangle is described by three inequalities:

$x \geq 2, y > 1$ and $x + y \leq 6$.

> **Quick Test**

1. Show $x < -4$ on a number line.
2. $-10 \leq n < -5$ and n is an integer. Write down all the possible values of n.
3. Solve the inequality $\dfrac{2x - 5}{3} \geq 8$. **[E]**
4. Show the region $y > x$ on a graph. **[E]**
5. On a graph show the region where $3 < x < 5$ and $2 \leq y \leq 4$. **[E]**

Sequences

Syllabus links:
C2.7; E2.7

Learning aims:

- Extend a sequence of numbers
- Term-to-term rules for sequences
- Understand the meaning of the nth term of a sequence

Rules for sequences

Here is a sequence of numbers:

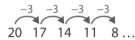

$$20 \quad 17 \quad 14 \quad 11 \quad 8 \ldots$$

Each **term** is 3 less than the term before it. The **term-to-term rule** is subtract 3.

The 6th term is $8 - 3 = 5$.

The nth term is $23 - 3n$.

The first term is $23 - 3 \times 1 = 20$; the 4th term is $23 - 3 \times 4 = 11$; the 12th term is $23 - 3 \times 12 = -13$.

Here are two useful sequences:

Square numbers:

$$1 \quad 4 \quad 9 \quad 16 \quad 25\ldots$$

with differences $+3 \quad +5 \quad +7 \quad +9$

The nth term is n^2.

Cube numbers: 1, 8, 27, 64, 125, ... The nth term is n^3.

Example 1   Find the next term and the nth term for each sequence:

a)   5, 7, 9, 11,...

b)   1, 4, 9, 16,...

c)   6, 11, 18, 27,...

....

a)   The next term is $11 + 2 = 13$.

The nth term is $2n + 3$.

The term-to-term rule is add 2.

$2 \times 1 + 3 = 5$; $2 \times 2 + 3 = 7$ and so on.

b)   The next term is $5^2 = 25$.

The nth term is n^2.

These are the square numbers.

c)   The next term is $27 + 11 = 38$.

The differences are 5, 7, 9 so the next difference is 11.

The nth term is $n^2 + 2n + 3$.

Add the terms of **a)** and **b)**:
$5 + 1 = 6$; $7 + 4 = 11$;
$9 + 9 = 18$.

Example 2   The nth term of a sequence is $2n^2 - 5$.

a)   Find the 4th term.

b)   A term in the sequence is 237. Which term is this?

....

a) $2 \times 4^2 + 5 = 32 + 5 = 37$ Substitute $n = 4$ in the expression.

b) $2n^2 - 5 = 237$ Form an equation and solve it.
          Add 5 to both sides.

$2n^2 = 242$

$n^2 = 121$ Divide both sides by 2.

$n = 11$ $11^2 = 121$

E More about sequences

T_n means the nth term of a sequence.

If $T_n = 3 \times 2^n$

$T_1 = 3 \times 2 = 6, T_2 = 3 \times 2^2 = 3 \times 4 = 12, T_3 = 3 \times 2^3 = 3 \times 8 = 24$ and so on.

The sequence is 6, 12, 24, 48,… and the term-to-term rule is multiply by 2.

Example 3   A sequence starts: $T_1 = 0, T_2 = 2, T_3 = 6, T_4 = 12$.

Find: **a)** T_5 **b)** T_n

....

a) $T_5 = 12 + 8 = 20$ The differences are 2, 4, 6 so the next difference is 8.

b)   Compare T_n with the square numbers: The differences between the square numbers increase by 2 each time. The same is true for T_n.

n	1	2	3	4
T_n	0	2	6	12
n^2	1	4	9	16

Look for a pattern.

$T_n = n^2 - n$ Middle row = third row – first row

> **Quick Test**

1. Find the next three terms in this sequence: 3, 11, 19, 27,…
2. The nth term of a sequence is $3(n + 5)$. Find the 11th term.
3. Find the nth term of this sequence: 25, 23, 21, 19,…
E 4.   A sequence is $T_n = n^3 + 2n$. Find the first term that is greater than 100.
E 5. $T_1 = 5, T_2 = 8, T_3 = 13, T_4 = 20$. Find T_n.

E Proportion

Learning aims:

- **E** Work with direct proportion and inverse proportion algebraically

Direct proportion

The perimeter p of an equilateral triangle is **directly proportional** to its height h. Write $p \propto h$ and the formula $p = kh$ where k is a constant.	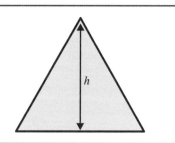
The diameter d of a circle is directly proportional to the square root of its area A. Write $d \propto \sqrt{A}$ and $d = k\sqrt{A}$.	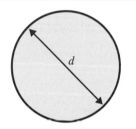
The volume V of a sphere is directly proportional to the cube of the diameter d. Write $V \propto d^3$ and $V = kd^3$.	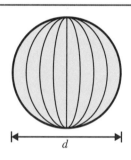

Use the formula to solve problems.

Example 1 y is directly proportional to $x^2 + 1$.

When $x = 3$, $y = 60$.

Find y when $x = 5$.

> **Key Point**
>
> The symbol $\propto$ means "is proportional to".

....

$y = k(x^2 + 1)$	Write down a formula for the proportionality.
$60 = k(3^2 + 1)$	Substitute values to get an equation. Solve the equation to find k.
$k = 60 \div 10 = 6$	
$y = 6(x^2 + 1)$	
$y = 6(5^2 + 1) = 156$	Put the value of k in the formula. Substitute $x = 5$.

Inverse proportion

If y is directly proportional to $\sqrt[3]{x}$ then $y \propto \sqrt[3]{x}$ and $y = k\sqrt[3]{x}$.

If y is **inversely proportional** to $\sqrt[3]{x}$ then $y \propto \dfrac{1}{\sqrt[3]{x}}$ and $y = \dfrac{k}{\sqrt[3]{x}}$.

The gravitational force F between two planets is inversely proportional to the distance d between them.

$F \propto \dfrac{1}{d^2}$ and $F = \dfrac{k}{d^2}$.

Example 2 y is inversely proportional to the square root of x.

When $x = 25, y = 6$. Find y when $x = 225$.

$y \propto \dfrac{1}{\sqrt{x}}$ and so $y = \dfrac{k}{\sqrt{x}}$.   Write down the equation.

$6 = \dfrac{k}{\sqrt{25}}$ and so $k = 6 \times 5 = 30$.   Substitute to find k.

$y = \dfrac{30}{\sqrt{x}}$

$y = \dfrac{30}{\sqrt{225}} = \dfrac{30}{15} = 2$ Use the equation to solve the problem.

Quick Test

1. $y \propto x^3$ and $y = 120$ when $x = 2$. Find y when $x = 3$.
2. y is directly proportional to $60 - x$ and when $x = 40, y = 5$. Find y when $x = 30$.
3. y is directly proportional to x^2 and when $x = 4, y = 400$.
   a) Find y when $x = 8$.
   b) Find x when $y = 900$.
4. y is inversely proportional to x^3. When $x = 5, y = 8$. Find y when $x = 2$.
5. $y \propto \dfrac{1}{\sqrt{x-4}}$. When $x = 10, y = 5$. Find y when $x = 20$.

Graphs in practical situations

Learning aims:

- Interpret travel graphs
- Use conversion graphs

Syllabus links:
C2.9; E2.9

Conversion graphs

This graph shows the cost of hiring a chainsaw.

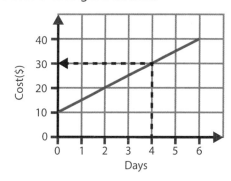

From the graph you can see that:

- there is a fixed charge of $10.00
- there is a charge of $5.00 per day
- the cost for 4 days is $30.00.

Distance–time graphs

This graph shows a journey.

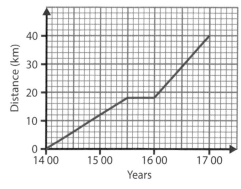

> **Key Point**
>
> The gradient shows the speed. The steeper the line, the greater the speed.

The journey is in three parts.

- 18 km from 14 00 to 15 30, that is 1.5 hours. The average speed is
  $18 \div 1.5 = 12$ km/h.
- A rest period from 15 30 to 16 00. The graph is flat. The distance travelled stays at 18 km.
- 22 km from 16 00 to 17 00. The average speed is 22 km/h.

The whole journey was 40 km in 3 hours so the average speed was
$40 \div 3 = 13.3$ km/h.

E Speed–time graphs

The area between the line and the time axis is the distance travelled.

> **Key Point**
>
> The gradient of a speed–time graph is the acceleration.

Example 1   This graph shows the speed of a cyclist.

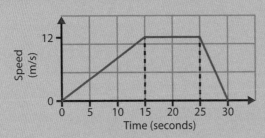

Find:

a)   the acceleration in the first 15 seconds

b)   the deceleration in the last 5 seconds

c)   the distance travelled by the cyclist.

....

a)   In the first 15 seconds the speed increases from 0 m/s to 12 m/s.

The acceleration is the gradient of the line.

$$\text{Acceleration} = \frac{12}{15} = 0.8 \text{ m/s}^2$$

b)   In the last 5 seconds the speed decreases from 12 m/s to 0 m/s.

$$\text{Deceleration} = \frac{12}{5} = 2.4 \text{ m/s}^2$$

c) $\text{Distance} = \frac{1}{2} \times 15 \times 12 + 10 \times 12 + \frac{1}{2} \times 5 \times 12$
$= 90 + 120 + 30 = 240 \text{ m}$

The area between the line and the time axis is the distance travelled.

> **Quick Test**
>
> 1. The exchange rate is 100 dollars = 91 euros. Sketch a conversion graph for dollars and euros.
> 2. A car drives for 2 hours at an average speed of 50 km/h. It stops for 90 minutes. Then it continues for another 90 minutes at 40 km/h. Sketch a distance–time graph of the journey.
> **E 3.** Sami runs for 30 s at 5 m/s. Sami then slows to a stop in 10 seconds.
>   **a)** Sketch a speed–time graph.   **b)** Work out the distance Sami travels.

Graphs of functions

Syllabus links:
C2.10; E2.10

Learning aims:

- Construct tables of values and draw graphs
- Solve equations graphically

Using tables of values

To draw a graph of a function, first draw up a table of coordinates. Choose values of x and calculate corresponding values of y.

Example 1

a) Copy and complete this table of values for $y = x^2 - 3x - 1$.

x	-2	-1	0	1	2	3	4	5
y		3			-3			

b) Use the table to draw a graph of $y = x^2 - 3x - 1$.

c) Use the graph to solve the equation $x^2 = 3x + 1$.

· ·

a)

x	-2	-1	0	1	2	3	4	5
y	9	3	-1	-3	-3	-1	3	9

When $x = 5$ then
$y = 5^2 - 3 \times 5 - 1 = 9$ and so on for the other values.

b)

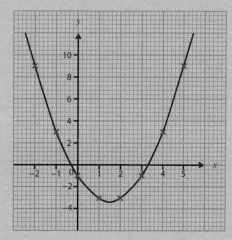

Plot the points and join them with a smooth curve.

c) If $x^2 = 3x + 1$ then $x^2 - 3x - 1 = 0$.

These are the values of x where the graph crosses the x-axis.

If $y = 0$ then $x = 3.3$ or -0.3

E A more complicated example

Sometimes you can solve an equation by drawing two graphs.

Example 2

a) Draw a graph of $y = \frac{12}{x}$.

b) By drawing a suitable straight line, solve the equation $\frac{12}{x} - 3 = 5x$.

· ·

a) Draw a table of values.

x	−6	−5	−4	−3	−2	−1	1	2	3	4	5	6
y	−2	−2.4	−3	−4	−6	−12	12	6	4	3	2.4	2

The graph of $y = \dfrac{12}{x}$ is in two parts with the y-axis between them.

b) Rewrite $\dfrac{12}{x} - 3 = 5x$ as $\dfrac{12}{x} = 5x + 3$.

Draw the line $y = 5x + 3$ and the solution will be the x-coordinate where the two lines cross.

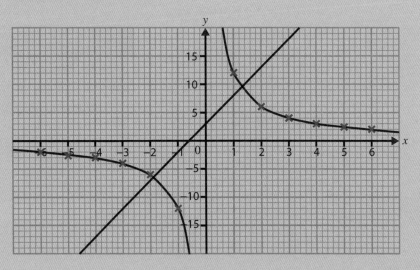

The solution is $x = 1.3$ or $−1.9$.

Quick Test

1. Copy and complete this table.

x	−2	−1	0	1	2	3
$x^2 + 2x - 4$		−5			4	

2. Copy and complete this table.

x	−6	−3	3	6	9
$\dfrac{36}{x}$	−6			6	

E 3. Copy and complete this table.

x	−2	−1	0	1	2	3
2^x	0.25				4	

E 4. Copy and complete this table.

x	−2	−1	0	1	2	3
$x^3 + 2x^2 - 4$		−3			12	

Sketching graphs

Learning aims:

Syllabus links:
C2.11; E2.11

- Sketch graphs of linear functions

- **E** Sketch graphs of quadratic, cubic, reciprocal and exponential functions

Linear graphs

$$y = 2x - 7 \qquad 3x + 5y = 30 \qquad x = 5y - 1$$

These are all examples of linear graphs. The graph of each one is a straight line.

Example 1   Sketch the graph of $2x - 3y = 18$.

....

When $x = 0$ then $-3y = 18$ and $y = -6$.   The line crosses the y-axis at -6.

When $y = 0$ then $2x = 18$ and $x = 9$.   The line crosses the x-axis at 9.

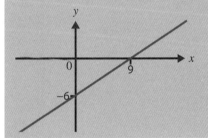

> **Key Point**
>
> A sketch does not need graph paper. Show the coordinates of special points, such as where the graph crosses the axes.

E Quadratic graphs

A quadratic graph is symmetrical with one turning point.

Example 2

a)   Solve the equation of $x^2 - 3x - 4 = 0$.   **b)**   Find the turning point of the graph of $y = x^2 - 3x - 4$.

c)   Sketch the graph of $y = x^2 - 3x - 4$.   **d)**   Write down the equation of the line of symmetry.

....

a) $(x - 4)(x + 1) = 0$ Factorise.

Either $x - 4 = 0$ and $x = 4$ or $x + 1 = 0$ and $x = -1$

b) $y = x^2 - 3x - 4$ Write the quadratic expression in completed square form

$y = (x - 1.5)^2 - 2.25 - 4 \qquad y = (x - 1.5)^2 - 6.25$

The turning point is at $(1.5, -6.25)$.   When $x = 1.5, x - 1.5 = 0$ and the value of y is a minimum.

c)

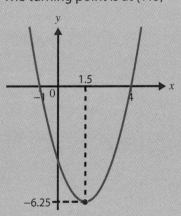

From part **a)** the graph crosses the x-axis at -1 and 4.

When $x = 0, y = -4$ so this is where the graph crosses the y-axis.

d) $x = 1.5$ The vertical line through the lowest point.

E Cubic graphs

Cubic graphs can have two turning points and cross the x-axis at three points.

Example 3

a) The points $(8, a)$ and $(-5, b)$ are on the graph of $y = x(x - 5)(x + 2)$.

 Find the values of a and b.

b) Sketch the graph of $y = x(x - 5)(x + 2)$.

....

a) When $x = 8$ then $y = 8 \times 3 \times 10 = 240$ $a = 240$

 When $x = -5$ then $y = -5 \times -10 \times -3 = -150$ $b = -150$

b)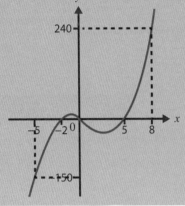

It crosses the x-axis
where $y = x(x - 5)(x + 2)$
So $x = 0, 5$ or -2.

E Reciprocal graphs

Here is a sketch of the graph of $y = \dfrac{10}{x} + 2$.

The lines $y = 2$ and $x = 0$ are **asymptotes**.

When x is a large positive or negative number then y is close to 2.

When x is positive and close to 0 then y is a large positive number.

When x is negative and close to 0 then y is a large negative number.

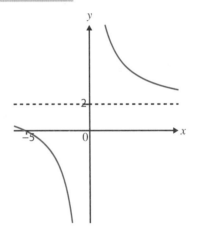

Exponential graphs

Here is a sketch of the graph of $y = 1.5^x$.

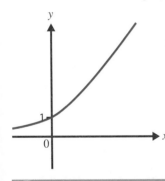

Graphs of the form $y = a^x$ are always this shape.

> **Quick Test**

1. Sketch the graph of $y = 5x + 60$.

 E 2. Sketch the graph of $y = x^2 + 8x$.

 E 3. Sketch the graph of $y = x(x - 3)(x - 6)$.

 E 4. Sketch the graph of $y = \dfrac{1}{x} + 4$.

E Differentiation

Syllabus links:
E2.12

Learning aims:

- E Use tangents to estimate gradients of curves
- E Differentiate polynomial expressions
- E Find gradients and stationary points using differentiation
- E Discriminate between maxima and minima

Gradient of a curve

To estimate the **gradient** of a curve at any point:

- Draw a tangent to the curve at that point
- Calculate the gradient of the **tangent**

The gradient at P is $\dfrac{a}{b}$ and it is negative.

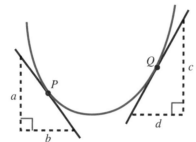

The gradient at Q is $\dfrac{c}{d}$ and it is positive.

Differentiation

You can use **differentiation** to calculate the gradient from the equation of a curve.

> **Key Point**
>
> If $y = ax^n$ where n is a positive integer,
> then $\dfrac{dy}{dx} = anx^{n-1}$.
>
> If $y = mx + c$
> then $\dfrac{dy}{dx} = m$.

If $y = x^n$ where n is a positive integer,

then the **derivative** $\dfrac{dy}{dx} = nx^{n-1}$.

y	x^2	$3x^4$	$6x - 3$	$2x^3 - 4x^2 - 9$
$\dfrac{dy}{dx}$	$2x$	$12x^3$	6	$6x^2 - 8x$

Example 1 The equation of a curve is $y = x^3 - 4x^2 + 2x$.

a) Find the gradient at $(2, -4)$.

b) Find the equation of the tangent to the curve at $(2, -4)$.

....

a) $\dfrac{dy}{dx} = 3x^2 - 8x + 2$ Differentiate each term.

If $x = 2$ then $\dfrac{dy}{dx} = 12 - 16 + 2 = -2$

The gradient at $(2, -4)$ is -2.   Substitute the value of x to find the gradient.

b) The equation of the tangent is $y = 2x + c$.   The gradient of the tangent is 2.

$(2, -4)$ is on the tangent so $-4 = 2 \times 2 + c$.   Substitute the coordinates of the point.

$c = -8$ Solve the equation to find c.

The equation of the tangent is $y = 2x - 8$.

Stationary points

A **stationary point** is a point where the gradient of the curve is zero. A and B are stationary points.

A is a **maximum point**. The value of y is larger than for points on each side.

B is a **minimum point**. The value of y is less than for points on each side.

A and B are also called **turning points**.

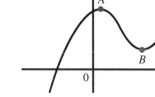

There are three ways to decide whether a stationary point is a maximum or a minimum. You can use any of these methods.

- Find the value of y at nearby points on each side.
- Make a sketch of the curve.
- Differentiate $\dfrac{dy}{dx}$ to find the second derivative $\dfrac{d^2y}{dx^2}$. If this is positive the point is a minimum, if it is negative the point is a maximum.

Example 2

a) Find the coordinates of the stationary points on the curve with the equation $y = 2x^3 - 3x^2 - 12x$.

b) Determine whether each stationary point is a minimum or a maximum. Give a reason for your answer.

···

a) $\dfrac{dy}{dx} = 6x^2 - 6x - 12$ Differentiate.

When $6x^2 - 6x - 12 = 0$

$x^2 - x - 2 = 0$ The derivative = 0 at a stationary point.

$(x - 2)(x + 1) = 0$ Divide by 6 to simplify the equation.

$x = 2$ or -1

When $x = 2$ then $y = 16 - 12 - 24 = -20$ Factorise and solve.

When $x = -1$ then $y = -2 - 3 + 12 = 7$

The stationary points are $(2, -20)$ and $(-1, 7)$.   Calculate the y-coordinates.

b) $\dfrac{d^2y}{dx^2} = 12x - 6$ Differentiate $\dfrac{dy}{dx}$ to find the second derivative.

When $x = 2$, $\dfrac{d^2y}{dx^2} = 18 > 0$ so $(2, -20)$ is a maximum.   Show whether $\dfrac{d^2y}{dx^2}$ is positive or negative.

When $x = -1$, $\dfrac{d^2y}{dx^2} = -18 < 0$ so $(-1, 7)$ is a minimum.   You could also answer part **b)** by finding values of y near $x = 2$ and $x = -1$ or by sketching the graph.

Quick Test

1. $y = x^4 + 3x^2 - 2$. Find $\dfrac{dy}{dx}$.

2. $y = ax^n$ and $\dfrac{dy}{dx} = 20x^4$. Find a and n.

3. The equation of a curve is $y = x^3 - 12x$. Find the coordinates of the stationary points.

4. A curve has the equation $y = x^4 - 18x^2 + 21$.
   Show that $(3, -60)$ is a stationary point. Is it a maximum or a minimum?

E Functions

Syllabus links:
E2.13

Learning aims:

- **E** Understand functions and function notation
- **E** Understand domain and range of a function
- **E** Find composite functions and inverse functions

Function notation

$$f(x) = 5x + 6 \qquad g(x) = \frac{3x-2}{4} \qquad h(x) = x^2 + 3$$

These are three examples of **functions**. You can evaluate a function for different values of x.

$$f(2) = 5 \times 2 + 6 = 16; \ g(7) = \frac{3 \times 7 - 2}{4} = 4.75; \ h(-10) = (-10)^2 + 3 = 103$$

The **domain** of a function $f(x)$ is the set of possible values of x.

The **range** of a function $f(x)$ is the set of possible values of $f(x)$.

If the domain of $f(x) = 8x - 3$ is $\{x: 0 \le x \le 10\}$ then the range is $\{y: -3 \le y \le 77\}$.

Inverse functions

The **inverse** of $f(x)$ is $f^{-1}(x)$ and it has the opposite effect to $f(x)$.

If $f(x) = 2x - 5$ then $f(4) = 3$ and $f^{-1}(3) = 4$; $f(-1.5) = -8$ and $f^{-1}(-8) = -1.5$.

To find an expression for $f^{-1}(x)$ when $f(x) = 2x - 5$:

Write $y = f(x)$: that is $y = 2x - 5$

Rearrange to make x the subject:
$$x = \frac{y + 5}{2}$$

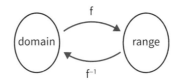

Replace y with x and write
$$f^{-1}(x) = \frac{x + 5}{2}.$$

Composite functions

If $f(x) = x^2 + 3$ and $g(x) = 2x - 1$ then $f(3) = 12$ and $g(3) = 5$

$fg(x)$ and $gf(x)$ are **composite functions**.

$fg(3) = f(g(3)) = f(5) = 28$ and $gf(3) = g(f(3)) = g(12) = 23$

$fg(x) = f(g(x)) = f(2x - 1)$

$= (2x - 1)^2 + 3$ Replace x in $f(x)$ by the expression for $g(x)$.

$= 4x^2 - 4x + 1 + 3$

$= 4(x^2 - x + 1)$

$gf(x) = g(f(x)) = g(x^2 + 3)$

$= 2(x^2 + 3) - 1$ Replace x in $g(x)$ by the expression for $f(x)$.

$= 2x^2 + 5$

> **Key Point**
>
> $fg(x)$ means first apply g then apply f.

Example 1 $f(x) = (x - 2)^2$ and $g(x) = \dfrac{2x + 6}{3}$

a) Find $f(-5)$.

b) Find $gf(8)$.

c) Find $g^{-1}(x)$.

d) Find $fg(x)$ writing your answer as simply as possible.

e) When the domain of $f(x)$ is $\{x: -4 \leq x \leq 4\}$ find the range of $f(x)$.

....

a) $f(-5) = (-5 - 2)^2 = 49$ Substitute -5 for x.

b) $gf(8) = g(36) = \dfrac{78}{3} = 26$ $f(8) = 36$

c) $y = \dfrac{2x + 6}{3}$ so $3y = 2x + 6$

$x = \dfrac{3y - 6}{2}$ Make x the subject.

So $f^{-1}(x) = \dfrac{3x - 6}{2}$ Replace y by x.

d) $fg(x) = f\left(\dfrac{2x + 6}{3}\right)$

$= \left(\dfrac{2x + 6}{3} - 2\right)^2 = \left(\dfrac{2x}{3}\right)^2$ Put the expression for $g(x)$ into f.

Because $\dfrac{2x + 6}{3}$

$-2 = \dfrac{2x + 6 - 6}{3}$

e) The range is $\{y: 0 \leq y \leq 36\}$.   The smallest value is f$(2) = 0$ and the largest is $f(-4) = 36$.

> **Quick Test**

1. $f(x) = 10 - 2x$ and the domain is $\{0 \leq x \leq 8\}$. Find the range.

2. $g(x) = \dfrac{3x - 1}{4}$. Find $g^{-1}(x)$.

3. $f(x) = x^3 + 1$ and $g(x) = \dfrac{36}{x}$. Find $fg(12)$ and $gf(2)$.

4. $g(x) = 4x - 1$ and $h(x) = 2 - 3x$. Write $gh(x)$ as simply as possible.

Introduction to algebra

1 When $n = 3$ find the value of:

a $4n - 2$ [1]

b $(n + 1)(2n + 1)$ [2]

2 Find the value of $\frac{1}{2}(xy + 2)^2$ when:

a $x = 3$ and $y = 4$ [2]

b $x = 2$ and $y = -3$ [2]

3 Find the value of $\frac{3a + 2b}{2a - b}$ when $a = 10$ and $b = 4$. [2]

4 Evaluate $\frac{v^2 - u^2}{uv}$ when $u = 5$ and $v = 20$. [2]

> Evaluate means find the value of.

5 The formula for the volume V of a sphere with a diameter d is $V = \frac{1}{6}\pi d^3$

Calculate the volume of a sphere of radius 2.4 cm. Round your answer to 3 s.f. [2]

6 The formula for the surface area S of a cuboid with sides a, b and c is $S = 2(ab + bc + ca)$.

Find the surface area of a cuboid with sides 2 cm, 3 cm and 5 cm. [2]

7 Copy and complete this table of values using the formula $y = 8x - 5$. [2]

x	−2	0	2	5
y			11	

8 Copy and complete this table of values using the formula $y = x^2 + 3x - 2$. [3]

x	−4	−2	0	2	4
y		−4			

Algebraic manipulation

1   Simplify $2x + 5x^2 + 3 - 6x^2 + 3x$ **[2]**

2   Expand:

a $4a(2a + 3b)$ **[2]**

b $(2x + y)(2x - 3y)$ **[2]**

3   Expand and simplify $3a(a + b) - b(a - 3b)$.   **[2]**

> The – sign before the second bracket will change the signs of the terms inside the bracket

4   Factorise each expression as much as possible.

a $4x^2 + 6x$ **[2]**

b $12xy - 9y^2 + 3y$ **[2]**

5   Expand $(x - 6)(x - 5)$.   **[2]**

6   Simplify as much as possible $2x(x + 3) + x(5x - 6)$.   **[2]**

7   Simplify as much as possible $(x + 2)(x - 2) - (x - 3)(x + 3)$.   **[3]**

8   Write $x^2 - 8x + 21$ in the form $(x - a)^2 + b$.   **[2]**

9   Factorise:

a $x^2 + 15x - 16$ **[2]**

b $x^2 - 8x + 16$ **[2]**

10   Factorise $x^3 - 3x^2 - 18x$.   **[2]**

11   Expand $(x + 3)(x - 1)(x + 2)$.   **[3]**

> **Show me**
>
> $(x + 3)(x - 1)(x + 2) = (x + 3)(x^2 + \ldots)$ Expand the last two brackets.
>
> $= x(x^2 + \ldots) + 3(x^2 \ldots)$ Expand the two brackets you have now.
>
> $= x^3 + \ldots x^2 + \ldots$ Group like terms together.

E Algebraic fractions

1 Write as a single fraction: $\dfrac{x}{3} + \dfrac{2x+1}{5}$. [2]

2 Write as a single fraction: $\dfrac{3}{a+3} - \dfrac{1}{a+1}$. [2]

3 Find $\dfrac{a}{4} \div \dfrac{a^2}{a+1}$. [3]

4 Simplify $\dfrac{4x}{x-1} \times \dfrac{x-3}{x+1}$. [3]

5 Write as a single fraction: $\dfrac{a+1}{a} - \dfrac{a+3}{a+2}$. [3]

6 Simplify $\dfrac{x^2 + 10x + 25}{x^2 + 6x + 5}$. [3]

7 Factorise and simplify $\dfrac{x^2 + 3x + 2}{x^2 - 1}$. [4]

8 Write as a single fraction: $\dfrac{x+1}{x-1} - \dfrac{x-4}{x+4}$. [4]

NC Further indices

1 **a** Write $\dfrac{1}{81}$ as a power of 9. [1]

b Write $\dfrac{1}{81}$ as a power of 3. [1]

2 **a** Write 5^{-2} as a decimal. [2]

b Find $\left(5^2\right)^0$. [2]

3 Simplify $\dfrac{c^6 \times c^5}{c^2}$. [2]

4 Simplify $24x^4 \div 2x^2$. [2]

5 Simplify $\left(3a^4\right)^{-2}$. [2]

6 Simplify $4x^6 y^2 \times 5x^{-5} y^3$. [2]

7 Solve the equation $2^x = 16$. [1]

E 8 Solve the equation $25^x = 125$. [2]

E 9 Simplify as much as possible $2x^{\frac{5}{4}} \times 5x^{-\frac{3}{4}}$. [2]

E 10 Find the value of $2^{\frac{1}{3}} \times 4^{-\frac{2}{3}}$. [3]

E 11 Simplify $\dfrac{2}{3} x^{\frac{3}{2}} \div \dfrac{4}{9} x^{-\frac{5}{2}}$. [2]

Equations

1 Solve the equation $\frac{x-3}{2} = 8$. [2]

2 Solve the equation $4(x-3) = 18 - x$. [2]

3 Rearrange the equation $y = 2x - 3z$ to make x the subject. [2]

4 Asher has x dollars. Bella has y dollars.

a Bella has 16 dollars more than Asher.

Write an equation to show this. [1]

b Bella has 3 times what Asher has.

Write an equation to show this. [1]

c Work out how much Asher has. [2]

5 Solve the simultaneous equations $x + 2y = 17$ and $3x + y = 21$. [4]

6 Solve the equation $x^2 - x = 11$. Give the answers to 3 d.p.

Use the formula $x = \dfrac{-b \pm \sqrt{b^2 - 4ac}}{2a}$ [4]

7 **a** Write the equation $x^2 = 4x + 1$ in the form $(x - a)^2 = b$. [2]

b Find the exact solution of the equation. [2]

8 Solve the equation $\frac{x}{2} + \frac{6}{x} = 4$. [4]

9 The sum of two numbers is 3.

The sum of the squares of the two numbers is 17.

Find the two numbers. [6]

> **Show me**

Call the numbers x and y

$x + y = \ldots$ and $x^2 + y^2 = \ldots$

From the first equation, $y = \ldots\ldots$

Substitute in the second equation: $x^2 + \ldots\ldots\ldots$

10 Here is a formula: $t = 2\sqrt{\dfrac{l}{g}}$.

Rearrange the formula to make g the subject. [2]

Inequalities

1 Show the inequality $x > -6$ on a number line. [1]

2

Use inequalities to represent this diagram. [1]

> A black dot means the end value is included

3 The number m is an even number and $20 < m < 30$.

List the possible values of m. [2]

4

The possible values of x are shown on this number line.

Use inequalities to show the possible values of x^2. [2]

E 5 Solve the inequality $5x - 7 \geq 2x + 11$. [2]

E 6 Solve the inequality $-13 < 4x - 7 \leq 13$. [3]

E 7 Show the region $3 \leq y \leq 7$ on a graph. [2]

E 8 **a** On a graph with positive axes only, draw the line $y = x + 1$. [2]

b On the same graph draw the line $x + y = 5$. [1]

c Show, by shading, the region where $y \geq 0$, $y \geq x + 1$ and $x + y \leq 5$. [2]

E 9 The vertices of a rectangle are (3, 4), (8, 4), (8, 7) and (3, 7).

Write down inequalities for x and y to represent the inside of the rectangle. [3]

Sequences

1 Here is a sequence: 6, 10, 14, x, y, 26, 30, …

a Write down the values of x and y. [1]

b Find the nth term of the sequence. [2]

c If the nth term is 98, find the value of n. [2]

2

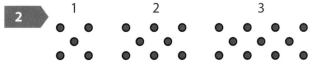

These are the first three patterns in a sequence.

a Draw the 4th pattern. [1]

b Write down the number of dots in each of the first four patterns. [2]

c Find the number of dots in the fifth pattern. [1]

d Find the number of dots on the nth pattern. [2]

e Which pattern has 50 dots? [2]

3 Here are two sequences.

Sequence A: 1, 4, 9, 16, 25,…   Sequence B: 3, 12, 27, 48, 75,…

a Find the 6th number in sequence A. [1]

b Find the 6th number in sequence B. [1]

c Find the nth term in sequence B. [2]

Here is another sequence.

Sequence C: 5, 14, 29, 50, 77,…

d Find the nth term in sequence C. [1]

4 Here is a sequence: 2, 3, 5, 8, 12,…

a Find the next three terms [2]

Two consecutive terms later in the series are 80 and 93.

b Find the term after 93. [1]

c Find the term before 80. [1]

5

These are the first three patterns in a sequence.

a Draw the next pattern. [1]

b Write down the number of crosses in each of the first four patterns. [1]

c Find the number of crosses in the nth pattern. [2]

d Which pattern has 110 crosses? [2]

6 A sequence is given by the formula $T_n = n(n - 8)$.

a Find T_1, T_2 and T_3. [2]

b Find the first positive number in the sequence. [2]

c Find the smallest number in the sequence. [2]

7 Here is a sequence: 11, 14, 19, 26, 35,…

a Find the next two terms. [2]

b Find the nth term. [2]

E Proportion

1 The mass of a coin is directly proportional to its diameter.

A coin with a diameter of 24 mm has a mass of 7.2 g.

Find the mass of a coin with a diameter of 20 mm. [3]

2 y is directly proportional to $\sqrt{2x+5}$. When $x = 2, y = 60$.

Find y when $x = 10$. [3]

> **Show me**

Write the inequality as an equation: $y = k\sqrt{}$

Substitute values of x and y: $60 = k\sqrt{}$..........

So k = ... and the equation is y = ...

When x = 10, y = ...

3 $y \propto x^3$. Find the values of a and b in this table. [5]

x	4	5	b
y	960	a	7680

4 y is inversely proportional to x^2. When $x = 0.2, y = 2.5$.

a Find y when $x = 0.4$. [3]

b Find x when $y = 0.4$. [2]

5 $y \propto \dfrac{1}{5x - 1}$. When $x = 1, y = 10$.

Find y when $x = 5$. [3]

NC 6 y is inversely proportional to the square root of x.

When $x = 2, y = 12$.

Find the exact value of y when $x = 16$. [3]

Graphs in practical situations

1 ▸ This graph can be used to convert from km/h to m/s.

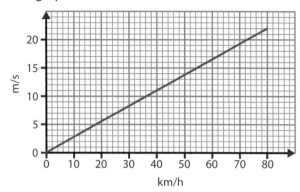

a Use the graph to convert 54 km/h to m/s. [1]

b Use the graph to convert 10 m/s to km/h. [1]

c Convert 60 m/s to km/h. [2]

2 ▸ This graph shows the journey of a cyclist from Acton to Corlon via Byfield.

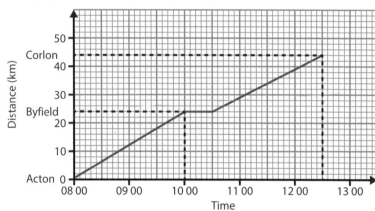

a Write down the time the journey started. [1]

b Find the average speed of the journey from Acton to Byfield. [2]

c How long did the cyclist stop at Byfield? [1]

d Work out the average speed from Byfield to Corlon. [3]

e Work out the average speed for the whole journey. [3]

3 ▸ This graph shows the speed of a car over a 15-second interval.

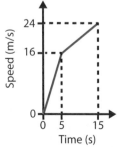

a Work out the acceleration for the first 5 seconds. [2]

Acceleration is the gradient of the speed-time graph

b   Work out the acceleration for the last 10 seconds.   [2]

c   Calculate the distance travelled.   [4]

Graphs of functions

1   **a**   Copy and complete this table of values of $y = 8 - x^2$ [2]

x	−4	−3	−2	−1	0	1	2	3	4
y		−1				7			

b   Use your table to draw a graph of $y = 8 - x^2$.

     Use a scale of 1 cm to 1 unit on the x-axis and 1 cm to 2 units on the y-axis.   [3]

c   On the same axes draw the line $y = x$.   [2]

d   Use the graph to solve the equation $8 - x^2 = x$.   [2]

2   **a**   Copy and complete this table of values of $y = \dfrac{10}{x}$.   [2]

x	1	2	3	4	5	6	7	8	9	10
y				2.5		1.67	1.43			

b   Draw a graph of $y = \dfrac{10}{x}$ for $1 \leq x \leq 10$. Use a scale of 1 cm to 1 unit on each axis.   [3]

c   On the same axes draw a graph of $y = \dfrac{5}{x}$.   [2]

E   **3**   **a**   Copy and complete this table of values of $y = x^3 - x^2 - 6x$.   [3]

x	−3	−2	−1	0	1	2	3	4
y			4		−6			

b   Use your table to draw a graph of $y = x^3 - x^2 - 6x$.

     Use a scale of 2 cm to 1 unit on the x-axis and 1 cm to 5 units on the y-axis.   [3]

c   On the same axes draw the line $y = 3x + 6$.   [3]

d   Use your graph to solve the equation $x^3 = x^2 + 9x + 6$.   [3]

E   **4**   **a**   Copy and complete this table of values of $y = x + 2\sqrt{x}$.   [3]

x	0	1	2	3	4	5
y			4.83			9.47

b   Use your table to draw a graph of $y = x + 2\sqrt{x}$.

     Use a scale of 2 cm to 1 unit on the x-axis and 1 cm to 1 unit on the y-axis.   [3]

c   Use the graph to solve the equation $\sqrt{x} = 3.5 - 0.5x$.   [3]

> **Show me**

If $\sqrt{x} = 3.5 - 0.5x$ then $y = x + 2\sqrt{x} = x + 2(\ldots\ldots\ldots\ldots) = \ldots\ldots$

From the graph, if $y = \ldots$ then $x = \ldots$

Sketching graphs

1 **a** Sketch the graph of $y = 10 - 2x$. [2]

   b Find the equation of this graph. [2]

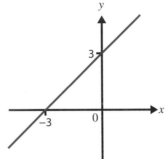

2 **a** Solve the equation $x^2 + 2x - 15 = 0$. [3]

   b Write $x^2 + 2x - 15$ in completed square form. [2]

   c Sketch the graph of $y = x^2 + 2x - 15$. [3]

3

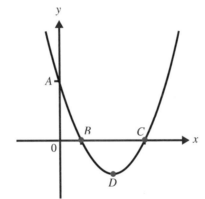

The equation of this curve is $y = x^2 - 8x + 7$.

Find the coordinates of A, B, C and D. [6]

4 **a** Factorise $x^3 - 4x$ as much as possible. [2]

   b Sketch the graph of $y = x^3 - 4x$. [3]

5 **a** $(10, a)$ and $(20, b)$ are on the graph of $y = 3 + \dfrac{4}{x}$. Find the values of a and b. [2]

   b Find the asymptotes of $y = 3 + \dfrac{4}{x}$. [2]

   c Sketch the graph of $y = 3 + \dfrac{4}{x}$. [3]

6 Sketch the graph of $y = 2^x$ for $-2 \leq x \leq 2$. [3]

E Differentiation

1
  a Draw the curve $y = \dfrac{6}{x}$ for $1 \le x \le 6$.

  Use a scale of 1 cm to 1 unit on each axis. [3]

  b Draw the tangent to the curve at $(3, 2)$. [2]

  c Use the tangent to estimate the gradient of the curve at $(3, 2)$. [2]

2 The equation of a curve is $y = x^3 - 2x^2 + 4x$.

  a Find $\dfrac{dy}{dx}$. [2]

  b Find the gradient of the curve where it crosses the y-axis. [2]

3 The equation of a curve is $y = 5x - x^2$.

  Find the equation of the tangent to the curve at the point where it crosses the positive x-axis. [5]

> **Show me**
>
> Where the curve crosses the x-axis $5x - x^2 = 0$
>
> Factorise, $x(\ldots\ldots\ldots) = 0$ so x = ... or ....
>
> The point required is $(\ldots, \ldots)$
>
> $\dfrac{dy}{dx} = \ldots\ldots\ldots$
>
> The gradient at $(\ldots, \ldots)$ is $\ldots\ldots$
>
> The equation of the tangent is $\ldots\ldots$

4 The equation of a curve is $y = x^3 - 6x^2 + 10x$.

  a Find $\dfrac{dy}{dx}$. [2]

  b Find the coordinates of the two points on the graph where the gradient is 1. [5]

5 The equation of a curve is $y = x^3 - 3x^2 + 3$.

  a Find $\dfrac{dy}{dx}$. [2]

  b Find the gradient at $(1, 2)$. [1]

  c Find the coordinates of the stationary points. [4]

  d State whether each stationary point is a maximum of a minimum.

  Give reasons for your answers. [3]

E Functions

1 $f(x) = \dfrac{12}{x} + 2$

   a   Find f(4).   **[1]**

   b   Find ff(3).   **[2]**

   c   Find $f^{-1}(x)$.   **[2]**

   d   When the domain of f(x) is $\{x : x \geq 1\}$ find the range of f(x).   **[2]**

2 $f(x) = 10 - 2x$ and $g(x) = (x - 3)^2$.

   a   Find f(3).   **[1]**

   b   Find fg(6).   **[2]**

   c   Find $f^{-1}(x)$.   **[2]**

   d   Solve the equation $g(x) = 4$.   **[2]**

3 $f(x) = 3x + 4$ and $g(x) = 5x - 2$.

   a   Find gg(2).   **[2]**

   b   Find fg(x). Write your answer as simply as possible.   **[2]**

   c   Find $fg(x) + gf(x)$.   **[2]**

   d   Solve the equation $f^{-1}(x) = 3$.   **[2]**

4 $h(x) = \dfrac{10}{x - 3}$

   a   Find h(−7).   **[1]**

   b   Find $h^{-1}(x)$.   **[2]**

   c   Solve the equation $h(x) = x$.   **[4]**

5 $f(x) = x^2 - 5$ and $g(x) = 2x + 3$.

   a   Find gf(4).   **[2]**

   b   Solve the equation $f(x) = 4$.   **[2]**

   c   Solve the equation $f(x) = g(x)$.   **[4]**

Linear graphs 1

Syllabus links:

C3.1; E3.1; C3.2;
E3.2; C3.3; E3.3;
C3.5; E3.5; C3.6;
E3.6

Learning aims:

- Draw straight-line graphs
- Find the gradient and the equation of a straight-line graph
- Find equations of parallel lines

The equation of a straight line

$y = 2x - 1$ is the equation of a straight line.

Here is a table of values:

x	−2	−1	0	1	2	3	4	5
y	−5	−3	−1	1	3	5	7	9

Here is a graph:

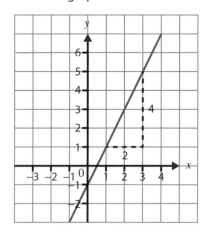

The **gradient** of the line is $\frac{4}{2} = 2$.

The **y-intercept** where the line crosses the y-axis is −1.

Both these numbers are in the equation $y = 2x - 1$

The gradient is 2.

The **y-intercept** is −1.

> **Key Point**
>
> $y = mx + c$ where m and c are numbers is the equation of a straight line. The gradient is m and the y-intercept is c.

Example 1

a) Find the gradient of this straight line.

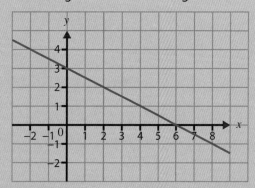

b) Write down the y-intercept.

c) Find the equation of the line.

....

a) gradient $= \frac{-3}{6} = -\frac{1}{2}$ 　　　Use the triangle formed by the axes.

b) The y-intercept is 3. 　　　Where the line crosses the y-axis.

c) $y = -\frac{1}{2}x + 3$ 　　　$y = $ (gradient) $x + $ (y-intercept)

Parallel lines

Parallel lines have the same gradient.

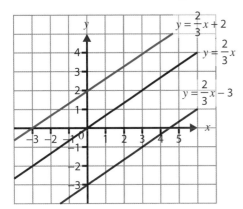

$$y = \frac{2}{3}x - 3 \qquad y = \frac{2}{3}x \qquad y = \frac{2}{3}x + 2$$

All these lines have a gradient of $\frac{2}{3}$. They are parallel.

Example 2 Find the equation of the line parallel to $y = 3x + 5$ that passes through $(4, 8)$.

The gradient is 3. | The coefficient of x.

The equation is $y = 3x + c$. | The equation always has this form.

$8 = 3 \times 4 + c$ | Substitute the coordinates $(4, 8)$.

$c = 8 - 12 = -4$

The equation is $y = 3x - 4$. | Solve the equation to find c.

> **Quick Test**

1. Find the gradient of the line $y = 6x - 8$.
2. **a)** Use this table of coordinates to draw a straight line.

x	0	2	4
y	−2	4	10

b) Find the gradient of the line.
c) Find the equation of the line parallel to $y = -x$ that passes through $(4, 2)$.

E Linear graphs 2

Syllabus links:
E3.1; E3.2; E3.3; E3.4;
E3.5; E3.6; E3.7

Learning aims:

- • **E** Straight-line graphs and their equations in various forms
- • **E** Gradient, length and midpoint of a line segment
- • **E** Parallel and perpendicular lines

Equation of a straight line graph

$y = -\frac{2}{3}x + 4$ is the equation of a straight line with a gradient of $-\frac{2}{3}$ and a y-intercept of 4.

The equation can be written in different ways such as:

$y = 4 - \frac{2}{3}x$ or $3y = -2x + 12$ or $2x + 3y = 12$

Example 1 The equation of a line is $4x + 5y = 20$.

a) Draw a graph of the line.

b) Find the gradient of the line.

....

a) If $x = 0$ then $5y = 20$ and $y = 4$ The easiest way is to find where the line crosses each axis.

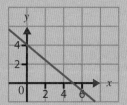

$(0, 4)$ is on the line.

If $y = 0$ then $4x = 20$ and $x = 5$

$(5, 0)$ is on the line.

b) $4x + 5y = 20$

You can find the gradient from the graph but you can also find it by rearranging the equation to make y the subject.

$5y = -4x + 20$

$y = -\frac{4}{5}x + 20$

Line segments

The gradient of the line through A and B is:

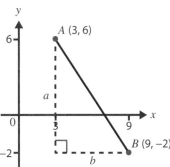

$$\frac{a}{b} = \frac{\text{difference between } y\text{-coordinates}}{\text{difference between } x\text{-coordinates}} = \frac{-2 - 6}{9 - 3} = \frac{-8}{6} = -\frac{4}{3}$$

Using Pythagoras's theorem, the length of the line segment
is $\sqrt{a^2 + b^2} = \sqrt{8^2 + 6^2} = 10$

The midpoint of the line segment $= \left(\frac{3 + 9}{2}, \frac{6 + -2}{2}\right) = (6, 2)$

> **Key Point**
>
> If $A_{(x_1, y_1)}$ and $B_{(x_2, y_2)}$ are two points:

- The gradient of the line through A and B is $\frac{y_2 - y_1}{x_2 - x_1}$

- The length of the line segment AB is $\sqrt{(x_2 - x_1)^2 + (y_2 - y_1)^2}$

- The midpoint of AB is $\left(\frac{x_1 + x_2}{2}, \frac{y_1 + y_2}{2}\right)$

Parallel and perpendicular lines

The line L has the equation $y = mx + c$. The gradient of the line is m.

A line parallel to L has the same gradient, m.

A line **perpendicular** to L has the gradient $-\frac{1}{m}$.

Example 2   A line L has the equation $2x + 5y = 40$.

Find the equation of the line perpendicular to L passing through (3, 4).

··

$5y = 40 - 2x \Rightarrow y = 8 - \frac{2}{5}x$ 　Rewrite the equation to make y the subject

Gradient of $L = -\frac{2}{5}$

Gradient of perpendicular line
$= \frac{5}{2} = 2.5$ 　The coefficient of x.

$y = 2.5x + c$

$4 = 2.5 \times 3 + c$ 　The equation of the perpendicular line

$c = 4 - 7.5 = -3.5$ 　Substitute the coordinates and find c.

The perpendicular line is
$y = 2.5x - 3.5$ 　This could be written as $2y = 5x - 7$

Here are the two lines in the worked example.

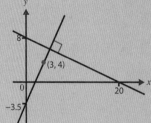

> ## Quick Test
>
> 1. Find the gradient of the line through $(-6, 0)$ and $(0, 9)$.
> 2. Find the gradient of the line with equation $6x + 5y = 12$.
> 3. Find the equation of a line perpendicular to $y = 10 - 2x$ that crosses the x-axis at $(6, 0)$.
> 4. P is $(-4, 2)$ and Q is $(1, 14)$.
>   a) Find the length of PQ.　b) Find the midpoint of PQ.

Linear graphs 1

1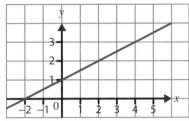

a Find the gradient of this line. [2]

b Find the equation of the line. [2]

> **Show me**

Two points on the line are (0, 1) and . . . . .

The gradient is $\dfrac{\ldots - 1}{\ldots - 0} = \ldots$

c Find the equation of the parallel line through (0, 4). [2]

2

x	1	3	7
y	5	3	−1

a Use this table of coordinates to draw a straight line. [3]

b Find the gradient of the line. [2]

c Find the y-intercept. [1]

d Write down the equation of the line. [1]

3 The equation of a straight line is $y = 4x + 10$.

a Find the gradient of the line. [1]

b Find the coordinates of the point where it crosses the y-axis. [1]

c Find the equation of a parallel line through the origin (0, 0). [1]

d Find the equation of a parallel line through (2, 0). [2]

4 a Find the equation of a straight line with a gradient of −2 and a y-intercept of 8. [2]

b Find the equation of a parallel line with a y-intercept of −4. [1]

c Find the equation of a parallel line through (1, 2). [2]

5 a Write down the y-intercept of this line. [1]

b Find the gradient. [2]

c When the line is extended it passes through (10, a). Find the value of a. [2]

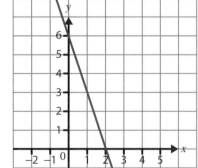

E Linear graphs 2

1 A is $(-10, 2)$ and B is $(-1, 14)$.

(a) Find the gradient of AB. [2]

(b) Find the length of AB. [2]

> Use Pythagoras' theorem to find the length.

(c) Find the midpoint of AB. [2]

2

(a) Find the gradient of this line. [2]

(b) Find the equation of this line. [2]

(c) Find the equation of a perpendicular line through $(2, 3)$. [3]

3 The equation of a line is $2x + 3y = 15$.

(a) The point $(a, 8)$ is on the line. Find the value of a. [2]

(b) Find the equation of a parallel line through $(6, 4)$. [3]

(c) Find the equation of a perpendicular line through $(6, 2)$. [3]

4 The line $3x + 4y = 18$ crosses the x-axis at A and the y-axis at B.

(a) Find the coordinates of A and B. [2]

(b) Find the length of AB. [2]

(c) Find the gradient of AB. [2]

(d) Find the equation of the line perpendicular to AB and passing through B. [3]

5 A line segment joins A (3, -5) and B (6, 7)

(a) Find the midpoint of the line segment AB [2]

(b) Find the equation of the straight line through A and B. [3]

6 The coordinates of P are (2, 5)

The coordinates of Q are (8, 1)

Work out the equation of the perpendicular bisector of PQ. [4]

Geometric terms and constructions

Syllabus links:
C4.1; E4.1; C4.2; E4.2

Learning aims:

- Geometrical terms for lines, angles and shapes
- Constructions using a ruler and compasses
- Nets

Geometrical terms

Angles

 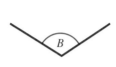 

acute angle	obtuse angle	reflex angle	right angle
$A < 90°$	$90° < B < 180°$	$C > 90°$	$90°$

Triangles

   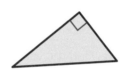

equilateral triangle	isosceles triangle	scalene triangle	right-angled triangle
3 equal sides	2 equal sides	all sides different	a 90° angle

Quadrilaterals

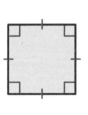 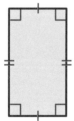 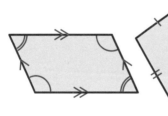 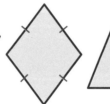

square   rectangle   parallelogram   kite   rhombus   trapezium

Polygons

  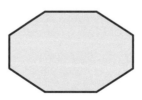 

pentagon	hexagon	octagon	decagon
(5 sides)	(6 sides)	(8 sides)	(10 sides)

> **Key Point**
>
> In a **regular polygon**:
> - all the sides and the same length
> - all the angles are the same size.

Solids

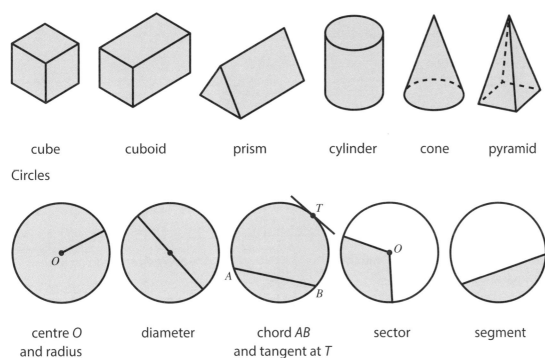

| cube | cuboid | prism | cylinder | cone | pyramid |

Circles

centre *O*   diameter   chord *AB*   sector   segment
and radius   and tangent at *T*

Nets

A net can be folded up to make a solid.

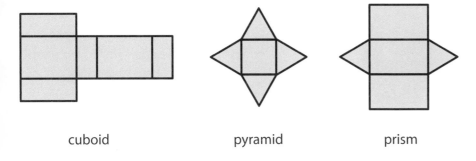

| cuboid | pyramid | prism |

Drawing a triangle

How to draw a triangle with sides 10.5 cm, 9 cm and 7.5 cm using a ruler and compasses.

- Draw a line 10.5 cm long.

- Use the compasses to draw an arc of radius 9 cm from one end.

- Draw an arc of radius 7.5 cm from the other end.

- Where the arcs cross is the third point of the triangle. Join it to the other two points.

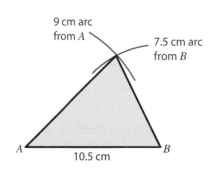

> **Quick Test**

1. Write down the number of sides in an octagon.
2. Write down the geometric name for a regular quadrilateral.
3. Write down the number of edges on a square-based pyramid.
4. Draw a circle with two perpendicular chords.

Scale drawings

Learning aims:

- Use scale drawings
- Use three figure bearings for directions

Syllabus links:
C4.3; E4.3

Scale drawings

Sam is making a **scale drawing** of a football pitch. Scale 1 cm to 5 m.

The length of the pitch is 108 m and the width is 55 m.

The length of the scale drawing is 108 ÷ 5 = 21.6 cm and the width is 55 ÷ 5 = 11 cm.

On Sam's drawing the width of the goal is 1.5 cm and the penalty spot is 2.2 cm from the goal-line.

On the pitch the width of the goal is 1.5 × 5 = 7.5 m and the penalty spot is 2.2 × 5 = 11 m away.

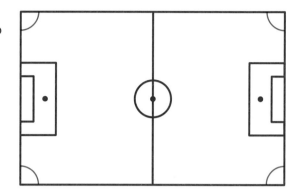

> **Key Point**
>
> Use the scale and be careful with the units.

Bearings

A **bearing** is used to give a direction.

It is an angle measured clockwise from north.

It is always given as three figures.

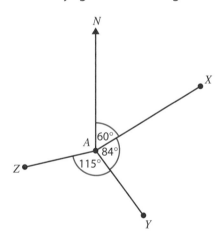

The bearing of X from A is 060°.

The bearing of Y from A is 60° + 84° = 144°.

The bearing of Z from A is 144° + 115° = 259°.

Example 1   A boat travels 2.5 km from A to B on a bearing of 168°.

It then changes direction and travels 3.6 km from B to C on a bearing of 291°.

a)   Make a scale drawing of the journey. Use the scale 1 cm to 0.5 km.

b)   Use measurements to find the distance and bearing of the return journey directly from C to A.

a)

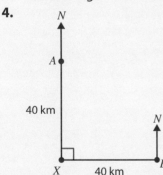

Start with a north line at A.

The length of AB on the drawing is 2.5 ÷ 0.5 = 5 cm. Draw the line with an angle of 168°.

Now draw a north line at B.

The length of BC is 3.6 ÷ 0.5 = 7.2 cm.

Draw the line at an angle of 291°.

b)   The bearing of A from C is 062°.   Draw a north line at C, draw the dashed line and measure the angle shown.

The distance is 5.6 × 0.5 = 2.8 km.   The distance on the drawing is 5.7 cm.

> **Quick Test**

1. A map has a scale of 1 cm to 4 km.
   Find the length on the ground when the map distance is 6.2 cm.
2. A window is 3.2 m wide and 1.8 m high.
   Find the size of the window on a scale drawing with the scale 1 cm to 50 cm.
3. The bearing of B from A is 260°. Work out the bearing of A from B.
4.

A is 40 km north of X. B is 40 km east of X.
Find the bearing of B from A.

Similarity

Syllabus links:
C4.4; E4.4

Learning aims:

* Calculate length in similar shapes
* **E** Understand the relationship between lengths and areas in similar shapes
* **E** Understand the relationship between lengths and volumes in similar solids

Similar shapes

These two shapes are **similar**.

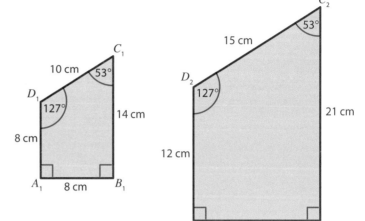

Corresponding angles are the same.

The ratio between corresponding sides is always the same:

$$\frac{A_2B_2}{A_1B_1} = \frac{12}{8} = 1.5$$

$$\frac{B_2C_2}{B_1C_1} = \frac{21}{14} = 1.5$$

$$\frac{C_2D_2}{C_1D_1} = \frac{15}{10} = 1.5$$

$A_2B_2C_2D_2$ is an enlargement of $A_1B_1C_1D_1$ with a scale factor of 1.5

Example 1

a) Explain why these triangles are similar.

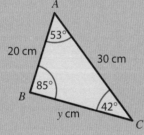

b) Find x.

c) Find y.

....

a) The angles of the triangles are the same. This is sufficient to show that to triangles are similar.

b) $\dfrac{XY}{AB} = \dfrac{25}{20} = 1.25$

XY and AB are corresponding sides because they are both opposite 42°.

$\dfrac{XZ}{AC} = \dfrac{x}{30} = 1.25$

XZ and AC are corresponding sides.

$x = 1.25 \times 30 = 37.5$

Solve the equation for x.

c) $\dfrac{YZ}{BC} = \dfrac{30}{y} = 1.25$

YZ and BC are corresponding sides.

$y = \dfrac{30}{1.25} = 24$

Solve the equation for y.

E Similar areas

If two shapes are similar with a length scale factor of k then the area scale factor is k^2.

The area of $A_1 B_1 C_1 D_1$ in the first diagram is $88 \, cm^2$.

The linear scale factor is 1.25 so the area scale factor is 1.25^2.

The area of $A_2 B_2 C_2 D_2$ is $88 \times 1.25^2 = 198 \, cm^2$.

The area of triangle ABC in the first worked example is $240 \, cm^2$.

The linear scale factor is 1.25

The area of DEF is $240 \times 1.25^2 = 375 \, cm^2$.

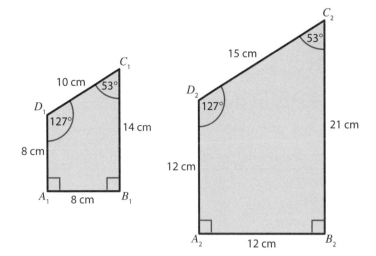

E Similar volumes

Two solids are similar when the ratio of corresponding sides are the same. One is an enlargement of the other.

Example 2

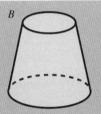

These two solids are similar. Complete this table.

Shape	Height (cm)	Area of base (cm²)	Volume (cm³)
A	20	300	
B	24		8640

> **Key Point**
>
> If the ratio of corresponding sides in two similar solids is k then the ratio of corresponding areas is k^2 and the ratio of the volumes is k^3.

....

The linear scale factor = $24 \div 20 = 1.2$ The heights are lengths.

Area scale factor = $1.2^2 = 1.44$

Area of base of B = $300 \times 1.44 = 432 \, cm^2$ Multiply by the area factor.

Volume scale factor = $1.2^3 = 1.728$

Volume of A = $8640 \div 1.728 = 5000 \, cm^3$ Divide the find the volume of A.

> **Quick Test**
>
> 1. The shortest side of a triangle is 24 mm and the longest side is 38 mm.
>   The shortest side of a similar triangle is 84 mm. Find the longest side.
>
> **E** 2. A trapezium 32 cm wide has an area of $1440 \, cm^2$.
>   Find the area of a similar trapezium 18 cm wide.
>
> **E** 3. A pyramid 15 cm high has a volume of $800 \, cm^3$.
>   Find the volume of a similar pyramid with a height of 45 cm.

Symmetry

Syllabus links:
C4.5; E4.5

Learning aims:

- Recognise lines of symmetry and rotational symmetry in two dimensions
- **E** Recognise planes of symmetry and rotational symmetry in three dimensions

Symmetry of shapes

Shapes can have reflection symmetry or rotation symmetry.

Here are the symmetries of some common shapes.

	Isosceles triangle 1 line of symmetry no rotational symmetry		Equilateral triangle 3 lines of symmetry rotational symmetry of order 3		Rectangle 2 lines of symmetry rotational symmetry of order 2
	Square 4 lines of symmetry rotational symmetry of order 4		Rhombus 2 lines of symmetry rotational symmetry of order 2		Parallelogram no lines of symmetry rotational symmetry of order 2
	Kite 1 line of symmetry no rotational symmetry		Regular pentagon 5 lines of symmetry rotational symmetry of order 5		Circle every diameter is a line of symmetry

E Symmetry of solids

Solids can have:

- reflection symmetry with a **plane of symmetry**
- rotation symmetry with an **axis of symmetry**.

	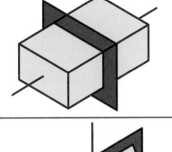	<ul><li>This is a cuboid.</li><li>There is a plane of symmetry through the midpoint of four parallel edges.</li><li>There is an axis of symmetry through the centre of two opposite faces. The order of rotational symmetry about this axis is 2.</li></ul>
	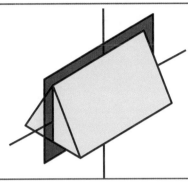	<ul><li>This is a triangular prism. The cross-section is an equilateral triangle.</li><li>There is a plane of symmetry that passes through a vertex and the midpoint of the opposite edge of each of the triangular faces.</li><li>An axis of symmetry passes through the centre of each triangular face. The order of rotational symmetry about this axis is 3.</li><li>An axis of symmetry passes through the midpoint of an edge and the centre of the opposite rectangular face. The order of rotational symmetry about this axis is 2.</li></ul>

Here are some more solids.

Cylinder		<ul><li>An axis of symmetry passes through the centre of each circular face.</li><li>A plane of symmetry passes thorough the centre of the cylinder parallel to the circular faces.</li></ul>
Cone		<ul><li>There is an axis of symmetry through the vertex and the centre of the base.</li><li>Any plane through the vertex of a cone and a diameter of the base is a plane of symmetry.</li></ul>
Square-based pyramid		<ul><li>There is an axis of symmetry through the vertex and the centre of the square base.</li><li>Any plane through a line of symmetry of the base and the vertex of the pyramid is a plane of symmetry.</li></ul>

> **Quick Test**

1. Find the number of lines of symmetry on a regular hexagon.
2. Find the order of rotational symmetry of a regular octagon.
E 3. Find the number of planes of symmetry for a square-based pyramid.

Angles

Learning aims:

Syllabus links:
C4.6; E4.6

- Calculate angles around a point
- Calculate angles of triangles and quadrilaterals
- Angles of regular polygons
- **E** Angles of irregular polygons

Angles around a point

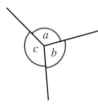

The sum of the angles at a point is 360°:

$$a + b + c = 360°$$

The sum of the angles on a straight line is 180°:

$$a + b + c = 180°$$

Vertically opposite angles are equal:

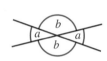

the angles marked a are equal

the angles marked b are equal.

Triangles and quadrilaterals

The sum of the angles of any triangle is 180°:

$$a + b + c = 180°$$

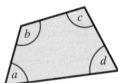

The sum of the angles of any quadrilateral is 360°:

$$a + b + c + d = 360°$$

Parallel lines

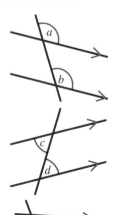

Corresponding angles are equal:

$$a = b$$

Alternate angles are equal:

$$c = d$$

The sum of **co-interior angles** is 180°:

$$e + f = 180°$$

Regular polygons

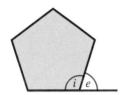

This is a **regular** pentagon.

All the sides are equal.

All the angles are equal.

i is an **interior angle** of this pentagon.

e is an **exterior angle**.

The sum of the exterior angles is 360°.

Exterior angle, $e = \dfrac{360}{5} = 72°$

Interior angle, $i = 180 - e = 108°$

A regular octagon has 8 sides.

- The exterior angle is $\dfrac{360}{8} = 45°$.
- The interior angle is $180 - 45 = 135°$.

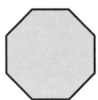

> ### Key Point
>
> If a regular polygon has n sides, the exterior angle is $\dfrac{360°}{n}$ and the interior angle is $180° - \dfrac{360°}{n}$.

E Irregular polygons

This is an **irregular** pentagon because the angles and the sides are not all equal.

It can be divided into three triangles. The angles of the triangle are the angles of the pentagon.

So the sum of the angles of the pentagon are $3 \times 180° = 540°$. This is true for any pentagon.

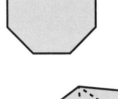

> ### Key Point
>
> If a polygon has n sides, the sum of the angles is $(n - 2) \times 180°$.

Shape	Sum of angles
pentagon (5 sides)	$3 \times 180° = 540°$
hexagon (6 sides)	$4 \times 180° = 720°$
octagon (8 sides)	$6 \times 180° = 1080°$

> ### Quick Test
>
> NC 1. Three angles of a quadrilateral are 80°. Find the fourth angle. Give a reason for your answer.
>
> NC 2. Find the values of a and b. Give reasons for your answers.
>
>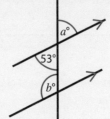
>
> 3. Find the interior angle of a regular 9-sided polygon.
>
> E 4. Find the sum of the angles of a 12-sided polygon.

Circle theorems

Syllabus links:
C4.7; E4.7; E4.8

Learning aims:

- Use geometrical properties of circles to find angles
- **E** Use symmetry properties of circles

Semicircles and tangents

O is the centre of the circle.

AB is a diameter.

ST is the **tangent** at A.

C is an angle in a **semicircle**.

- The angle in a semicircle at C is 90°.
- The angle between the tangent AT and the diameter AB is 90°.

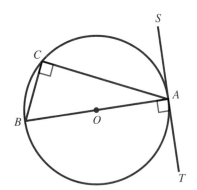

E Geometrical properties

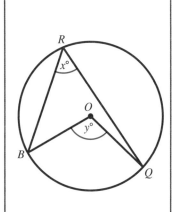	O is the centre of the circle. POQ is the angle at the centre. PRQ is the angle at the circumference. The angle at the centre is twice the angle at the circumference: $y = 2x$	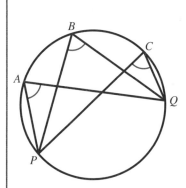	A, B and C are angles at the circumference from P and Q. The angles at A, B and C are all equal. Angles at the circumference in the same segment are equal.
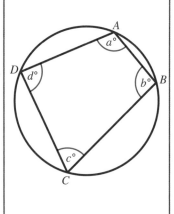	$ABCD$ is a **cyclic quadrilateral**. The vertices are all on a circle. The sum of opposite angles of a cyclic quadrilateral is 180°: $a + c = 180$ and $b + d = 180$	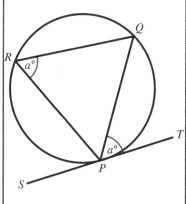	ST is a tangent to the circle at P. Angles TPQ and PRQ are angles in the same segment. Angles in the same segment are equal.

E Symmetry properties

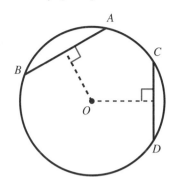

AB and CD are two chords of the circle.

If they are the same length, they are the same distance from the centre of the circle. The dashed lines are perpendicular bisectors of the chords. They pass through the centre O of the circle.

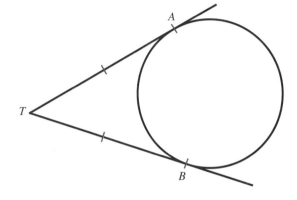

TA and TB are the two tangents from T to the circle.

TA and TB are the same length.

Example 1 Find x and y.

Give reasons for your answers.

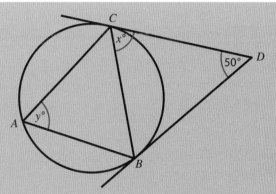

....

CD and BD are tangents so they are the same length and triangle BDC is isosceles.

$x = (180 - 50) \div 2 = 65°$

x and y are angles in the same segment so they are equal and $y = 65°$.

NC Quick Test

1. AB is a diameter of the circle.
   Work out the value of a.

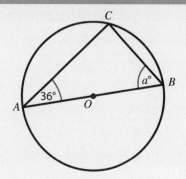

E 2. Two angles of a cyclic quadrilateral are 45° and 113°.
   Work out the other two angles.

Geometric terms and constructions

1 Write down the mathematical name for:

a a polygon with 10 sides [1]

b a quadrilateral with exactly one air of parallel sides [1]

c a regular triangle. [1]

2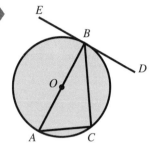

O is the centre of this circle.

Write down the mathematical name for:

a AB [1]

b BC [1]

c ED. [1]

3 This is the net of a cuboid.

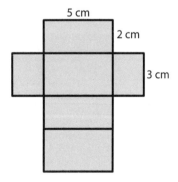

a Find the total area of all the faces of the cuboid. [2]

b Find the total length of all the edges of the cuboid. [2]

c Find the volume of the cuboid. [2]

4 **a** Using a ruler and compasses, draw a triangle with sides 7.9 cm, 8.6 cm and 6.1 cm. [4]

b Measure the largest angle. [1]

Scale drawings

1

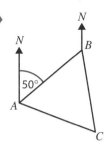

ABC is an equilateral triangle.

> A **bearing** is an angle measured clockwise from north. It is written with three figures.

a Find the bearing of B from A. [1]

b Find the bearing of C from A. [2]

c Find the bearing of C from B. [2]

2

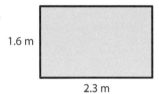

This is the frame of a large rectangular picture.

a Make a scale drawing. Scale 1 cm to 20 cm. [3]

b By measuring find the length of the diagonal of the picture frame. [2]

3

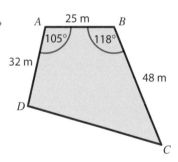

This is a sketch of a field ABCD.

a Make a scale drawing of the field. Start with side AB. Scale 1 cm to 5 m. [4]

b By measuring, find the length of the side CD. [2]

4

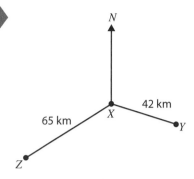

Y is 42 km from X on a bearing of 113°.

Z is 65 km from X on a bearing of 236°.

a Make a scale drawing of X, Y and Z. Use the scale 1 cm to 10 km. [4]

b By measuring find the distance from Y to Z. [2]

c By measuring find the bearing of Z from Y. [2]

Similarity

1

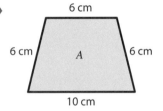

Not to scale

These two trapeziums are similar.

Find the missing length of trapezium B. [2]

2

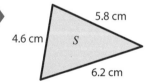

Triangle T is similar to triangle S.

The shortest side of triangle T is 11.5 cm.

Work out the perimeter of triangle T. [4]

> **Show me**
>
> *Shortest side of original triangle = ... cm so scale factor is 11.5 ÷ ... = ...*
>
> *Either other sides are 5.8 × ... = ... and 6.2 × ... = ... so perimeter = ... cm*
>
> *Or perimeter = (4.6 + 5.8 + ...) × ... = ... cm*

3

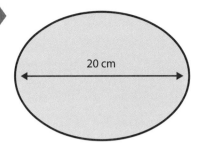

20 cm

This shape is an ellipse.

It is 20 cm long and the area is 250 cm^2.

Find the area of a similar ellipse 28 cm long. [3]

4

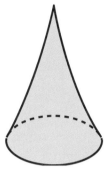

This solid is 15 cm high. Its volume is 400 cm^3.

A similar solid is 25 cm high.

a Find the volume of the similar solid. Round your answer to 3 significant figures. [3]

The area of the base of the similar solid is 278 cm^2.

b Find the area of the base of the original solid. [3]

Symmetry

1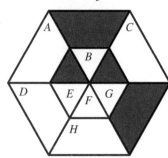

a Write down the letters of two regions that you can shade to make a shape with rotational symmetry of order 3. [2]

b Write down the number of lines of symmetry for this new shape. [2]

2

a Copy this shape. Shade one more square so that the shape has one line of symmetry. [1]

b Copy the shape again. Shade a different square so that the shape has one line of symmetry. [1]

c Copy the shape again. Shade one more square so that it has rotational symmetry. [1]

E 3 This is a cuboid with two square faces.

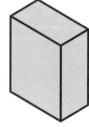

a Find the number of planes of symmetry. [2]

b The order of rotational symmetry about an axis of symmetry is 4.

Describe the position of this axis of symmetry. [2]

E 4 This is a cube.

a The order of rotational symmetry about an axis of symmetry is 2.

Describe the position of this axis of symmetry. [2]

b The order of rotational symmetry about a different axis of symmetry is 3.

Describe the position of this axis of symmetry. [2]

Angles

1

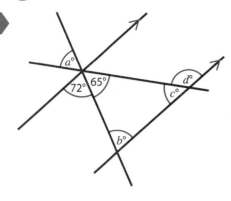

a   Find the value of a. Give a reason for your answer.   [2]

b   Find the value of b. Give a reason for your answer.   [2]

c   Find the value of c. Give a reason for your answer.   [2]

d   Find the value of d. Give a reason for your answer.   [2]

2   **a**   Two angles of a triangle are 63° and 54°. Show that the triangle is isosceles.   [2]

b   One angle of a different isosceles triangle is 112°. Find the other two angles.   [2]

3   **a**   Work out the exterior angle of a regular hexagon.   [2]

b   Find the interior angle of a regular 10-sided polygon.   [3]

4   **a**   The sum of the angles of a polygon is 2340°. Work out the number of sides.   [2]

b   The sides of a pentagon are $x°$, $(x + 10)°$, $(x + 20)°$, $(x + 30)°(x + 30)°$ and $(x + 40)°$.

Work out the value of x.   [3]

Circle theorems

NC **1** *AB* is a diameter of the circle. *PAQ* is the tangent at *A*.

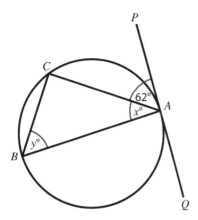

a Find *x*. Give a geometrical reason for your answer. **[2]**

A **geometrical reason** means stating the theorem you are using.

b Find *y*. Give a geometrical reason for your answer. **[2]**

NC **E** **2** *A*, *B*, *C* and *D* are points on a circle.

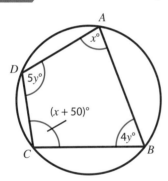

a Find the value of *x*. **[2]**

b Find the value of *y*. **[2]**

NC **E** **3** *EAF* is a tangent to the circle at *A*.

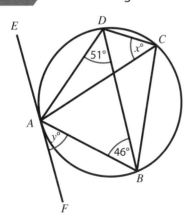

a Find *x*. Give a geometrical reason for your answer. **[2]**

b Find *y*. Give a geometrical reason for your answer. **[2]**

NC E 4

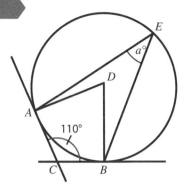

D is the centre of the circle.

AC and BC are tangents.

Work out the value of a. Give geometrical reasons.

[3]

Show me

Angle DAC = angle DBC = ...   Reason: ....

Angle ADB = 360 – .... = ...   Reason: ....

Angle AEB = ...   Reason: ....

Units of measure

Learning aims:

- Use metric units of length, area, volume, capacity and mass
- Convert between metric units

Syllabus links:
C5.1; E5.1

Units of length

Lengths can be measured in millimetres (mm), centimetres (cm), metres (m) and kilometres (km).

1 cm = 10 mm   1 m = 100 cm = 1000 mm   1 km = 1000 m

How to convert units of length:

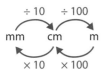 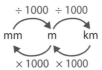

Units of area

Area is measured in square units: mm^2, cm^2, m^2 and km^2.

1 cm = 10 mm 1 cm = 10 mm (square)	$1\ cm^2 = 10\ mm \times 10\ mm = 100\ mm^2$
1 m = 100 cm 1 m = 100 cm (square)	$1\ m^2 = 100\ cm \times 100\ cm = 10\ 000\ cm^2$
1 km = 1000 m 1 km = 1000 m (square)	$1\ km^2 = 1000\ m \times 1000\ m = 1\ 000\ 000\ m^2$

Units of volume

Volume is measured in cube units: mm^3, cm^3, m^3 and km^3.

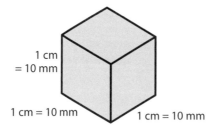

$1\ cm^3 = 10\ mm \times 10\ mm \times 10\ mm = 1000\ mm^3$

$1\ m^3 = 100\ cm \times 100\ cm \times 100\ cm = 1\ 000\ 000\ cm^3$

Example 1 The sides of this cuboid are 20 mm, 35 mm and 52 mm

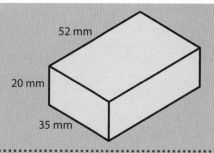

52 mm

20 mm

35 mm

a) Find the area of the smallest face in cm^2.

b) Find the volume of the cuboid in cm^3.

....

a) There are two methods:

$20 \times 35 = 700$ mm^2 = 7 cm^2

or

$2 \times 3.5 = 7$ cm^2

Use either method

Find the answer in mm^2 and divide by 100.

Change the lengths to cm and multiply.

b) There are two methods:

$20 \times 35 \times 52 = 36\ 400$ mm^2 = 36.4 cm^3

or

$2 \times 3.5 \times 5.2 = 36.4$ cm^3

Use either method

Find the answer in mm^3 and divide by 1000.

Change the lengths to cm and multiply.

Units of capacity

Measure capacity in litres (*l*). Use it for liquids.

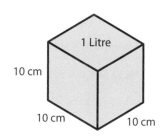

1 Litre

10 cm

10 cm   10 cm

A litre is the same as a cube with a side of 10 cm.

$1\ l = 10 \times 10 \times 10 = 1000$ cm^3

1 m$^3 = 1000\ l$

Units of mass

Measure mass in grams (g) or kilograms (kg)

1 kg = 1000 g

SUGAR

A paper clip has a mass of about 1 g.   A bag of sugar has a mass of 1 kg.

> **Quick Test**

1. Which of these could be the mass of a man?
   9 kg   80 kg   700 kg   6000 g
2. Change 4520 mm to m.
3. The capacity of a tank is 6.2 m^3. Find the capacity in litres.
4. Write 90 m in km.

Perimeter and area

Syllabus links:
C5.2; E5.2

Learning aims:

- Finding the perimeter and area of a rectangle, triangle, parallelogram and trapezium
- Perimeter and area of compound shapes

Four common shapes

The perimeter of a shape is the distance around the outside.

The area of a shape is the amount of space it covers.

Rectangle	Triangle
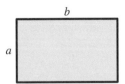	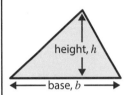
Perimeter = $2(a + b)$ Area = ab	Area = $\frac{1}{2} \times$ base $\times$ height $= \frac{1}{2}bh$
Parallelogram	Trapezium
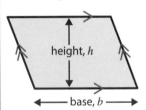	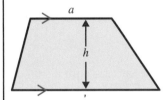
Area = base $\times$ height $= bh$	Area = mean of parallel sides $\times$ height $= \frac{a + b}{2} \times h$

Example 1   This shape is made by putting together two identical rectangles.

a)   Find the area of the shape.

b)   Find the perimeter of the shape.

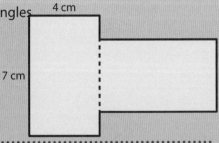

....

a) $2 \times 4 \times 7 = 56 \text{ cm}^2$

Each rectangle is 4 cm by 7 cm with an area of 28 cm^2.

Write the missing lengths on the diagram.

b)

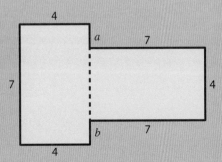

You do not know a and b but $a + b = 7 - 4 = 3$

$7 + 4 + 3 + 7 + 4 + 7 + 4 = 36$ cm   Going clockwise from the left hand side. The 3 is $a + b$.

> **Quick Test**

1. The area of a square is 81 cm² . Find the perimeter.
2. The area of this right-angled triangle is 42 cm² . Find the value of x.

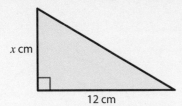

3.

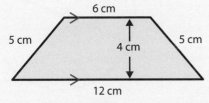

   a) Find the perimeter of this trapezium.
   b) Find the area of the trapezium.

4. A square is removed from a rectangle to make this shape.

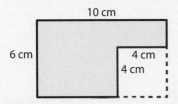

   Find:
   a) the perimeter
   b) the area.

Circles, arcs and sectors

Syllabus links:
C5.3; E5.3

Learning aims:

- Calculating the circumference and area of a circle
- Calculating the length of an arc and the area of a sector

Circumference and area

The diagram shows the diameter, d, and the radius, r, of a circle.

The perimeter of a circle is called the **circumference**.

A formula for the circumference, C, of a circle is $C = \pi d$ or $C = 2\pi r$.

A formula for the area, A, of a circle is $A = \pi r^2$.

The value of π is 3.14159…. You will find it on your calculator.

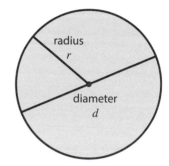

Sectors 1

This is a sector.

It is part of a circle.

OA and OB are radii.

The curved line AB is an **arc** of the circle.

Example 1   This is a sector of a circle of radius 12 cm.

The angle of the sector is 45°.

Calculate:

a)   the perimeter of the sector

b)   the area of the sector.

Give your answer to a in terms of π.

> **Key Point**
>
> The instruction "give your answer in terms of π" means leaving the answers in exact form instead of using your calculator and rounding the answer.

....

a)   The fraction of the circle is $\dfrac{45}{360} = \dfrac{1}{8}$ A circle is 360°.

The arc length is $\dfrac{1}{8} \times 2 \times \pi \times 12 = 3\pi$ cm   Use the formula $2\pi r$ where $r = 12$.

The perimeter is $12 + 12 + 3\pi = 24 + 3\pi$ This is the exact answer in terms of π.

b)   The area of the sector is $\dfrac{1}{8} \times \pi \times 12^2$ The same fraction as in **(a)**.

Use the formula πr^2 where $r = 12$.

$= 18\pi$ cm^2 This is the exact answer in terms of π.

$= 56.5$ cm^2 to 3 s.f.   Use a calculator and round your answer.

E Sectors 2

This circle has been divided into two sectors.

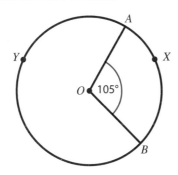

There are two arcs.

The shorter arc AXB is the **minor arc**.

The longer arc AYB is the **major arc**.

The length of the minor arc is $\frac{105}{360} \times 2 \times \pi \times 8.6 = 15.8$ cm to 3 s.f.

The angle of the major arc is $360 - 105 = 255°$

so the length of the major arc is $\frac{255}{360} \times 2 \times \pi \times 8.6 = 38.3$ cm to 3 s.f.

Use the same fractions to find the areas of the minor and major arcs.

> ### Quick Test
>
> 1. The circumference of a circle is 250 cm. Calculate the diameter.
> 2. The area of a circle is 100 cm^2. Calculate the radius.
>
> **NC** 3. This is a quarter of a circle of radius 10 cm.
>
>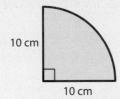
>
> 10 cm
>
> Find the area. Give your answer in terms of π.
>
> **E** 4. A sector of angle 130° is removed from a circle of radius 19 cm.
> Calculate the area of the remaining sector.

Surface area and volume

Learning aims:

- Calculate the surface areas and volumes of common solids

Common solids

The volume of a solid is the amount of space it occupies.

The surface area of a solid is the total area of all the surfaces.

Cuboid

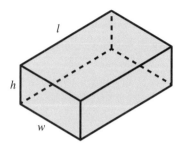

Volume = length × width × height = lwh

Surface area = total area of six faces

= $2lw + 2wh + 2hl$

Prism

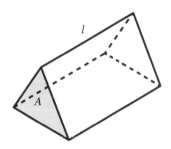

Volume = cross-sectional area × length = Al

Cylinder

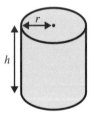

Area of base = πr^2

Volume = area of base × height = $\pi r^2 h$

Area of curved surface = $2\pi rh$

Pyramid

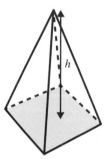

Volume = $\frac{1}{3}$ × area of base × height = $\frac{1}{3}Ah$

Cone

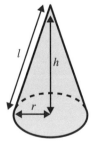

Area of base = πr^2

Volume = $\frac{1}{3}$ × area of base × height = $\frac{1}{3}\pi r^2 h$

Area of curved surface = πrl

Sphere

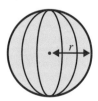

Volume = $\frac{4}{3}\pi r^3$

Area of curved surface = $4\pi r^2$

Example 1 The volume of a sphere is 1000 cm^3.

Find the diameter of the sphere.

....

$\frac{4}{3}\pi r^3 = 1000$

$r^3 = \dfrac{3000}{4\pi}$ The formula for the volume of a sphere.

$r = \sqrt[3]{\dfrac{3000}{4\pi}} = 6.203\ldots$

diameter $= 2r = 12.407\ldots = 12.4$ cm to 3 s.f.   Solve it to find the radius.

The diameter is twice the radius.

Do not round the answer until the end.

> **Quick Test**

1. The sides of a cuboid are x cm, $2x$ cm and $3x$ cm. The volume of the cuboid is 384 cm^3.
   Find the value of x.
2. A pyramid is 2.4 m high, and the volume is 12 m^3.
   Find the area of the base of the pyramid.
3. The diameter of the base of a cylinder is 24 cm. The height is 30 cm.
   a) Find the volume of the cylinder.
   b) Find the area of the curved surface.
   Round your answers to 3 significant figures.
4. The surface area of a sphere is 100 cm^2.
   Calculate the radius.

Compound shapes and solids

Syllabus links:
C5.5; E5.5

Learning aims:

- Find the perimeters and areas of compound solids or parts of solids
- Find the surface areas and volumes of compound solids or parts of solids

Compound shapes

Compound shapes are formed by putting together two or more different shapes.

You can find the perimeter or the area by using the perimeter or the area of the separate shapes.

Example 1 This shape is made from a rectangle and semicircle.

Work out:

a) the perimeter of the shape

b) the area of the shape.

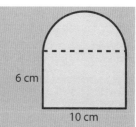

6 cm

10 cm

a) The diameter of the semicircle is 10 cm.   The diameter is the side of the rectangle.

Perimeter of semicircle is $\frac{1}{2} \times \pi \times 10 = 5\pi$ cm

Perimeter of shape = $6 + 10 + 6 + 5\pi$ Circumference = $\pi \times$ diameter

$= 22 + 5\pi = 37.7$ cm

Add the four sides.

b) Area of semicircle = $\frac{1}{2} \times \pi \times 5^2 = 12.5\pi$ cm^2

Area of rectangle = $6 \times 10 = 60$ cm^2 The radius of the circle is 5 cm.

Area of shape = $60 + 12.5\pi = 99.3$ cm^2

Parts of solids

You can form a new solid by removing part of another solid.

Use facts about the original solid to find the surface area and volume of the new solid.

Example 2 This is half a sphere of radius 1.50 m.

Find the total surface area.

Curved surface = $\frac{1}{2} \times 4 \times \pi \times 1.50^2 = 14.14$ cm^2 Surface area of a whole sphere = $4\pi r^2$

Area of circle = $\pi \times 1.5^2 = 7.07$ cm^2 Add the area of the curved surface and the

Total surface area = $14.14 + 7.07$ circle for the total surface area.

$= 21.2$ cm^2 to 3 s.f.

Compound solids

Compound solids are formed by putting together two or more different solids.

You can find the perimeter or the area by using the perimeter or the area of the separate shapes.

Example 3 This solid is a cube of side 12 cm with a pyramid on top.

The total height is 20 cm.

Calculate the volume of the shape.

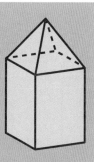

Volume of cube = $12 \times 12 \times 12 = 1728$ cm^3

Area of base of pyramid = $12 \times 12 = 144$ cm^2 This is one face of the cube.

Height of pyramid = $20 - 12 = 8$ cm   Total height – height of cube

Volume of pyramid = $\frac{1}{3} \times 144 \times 8 = 384$ cm^3 Volume of a pyramid = $\frac{1}{3}Ah$

Total volume = $1728 + 384 = 2112$ cm^3

> **Quick Test**

1. This shape is made by removing one rectangle from another.
   a) Find the area of the shape.
   b) Find the perimeter of the shape.

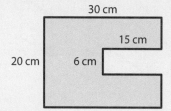

NC 2. This shape is made from three semicircles.

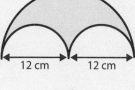

   Find the perimeter of the shape.
   Leave π in your answer.

3. This solid is made from a cone and a cylinder.
   The radius of the cylinder is 5 cm.
   Height of the cylinder = height of the cone = 8 cm
   Find the total volume of the shape.

Units of measure

NC **1** One lap of a running track is 400 m.

Find the total length of 20 laps. Give your answer in kilometres. [2]

NC **2** The mass of 20 books is 6.4 kg.

Find the mass of one book. Give your answer in grams. [2]

NC **3**

50 mm

25 mm

a Find the perimeter of this rectangle in cm. [2]

b Find the area of the rectangle in cm². [2]

NC **4** The area of a shape is 420 000 mm²

a Write the area in cm². [1]

b Write the area in m². [1]

5 The end of this cuboid is a square of side 25 mm. It is 8 cm long.

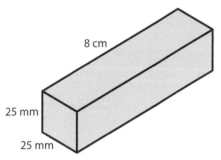

8 cm

25 mm

25 mm

a Find the volume in mm³. [1]

b Find the volume in cm³. [1]

6 A snail moves 145 mm in one minute.

If it continues at the same speed, work out how many metres it moves in one hour. [2]

NC **7** The capacity of a tank is 360 litres.

a Find the capacity in cm³. [1]

b Find the capacity in m³. [1]

1 litre = 1000 cm³

Perimeter and area

1

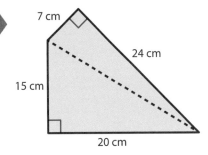

This quadrilateral is made from two right-angled triangles.

Find the area of the quadrilateral. [3]

2

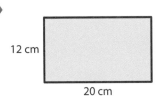 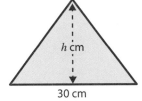

The rectangle and the triangle have the same area. Work out the value of h. [3]

3 The hexagon is made from three identical trapeziums.

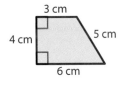 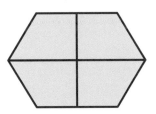

a Find the area of the hexagon. [3]

b Find the perimeter of the hexagon. [2]

4 All the angles in this shape are right angles.

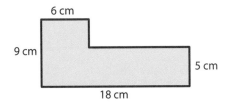

a Find the perimeter of the shape. [2]

b Find the area of the shape. [2]

> **Show me**
>
> **a** Missing lengths are 18 − .... = ... and 9 − .... = ...
>
> So the perimeter is 9 + 6 + ... = ... cm
>
> **b** *Either* divide into rectangles and add, such as (9 × 6) + (............ × ....) = ... cm²
>
> *Or* subtract one rectangle from another (9 × 18) − (............ × .... = ... cm²

Circles, arcs and sectors

1 The diameter of a circle is 23 cm.

a Calculate the circumference of the circle. [2]

b Calculate the area of the circle. [2]

2

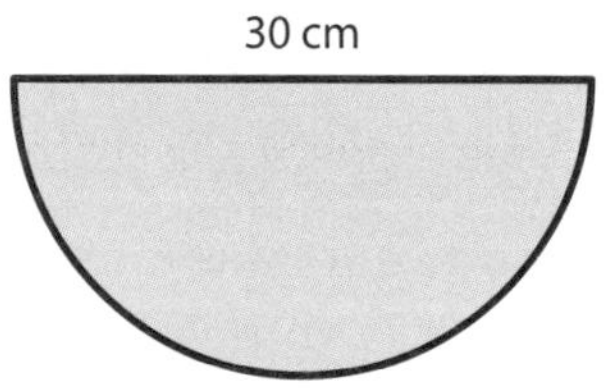

30 cm

This is a semicircle.

a Calculate the perimeter. [3]

b Calculate the area. [2]

3

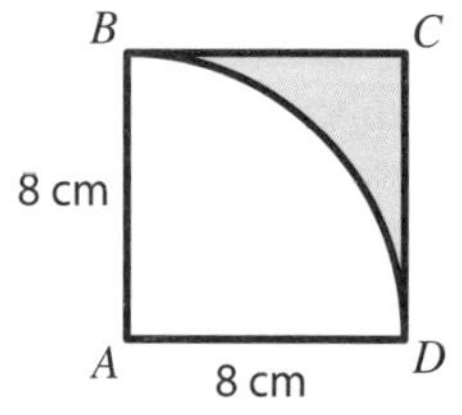

$ABCD$ is a square of side 8 cm.

BD is the arc of a circle with a centre at A.

a Calculate the area of the sector ABD. [2]

b Calculate the shaded area. [2]

E 4

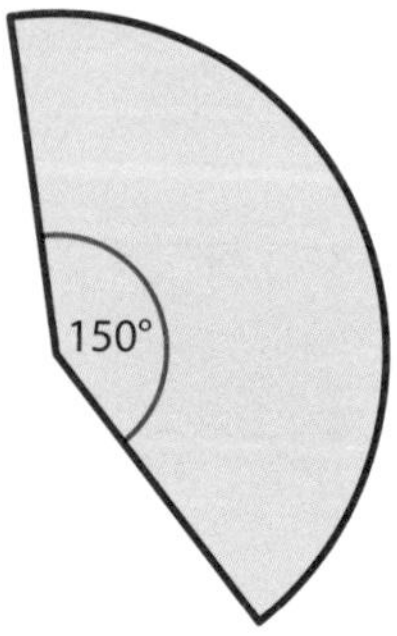

150°

This is the sector of a circle.

The area of the sector is 1100 cm^2.

Calculate the radius of the circle. [4]

Surface area and volume

1 The sides of a cuboid are 4 cm, 5 cm and 6 cm.

a Find the volume of the cuboid. [1]

b Find the surface area of the cuboid. [3]

> **Show me**
>
> There are 6 rectangular faces
>
> Area = 2 × (4 × 5) + 2 × (............ × .... + 2 × (............ × ....) = ... cm²

2 This solid is a prism.

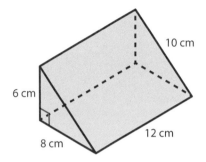

a Find the volume of the prism. [3]

b Find the surface area of the prism. [4]

3

The height of this cone is 4 cm. The radius of the base is 3 cm. The length of the sloping edge is 5 cm.

Find the **total** surface area of the cone. Leave π in your answer. [4]

4 Each side of a cube is 10 cm.

a Find the volume of the cube. [2]

b Find the surface area of the cube. [2]

A sphere has the same volume as the cube.

c Calculate the radius of the sphere. [3]

d Calculate the surface area of the sphere. [2]

Round your answers to 3 significant figures unless you are given other instructions.

Compound shapes and solids

1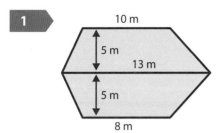

This shape is made from two trapezia.

Calculate the area. [3]

2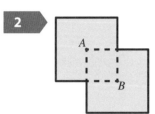

This shape is made from two squares of side 24 cm.

A and B are the centres of the squares.

a Find the perimeter of the shape. [2]

b Find the area of the shape. [3]

3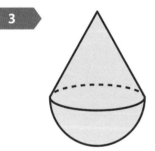

This solid is a cone on top of half a sphere.

The radius of the sphere is 4 cm.

The height of the cone is 5 cm.

Calculate the total volume. [4]

4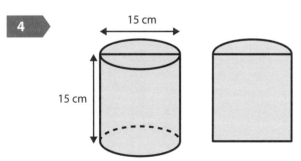

A cylinder is cut in half as shown.

The height of the cylinder is 15 cm and the diameter of the top is 15 cm.

(a) Find the volume of the half cylinder. [3]

(b) Find the area of the rectangular face of the half cylinder. [1]

(c) Find the total surface area of the half cylinder. [3]

Right-angled triangles

Syllabus links:
C6.1; E6.1; C6.2; E6.2

Learning aims:

- Use Pythagoras' theorem
- Use the sine, cosine and tangent of an acute angle
- Solve problems in two dimensions
- **E** The shortest distance from a point to a line
- **E** Angles of elevation and depression

Pythagoras' theorem

The sides of this right-angled triangle are a, b and c.

The **hypotenuse** is c, the side opposite the right-angle.

Pythagoras' theorem says that $a^2 + b^2 = c^2$

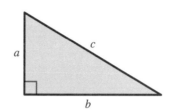

Example 1

a) Find x.

b) Find y.

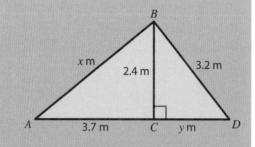

a) $x^2 = 3.7^2 + 2.4^2$ Use Pythagoras' theorem in triangle ABC.

$x = \sqrt{3.7^2 + 2.4^2} = 4.41$

b) $y^2 + 2.4^2 = 3.2^2$ Use Pythagoras' theorem in triangle BCD. The hypotenuse is BD.

$y^2 = 3.2^2 - 2.4^2$

$y = \sqrt{(3.2^2 - 2.4^2)} = 2.12$ Rearrange the equation and subtract the squares.

Sine, cosine and tangent

The hypotenuse is the longest side of the triangle.

The opposite is the side opposite angle θ.

The adjacent is the side next to angle θ.

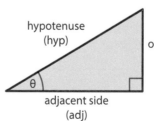

The **sine**, **cosine** and **tangent** ratios of angle θ are:

$$\sin\theta = \frac{\text{opp}}{\text{hyp}} \qquad \cos\theta = \frac{\text{adj}}{\text{hyp}} \qquad \tan\theta = \frac{\text{opp}}{\text{adj}}$$

> **Key Point**
>
> You must memorise these three formulas.

Example 2

a) Find angle *QPS*.

b) Find *x*.

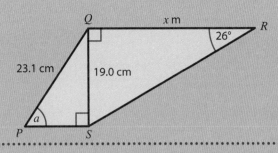

a) $\sin a = \dfrac{19.0}{23.1}$ Use triangle *PQS*. The hypotenuse is 23.1 and the side opposite *a* is 19.0

$a = \sin^{-1}\left(\dfrac{19.0}{23.1}\right) = 55.3°$ Use $\sin = \dfrac{\text{opp}}{\text{hyp}}$

b) $\tan 26° = \dfrac{19.0}{x}$ Use triangle *QRS*. The side opposite 26° is 19.0 and the side adjacent to 26° is *x*.

$x = \dfrac{19.0}{\tan 26°} = 39.0$ to 3 s.f.   Use $\tan = \dfrac{\text{opp}}{\text{adj}}$

E The shortest distance from a point to a line

The shortest distance from B to AC is the perpendicular line BX.

Using triangle *ABX*, $\sin 40° = \dfrac{BX}{20}$ so $BX = 20 \times \sin 40° = 12.9$ m to 3 s.f.

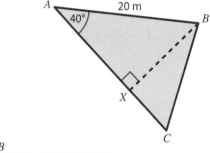

E Angle of elevation and depression

AB is a flagpole. P is a point 13.5 m away from the flagpole.

From P, the **angle of elevation** of the top of the flagpole is 15°.

From B the **angle of depression** of point P is 15°.

The height of the flagpole $AB = 13.5 \times \tan 15° = 3.62$ m to 3 s.f.

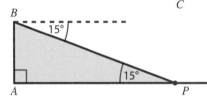

> ### Quick Test

1. In triangle *ABC*, angle *A* is a right angle. $BC = 36$ cm and $AB = 27$ cm.
   Calculate the length of *AC*.

2. Calculate angle *Z*.

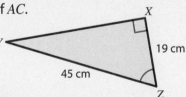

3. Calculate *x*.

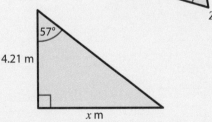

E 4. Calculate the shortest distance from *A* to *BC*.

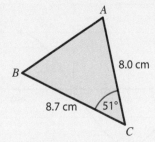

E Trigonometric functions

Syllabus links:
E6.3; E6.4

Learning aims:

- E Know exact values of trigonometric functions for particular angles
- E Know and use trigonometric graphs for angles between 0° and 360°

Exact trigonometric values

You need to know the exact values of the sine cosine and tangent of 0°, 30°, 45°, 60° and 90°.

These triangles will help you to remember them.

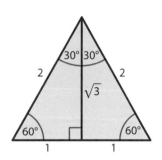 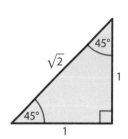

angle	0°	30°	45°	60°	90°
sine	0	$\dfrac{1}{2}$	$\dfrac{1}{\sqrt{2}}$	$\dfrac{\sqrt{3}}{2}$	1
cosine	1	$\dfrac{\sqrt{3}}{2}$	$\dfrac{1}{\sqrt{2}}$	$\dfrac{1}{2}$	0
tangent	0	$\dfrac{1}{\sqrt{3}}$	1	$\sqrt{3}$	–

Trigonometric graphs

The graph of $y = \sin x$ for $0° \le x \le 360°$

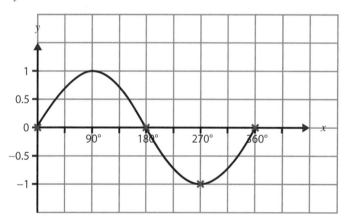

The graph has rotational symmetry about (180°,0).

$y = 90°$ is a line of symmetry for the section $0° \le x \le 180°$.

The graph of $y = \cos x$ for $0° \le x \le 360°$

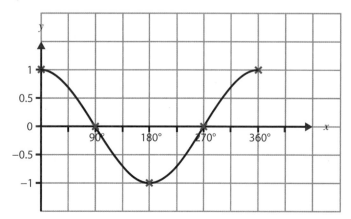

The sine graph and the cosine graph have similar shapes and symmetries.

The graph of $y = \tan x$ for $0° \leq x \leq 360°$

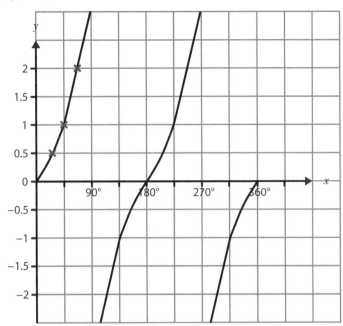

The section $0° \leq x \leq 180°$ and the section $180° \leq x \leq 360°$ have similar shapes.

Example 1 Without using a calculator, solve the equation

$2\cos x + \sqrt{3} = 0$ for $0° \leq x \leq 360°$

••

$\cos x = -\dfrac{\sqrt{3}}{2}$ Rearrange to make $\cos x$ the subject.

$\cos 30° = \dfrac{\sqrt{3}}{2}$ Remember this or use the equilateral triangle.

$x = 180° - 30°$ or $180° + 30°$ This comes from the symmetry of the graph

$x = 150°$ or $210°$

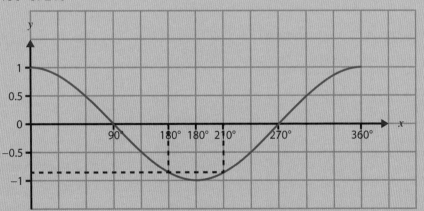

> **Quick Test**
>
> **NC** 1. Find the value of $(\sin 30°)^2 + (\sin 60°)^2$.
>
> **NC** 2. Solve the equation $\sin x = \dfrac{1}{2}\sqrt{2}$ for $0° \leq x \leq 180°$.
>
> 3. Solve the equation $\tan x = 1.3$ for $0° \leq x \leq 360°$.
>
> **NC** 4. $\tan 60° = k\tan 30°$. Find the value of k.

E Non right-angled triangles

Learning aims:

* E The sine rule and the cosine rule
* E The formula for the area of a triangle

The sine rule and the cosine rule

The vertices of a triangle are A, B and C.

The sides a, b and c are opposite the corresponding angles.

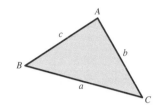

The **sine rule**: $\dfrac{a}{\sin A} = \dfrac{b}{\sin B} = \dfrac{c}{\sin C}$

The **cosine rule**: $a^2 = b^2 + c^2 - 2bc \cos A$

Use these rules when you know three of the sides and angles and you want to find a fourth.

* Use the sine rule if you know a side and the angle opposite it.
* Use the cosine rule if you know three sides, or two sides and the angle between them.

To find an angle you can use the sine rule or cosine rule:

The sine rule: $\dfrac{\sin A}{a} = \dfrac{\sin B}{b} = \dfrac{\sin C}{c}$ The cosine rule: $\cos A = \dfrac{b^2 + c^2 - a^2}{2bc}$

> **Key Point**
>
> In the cosine rule always add the squares of the two sides adjacent to the angle.

Example 1 A boat sails 25 km from X to Y at a bearing of 060° followed by 30 km from Y to Z at a bearing of 124°.

Find the distance and bearing of Z from X.

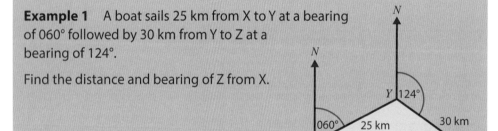

...

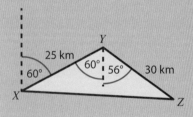

Use triangle XYZ.

Angle Y is $60° + 56° = 116°$.

$XZ^2 = 25^2 + 30^2 - 2 \times 25 \times 30 \cos 116°$

$XZ = 46.7178... = 46.7$ km to 3 s.f.   Use the cosine rule to find XZ.

$\dfrac{\sin Z}{30} = \dfrac{\sin 116°}{46.7}$

Don't round the answer until the end of the calculation.

$Z = \sin^{-1}\left(\dfrac{30 \sin 116°}{46.7}\right) = 35.3°$ to 1 d.p   Use the sine rule to find Z.

The bearing of X from Z is $60 + 35.3 = 095.3°$.

The area of a triangle

The area of this triangle is $\frac{1}{2}ab \sin C$

Use this formula if you know an angle and the two adjacent sides.

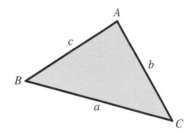

Example 2 Find the area of this triangle.

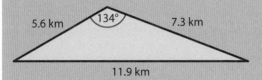

11.9 km

Area $= \frac{1}{2} \times 5.6 \times 7.3 \times \sin 144°$ Use the two sides next to the angle.

$= 14.7 \text{ km}^2$ to 3 s.f.

> **Quick Test**

1. The sides of a triangle are 10 cm, 15 cm and 20 cm. Calculate the largest angle.
   Hint: The largest angle is opposite the longest side.
2. Find the area of the triangle in question 1.
3. In triangle DEF, $DE = 4.30$ m, angle $D = 56°$ and angle $F = 79°$. Find EF.

E Trigonometry in three dimensions

Learning aims:

- **E** Use trigonometry to solve problems in three dimensions
- **E** Find the angle between a line and a plane

Finding right-angled triangles

To calculate lengths and angles on three dimensions, look for right-angled triangles.

The cuboid can be used to show how to do this.

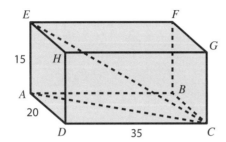

EC is a diagonal joining opposite vertices of the cuboid.

To calculate the length of EC:

1   Find AC using triangle ADC and Pythagoras' theorem:

$$AC^2 = AD^2 + DC^2 = 20^2 + 35^2$$

$$AC = \sqrt{1625}$$

2   Find EC using triangle EAC and Pythagoras' theorem:

$$EC^2 = AC^2 + AE^2 = 1625 + 15^2$$

$$EC = \sqrt{1850} = 43.0 \text{ to 3 s.f.}$$

The angle between a line and a plane

The angle between EC and the base ABCD is ECA.

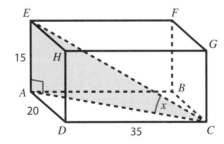

It is labelled x.

To find x, use triangle ECA where the angle at E is 90°:

$$\sin x = \frac{EA}{EC} = \frac{15}{\sqrt{1850}}$$

$$x = \sin^{-1}\left(\frac{15}{\sqrt{1850}}\right) = 20.4° \text{ to 1 d.p.}$$

The angle between EC and the face of AEHD is angle *CED*.

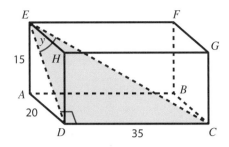

It is labelled *y*.

To find *y*, use triangle *EDC* where the angle at *D* is 90°:

$$\sin y = \frac{CD}{EC} = \frac{35}{\sqrt{1850}}$$

$$y = \sin^{-1}\left(\frac{35}{\sqrt{1850}}\right) = 54.5° \text{ to 1 d.p.}$$

> **Quick Test**
>
> 1. The sides of a cuboid are 7 cm, 8 cm and 9 cm.
>   Find the length of the diagonal of the cuboid.
> 2. The height of this cone is 10 cm.
>
>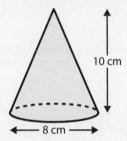
>
> The diameter of the base is 8 cm.
> a) Calculate the length of the sloping edge.
> b) Calculate the angle between the sloping edge and the base.

Right-angled triangles

1 This is a rectangle.

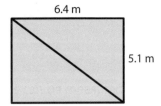

a Calculate the length of the diagonal. [2]

b Calculate the angle between the diagonal and the longer side. [3]

2

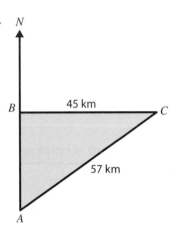

B is due north of A.

C is 45 km due east of B.

The distance from A to C is 57 km.

Find the bearing of C from A. [3]

3

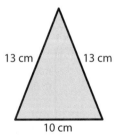

This is an isosceles triangle.

Find the area of the triangle. [4]

E **4**

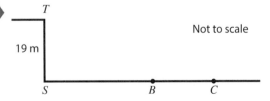

ST is a cliff. It is 19 m high.

A boat at B is 45 m from the foot of the cliff.

The angle of elevation of B from A is the same as the angle of depression of A from B

a Calculate the angle of depression of the boat from the top of the cliff. [3]

Another boat is at C.

The angle of elevation of the top of the cliff from this boat is 9.5°.

b Calculate the distance SC. [3]

E Trigonometric functions

1

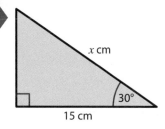

Find the **exact** value of x. [2]

2 **a** Sketch a graph of $y = \sin x$ for $0° \leq x \leq 360°$. [2]

b Solve the equation $2\sin x + 1 = 0$ for $0° \leq x \leq 360°$. [2]

3 Solve the equation $\sin x = \cos x$ for $0° \leq x \leq 360°$. [3]

4 **a** Sketch the graph of $y = \cos x$ for $0° \leq x \leq 360°$. [2]

b Solve the equation $8\cos x = 5$ for $0° \leq x \leq 360°$. [3]

5 Solve the equation $10 + 3\tan x = 2$. [3]

6

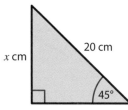

Find the exact value of x in the form $a\sqrt{b}$. [4]

E Non right-angled triangles

1

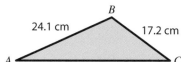

The area of this triangle is 161 cm^2 and angle B is obtuse.

Find angle B. [4]

2

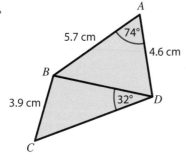

ABCD is made from two triangles.

Angle *BAD* = 74°, angle *BDC* = 32°, *AB* = 5.7 m, *AD* = 4.6 m and *BC* = 3.9 m.

a Find the length of *BD*. [3]

b Find angle *BCD*. [3]

c Find the area of triangle *BCD*. [3]

3

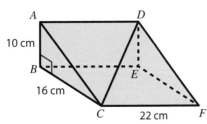

A is 57 m from P on a bearing of 324°.

B is 83 m from P on a bearing of 075°.

a Find the area of triangle *APB*. Round your answer to 3 s.f. [3]

b Find the distance from A to B. [3]

c Find the bearing of B from A. [4]

E Trigonometry in three dimensions

1

The diagram shows a triangular prism.

The cross section is a right-angled triangle.

CD is the diagonal of face ADFC.

a Calculate the length of CD. [3]

> **Show me**

Use Pythagoras' theorem in triangle CFE: CE=$\sqrt{\ldots^2 + \ldots^2}$ = ...

From triangle CDE: CD = $\sqrt{\ldots^2 + \ldots^2}$ = ...

b   Calculate the angle between CD and the base BCEF.   [3]

2

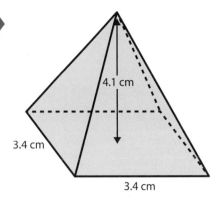

The base of this pyramid is a square of side 3.4 m.

The height of the pyramid is 4.1 m.

a   Calculate the length of a sloping edge.   [3]

b   Calculate the angle between the sloping edge and the base.   [3]

3

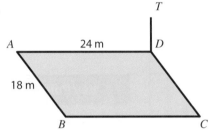

ABCD is a rectangle of flat ground. $AB = 18$ m and $AD = 24$ m.

DT is a tower at T.

The angle of elevation of the top of the tower from A is 15.6°.

Calculate the angle of elevation of the top of the tower from B.   [5]

Transformations

Learning aims:

Syllabus links:
C7.1; E7.1

- Reflect a shape in a line
- Rotate a shape through multiples of 90°
- Enlarge a shape from a centre of enlargement
- Translate a shape by a vector

Reflections

T is a reflection of S in the line $x = -1$.

U is a reflection of S in the line $y = 3$.

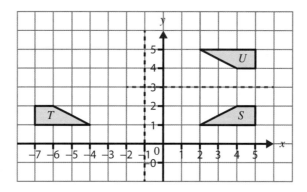

> **Key Point**
>
> To describe a reflection you must give a mirror line.

Rotations

Q is a 90° clockwise rotation of P about the vertex at (1, 1).

R is a 90° anticlockwise rotation of P about the origin.

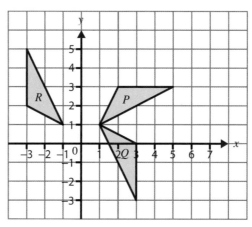

> **Key Point**
>
> To describe a rotation you must give the centre and the angle of the rotation.

Enlargements

B is an enlargement of A, centre (3, 0), scale factor 3.

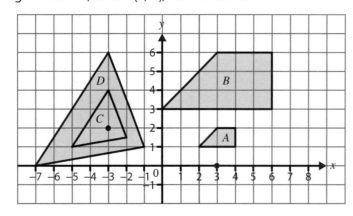

> **Key Point**
>
> To describe an enlargement you must give a centre and a scale factor.

C is an enlargement of D, centre (−3, 2), scale factor $\frac{1}{2}$.

Translations

The vector of the translation from X to Y is $\begin{pmatrix} 5 \\ 1 \end{pmatrix}$.

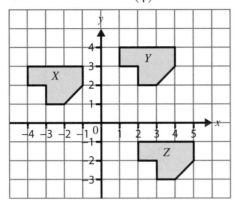

> **Key Point**
>
> To describe a translation you must give the vector.

The vector of the translation from Y to Z is $\begin{pmatrix} 1 \\ -5 \end{pmatrix}$.

The vector of the translation from Z to X is $\begin{pmatrix} -6 \\ 4 \end{pmatrix}$.

E Further transformations

A reflection can be in any line.

B is a reflection of A in the line $y = x + 1$.

The centre of a rotation can be any point. D is a 180° rotation of A about $(-1, 3)$.

An enlargement can have a negative scale factor. C is an enlargement of A with scale factor –2 and centre of enlargement $(1, 1)$.

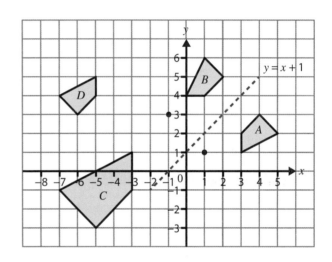

> **Key Point**
>
> A negative enlargement is the same as a positive enlargement and a rotation of 180°.

> **Quick Test**
>
> 1. Describe the transformation from A to B.
> 2. Describe the transformation from A to C.
> 3. Describe the transformation from B to F.
> 4. Describe the transformation from B to D.
>
> E 5. Describe the transformation from E to C.

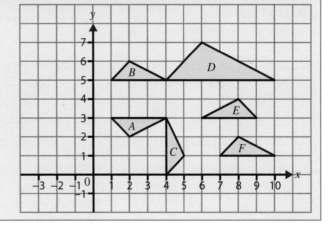

E Vectors

Syllabus links:
E7.2; E7.3; E7.4

Learning aims:

- E Represent vectors in different ways
- E Find the magnitude of a vector
- E Use vectors to solve geometric problems

Representing vectors

Vectors can be represented by the end points of a line segment or by two numbers in a vertical bracket.

$$\overrightarrow{AB} = \begin{pmatrix} 6 \\ 1 \end{pmatrix}, \overrightarrow{AC} = \begin{pmatrix} 3 \\ -4 \end{pmatrix}, \overrightarrow{AD} = \begin{pmatrix} -2 \\ -3 \end{pmatrix}$$

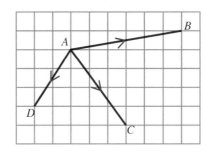

Vectors can also be represented by lower case letters in bold type.

$$\mathbf{a} = \begin{pmatrix} 2 \\ 4 \end{pmatrix}, \mathbf{b} = \begin{pmatrix} -5 \\ -1 \end{pmatrix}, \mathbf{c} = \begin{pmatrix} 2 \\ -2 \end{pmatrix}$$

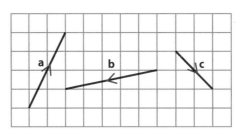

> **Key Point**
>
> When you hand write a vector as a lower case letter, you cannot write in **bold** so underline it instead. Write **a** as a̲, write **b** as b̲ and so on.

Magnitude of a vector

The **magnitude of a vector** is the length of a vector.

For vector $\overrightarrow{AB} = \begin{pmatrix} 6 \\ 1 \end{pmatrix}$, the magnitude $|\overrightarrow{AB}| = \sqrt{(1^2 + 6^2)} = \sqrt{37}$.

For $\mathbf{b} = \begin{pmatrix} -5 \\ -1 \end{pmatrix}$, $|\mathbf{b}| = \sqrt{(-5)^2 + (-1)^2} = \sqrt{26}$.

> **Key Point**
>
> The magnitude of vector
> $\begin{pmatrix} a \\ b \end{pmatrix}$ is $\left| \begin{pmatrix} a \\ b \end{pmatrix} \right| = \sqrt{a^2 + b^2}$.

Adding and subtracting vectors

Vectors can be added by joining line segments.

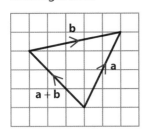

Add the corresponding elements:

$$\mathbf{a} + \mathbf{b} = \begin{pmatrix} 2 \\ 4 \end{pmatrix} + \begin{pmatrix} -5 \\ -1 \end{pmatrix} = \begin{pmatrix} -3 \\ 3 \end{pmatrix}$$

You can multiply a vector by a constant.

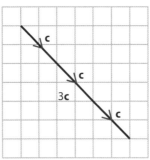

Multiply each element by the constant:

$$3\mathbf{c} = 3\begin{pmatrix} 2 \\ -2 \end{pmatrix} = \begin{pmatrix} 6 \\ -6 \end{pmatrix}$$

You can subtract a vector by adding the inverse.

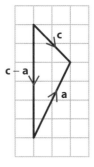

Subtract the corresponding elements:

$$\mathbf{c} - \mathbf{a} = \begin{pmatrix} 2 \\ -2 \end{pmatrix} - \begin{pmatrix} 2 \\ 4 \end{pmatrix} = \begin{pmatrix} 0 \\ -6 \end{pmatrix}$$

Solving geometric problems

$\overrightarrow{PA} = \mathbf{a}, \overrightarrow{PB} = \mathbf{b}$

X divides PA in the ratio 1 : 2.

Y divides BA in the ratio 1 : 2.

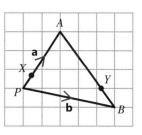

You can write other vectors in terms of **a** and **b**.

So $\overrightarrow{PX} = \frac{1}{3}\mathbf{a}$ and $\overrightarrow{XA} = \frac{2}{3}\mathbf{a}$

$\overrightarrow{AB} = \overrightarrow{AP} + \overrightarrow{PB} = -\mathbf{a} + \mathbf{b} = \mathbf{b} - \mathbf{a}$ and $\overrightarrow{AY} = \frac{2}{3}(\mathbf{b} - \mathbf{a})$

So $\overrightarrow{XY} = \overrightarrow{XA} + \overrightarrow{AY} = \frac{2}{3}\mathbf{a} + \frac{2}{3}(\mathbf{b} - \mathbf{a}) = \frac{2}{3}\mathbf{a} + \frac{2}{3}\mathbf{b} - \frac{2}{3}\mathbf{a} = \frac{2}{3}\mathbf{b}$

Since $\overrightarrow{PB} = \mathbf{b}$, this shows two things:

line segment XY is parallel to PB

line segment XY is two-thirds the length of PB.

Do not confuse AB which is a line segment with $\overrightarrow{AB}$ which is a vector.

> **Key Point**
>
> Two vectors are parallel if one is a scalar multiple of the other.

> **Quick Test**
>
> 1. Find $2\begin{pmatrix} 3 \\ -2 \end{pmatrix} - 3\begin{pmatrix} -1 \\ 4 \end{pmatrix}$.
>
> 2. Work out $\left|\begin{pmatrix} -8 \\ 15 \end{pmatrix}\right|$.
>
> 3. ABC is a triangle. X is the midpoint of BC.
> $\overrightarrow{AB} = \mathbf{s}$ and $\overrightarrow{AC} = \mathbf{t}$.
>
>   Write $\overrightarrow{AX}$ in terms of **s** and **t**. as simply as possible.

Transformations

1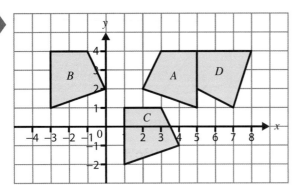

Describe the transformation:

a   from A to B. [2]

b   from B to C. [3]

c   from A to D. [3]

A transformation is described by a two numbers in brackets in a vertical column

2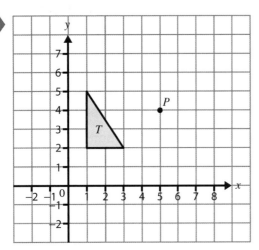

a   Copy the diagram and write down the coordinates of P. [2]

b   Draw an enlargement of T with centre P and scale factor 1.5 [3]

c   Rotate T 90° clockwise about the point (3, 2). [3]

E **3**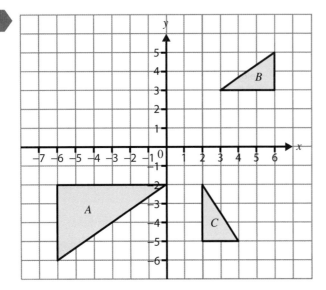

a Describe the transformation from A to B. [3]

b Describe the transformation from B to C. [3]

E Vectors

1 $r = \begin{pmatrix} 6 \\ 4 \end{pmatrix}$, $s = \begin{pmatrix} -3 \\ -5 \end{pmatrix}$ and $t = \begin{pmatrix} -2 \\ 7 \end{pmatrix}$.

a Work out:

   i) $r + s$ [1]

   ii) $4s$ [1]

   iii) $|t|$ [1]

b If $r + x = t$, find x. [2]

2 $\overrightarrow{PQ} = a$, $\overrightarrow{PR} = b$, M is the midpoint of PR and QS : SR = 4 : 1.

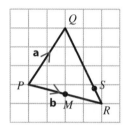

a Write $\overrightarrow{PS}$ in terms of **a** and **b**. [2]

> **Show me**

$\overrightarrow{PS} = \overrightarrow{PQ} + \overrightarrow{QS}$

$\overrightarrow{PQ} = a$ and $\overrightarrow{QS} = \dfrac{4}{5}\overrightarrow{QR} = \dfrac{4}{5}(\cdots\cdots\cdots) = \cdots\cdots\cdots$

So $\overrightarrow{PS} = a + \cdots\cdots\cdots = \cdots\cdots\cdots$

b Write $\overrightarrow{MS}$ in terms of **a** and **b**. [2]

Write your answers as simply as possible.

3 $\overrightarrow{AB} = 6s - 4t$ and $\overrightarrow{AC} = 9s - 6t$.

Write down two facts about the points A, B and C. [2]

4 X is the midpoint of OA.

Y is the midpoint of XA.

Z is the midpoint of AB.

$\overrightarrow{OA} = a$ and $\overrightarrow{OB} = b$.

a Find, in terms of **a** and **b** :

   i) $\overrightarrow{AB}$ [2]

   ii) $\overrightarrow{YZ}$ [2]

b Show that YZ is parallel to XB. [2]

Introduction to probability

Syllabus links:
C8.1; E8.1; C8.2; E8.2

Learning aims:

- Understand the probability scale
- Calculate simple probabilities
- Find the probability that an event does not occur
- **E** Understand probability notation

The probability scale

The **probability** of an event is a number between 0 and 1.

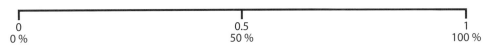

0	0.5	1
0 %	50 %	100 %

An event that is certain has a probability of 1.

An event that is impossible has a probability of 0.

A probability can be written as a fraction, a decimal or a percentage.

The probability of a single event

> **Key Point**
>
> The probability that an event does not happen = 1 – the probability it does happen.
> If the probability of rain tomorrow is 15%, the probability it will not rain is 100% – 15% = 85%.

Here are 10 cards. A card is chosen at random.

There is one A so the probability of choosing A is $\frac{1}{10}$ or 0.1 or 10%.

There are three Ts so the probability of choosing T is $\frac{3}{10}$ or 0.3 or 30%.

The probability the card is *not* an S is 1 – the probability it is an S

$= 1 - \frac{2}{10} = \frac{8}{10} = \frac{4}{5}$ or 0.8 or 80%.

E Notation

You can use letters to stand for events.

One of the digits 1, 2, 3, 4, 5, 6, 7, 8, 9 is chosen at random.

E is the event that it is an even number. M is the event that it is a multiple of four.

The probability of event E is $P(E) = \frac{4}{9}$; the probability of event M is $P(M) = \frac{2}{9}$.

M' is the event that the number is *not* a multiple of four.

$P(M') = 1 - \frac{2}{9} = \frac{7}{9}$ $P(E') = 1 - \frac{4}{9} = \frac{5}{9}$

Relative frequency

A cuboid has six faces, and one face is red.

If the cuboid is dropped the faces are not equally likely to be on the top.

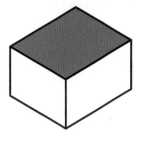

You cannot say that the probability that the cuboid lands with the red face on top is $\frac{1}{6}$.

Suppose that the cuboid is dropped 50 times and the red face is on top 12 times.

The **relative frequency** of a red face on top is $\frac{12}{50} = 0.24$.

An estimate of the probability of a red face is 0.24.

If you drop the cuboid more times you can get a better estimate.

> **Key Point**
>
> Relative frequency can be used to estimate probability.

Expected frequency

A computer game includes a spinner showing the integers from 1 to 5.

The probability of spinning a 1 is 0.35.

The probability of spinning a 5 is 0.1.

If the spinner spins 40 times:

- the **expected frequency** of 1 is $0.35 \times 40 = 14$
- the expected frequency of 5 is $0.1 \times 40 = 4$.

> **Key Point**
>
> relative frequency $\xrightarrow{\text{estimate}}$ probabilty $\xrightarrow{\text{calculate}}$ expected frequency

> **Quick Test**
>
> 1. A letter is chosen at random from the word FREQUENCY.
>   Find the probability that it is:
>   a) Q
>   b) E
>   c) A.
> 2. The probability that a plane will be late arriving is 5%.
>   Find the probability that it will not be late.
> 3. Ari plays chess with his father every week. After 20 weeks he has won 8 games. Estimate the probability that Ari wins a game.
> 4. A spinner is used in a game. The probability it shows an even number is 0.6.
>   Find the expected frequency of an even number in 60 spins.
> **E** 5. E is an event and $P(E') = \frac{7}{12}$. Find $P(E)$.

Probability of combined events

Syllabus links:
C8.3; E8.3; E8.4

Learning aims:

- Calculate probabilities using tables and tree diagrams
- **E** Calculate conditional probability

Sample space diagrams

Here are two sets of cards:

Set A $\boxed{2}\ \boxed{4}\ \boxed{4}$ Set B $\boxed{2}\ \boxed{3}\ \boxed{3}\ \boxed{5}$

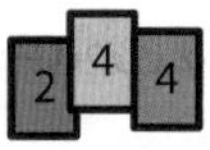

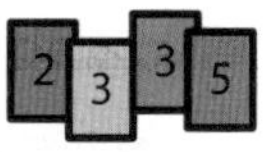

One card is taken at random from each set and the numbers are added.

The possible totals are shown in this table.

There are 12 equally likely pairs.

+		Set B		
+	**2**	**3**	**3**	**5**
2	4	5	5	7
4	6	7	7	9
4	6	7	7	9

(Set A labels rows 2, 4, 4)

From the table you can find the probabilities of different totals.

Total	4	5	6	7	8	9
Probability	$\frac{1}{12}$	$\frac{2}{12} = \frac{1}{6}$	$\frac{2}{12} = \frac{1}{6}$	$\frac{5}{12}$	0	$\frac{2}{12} = \frac{1}{6}$

Venn diagrams

You can find probabilities from Venn diagrams.

An integer between 11 and 20 is chosen at random.

The Venn diagram shows even numbers, E, and multiples of three, T.

$E \cap T$ is even multiple of 3.

The probability of an even multiple of $3 = \frac{2}{10} = \frac{1}{5}$.

$E \cup T$ is numbers that are even or multiples of three.

The probability of this is $\frac{6}{10} = \frac{3}{5}$.

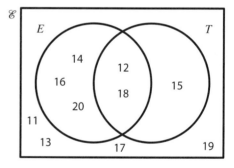

> **Key Point**
>
> The sum of the probabilities of the outcomes at the end of the tree is 1.

Tree diagrams

A bag contains 6 red balls and 4 blue balls.

One ball is taken out at random. The colour is noted, and the ball is replaced. Then a second ball is taken.

What is the probability they are both the same colour? What is the probability they are different colours? A tree diagram can be used to answer these questions.

Each time a ball is taken,

the probability of red $= \frac{6}{10} = \frac{3}{5}$

and the probability of blue $= \frac{4}{10} = \frac{2}{5}$.

These are the probabilities on the branches.

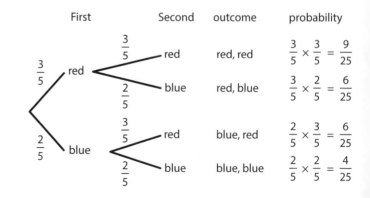

Multiply the numbers on the branches to find the probabilities of the outcomes.

The probability both balls are the same colour $= \dfrac{9}{25} + \dfrac{4}{25} = \dfrac{13}{25}$.

The probability the balls are different colours $= \dfrac{6}{25} + \dfrac{6}{25} = \dfrac{12}{25}$.

E Conditional probability

Look again at the tree diagram example.

If the first ball is *not* replaced then the probabilities on the second set of branches are different.

It the first ball is red, the probability that the second is red is $\dfrac{5}{9}$.

If the first ball is blue, the probability that the second ball is red is $\dfrac{2}{3}$.

First	Second	outcome	probability
$\frac{3}{5}$ red	$\frac{5}{9}$ red	red, red	$\frac{3}{5} \times \frac{3}{9} = \frac{15}{45} = \frac{1}{3}$
	$\frac{4}{9}$ blue	red, blue	$\frac{3}{5} \times \frac{4}{9} = \frac{12}{45} = \frac{4}{15}$
$\frac{2}{5}$ blue	$\frac{6}{9}$ red	blue, red	$\frac{2}{5} \times \frac{2}{3} = \frac{4}{15}$
	$\frac{3}{9}$ blue	blue, blue	$\frac{2}{5} \times \frac{1}{3} = \frac{2}{15}$

This time, the probability both balls are the same colour $= \dfrac{1}{3} + \dfrac{2}{15} = \dfrac{7}{15}$.

The probability the balls are different colours $= \dfrac{4}{15} + \dfrac{4}{15} = \dfrac{8}{15}$.

> **Key Point**
>
> On a tree diagram, *multiply* the probabilities on the branches; *add* the probabilities of the outcomes.

> **Key Point**
>
> **Conditional probability** means that the probability of an event depends on other events having already happened.

> **Quick Test**
>
> 1. A coin is spun twice. Find the probability of heads both times.
> 2. a) Copy the Venn diagram in the example above. Put in the integers from 1 to 10.
>   b) An integer between 1 and 20 is chosen at random. Find the probability that it is neither even nor a multiple of three.
> E 3. A bag contains 2 black pens and 3 blue pens. Two pens are taken out. Find the probability that they are not both black.

Introduction to probability

1 ▶ D I V I D E

Here are six cards. One card is chosen at random.

Find the probability that the card is:

a D [1]

b V or I [1]

c not E [1]

d C. [1]

2 ▶ A computer generates a random integer n where $1 \leq n \leq 15$.

Find the probability that the number is:

a even [1]

b a multiple of 5 [1]

c a prime number [1]

d less than 20. [1]

3 ▶ A bag contains red, blue and green counters. The numbers are in this table.

red	blue	green
5	7	8

a A counter is taken out at random. Find the probability that it is

i) blue [1]

ii) red or blue [1]

iii) not red. [1]

b Find the smallest number of counters you need to add to the bag so that each colour has the same probability of being taken. [1]

4 ▶ The probability that a seed of vegetable A will germinate is 70%.

a 120 seeds are planted. Find the expected number that will germinate. [2]

50 seeds of a vegetable B are planted and 23 germinate.

b Estimate the probability that a seed of vegetable B will germinate. [2]

A further 30 seeds of vegetable B are planted. 21 of these germinate.

c Find a better estimate of the probability that a seed of vegetable B will germinate. [2]

5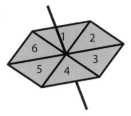

A fair spinner in the shape of a regular hexagon has the numbers 1, 2, 3, 4, 5, 6.

a Find the probability of scoring 3, 4, 5 or 6. [1]

b The spinner is spun 48 times. Find the expected frequency of 3, 4, 5 or 6. [2]

Probability of combined events

1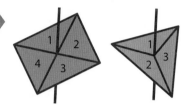

Here are two fair spinners. One has the numbers 1, 2, 3 and the other has the numbers 1, 2, 3, 4.

a Copy and complete this table to show the product of the two numbers. [2]

×	1	2	3	4
1				
2			6	
3				

b Find the probability that the product is:

i) 4 [1]

ii) an even number [1]

iii) less than 5. [1]

2 The probability that it will rain on Monday is 0.6.

The probability that it will rain on Tuesday is 0.8.

> To find the probability that two independent events will both happen, multiply their individual probabilities.

a Find the probability that it will rain on both days. [1]

b Find the probability that it will not rain on Monday. [1]

c Find the probability that it will not rain on either day. [2]

3 A bag contains 6 black counters and 18 white counters.

One counter is taken out at random.

a Show that the probability that it is black is $\frac{1}{4}$. [1]

b The first counter is replaced and a second counter is taken out at random.

Copy this tree diagram and complete the probabilities on the branches. [2]

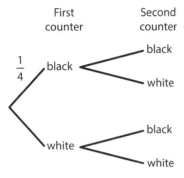

First counter   Second counter

$\frac{1}{4}$ black — black
black — white

white — black
white — white

c Find the probability that the two counters are:

i) both black [1]

ii) both white [1]

iii) different colours. [2]

> **Show me**

a Probability of outcome B, B is $\frac{1}{4} \times \ldots = \ldots$

b Probability of outcome W, W is $\frac{3}{4} \times \ldots = \ldots$

c Different colours could be B, W or W, B

Probability $= \left(\frac{1}{4} \times \frac{3}{4}\right) + (\ldots + \ldots) = \ldots$

4   A bag contains 2 red sweets, 5 green sweets and 1 yellow sweet.

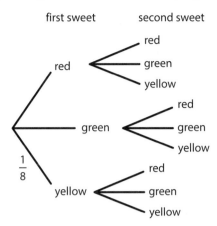

first sweet   second sweet

red

red

green

yellow

$\frac{1}{8}$

green

red

green

yellow

yellow

red

green

yellow

Two sweets are taken out at random.

a   Copy this tree diagram and put probabilities on the branches.

Find the probability that:

b   both sweets are red   [2]

c   both sweets are green   [2]

d   one of the sweets is yellow.   [2]

Statistical data

Syllabus links:
C9.1; E9.1; C9.2; E9.2

Learning aims:

- Classify statistical data
- Interpret tables and diagrams
- Compare sets of data

Tables and charts

Data can be shown in tables and charts.

On Monday morning Asa does a survey of the traffic where they live.

Asa starts with a tally chart and then puts the totals in a table.

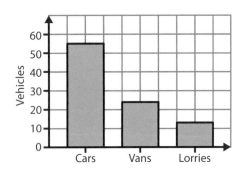

Type of vehicle	Frequency
Cars	55
Vans	24
Lorries	13

The data could be shown in a bar chart or a pie chart.

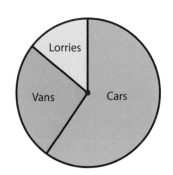

The pie chart shows the proportions clearly, but it does not show the number of vehicles.

Asa does another survey in the afternoon.

Here are the results of both surveys.

Type of vehicle	Morning	Afternoon	Total
Cars	55	38	93
Vans	24	16	40
Lorries	13	29	42
Total	92	83	175

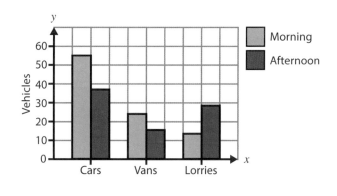

Asa draws a dual bar chart.

Then Asa works out percentages and draws a composite bar chart.

The percentage of cars in the morning $= \dfrac{55}{92} \times 100 = 60\%$ and so on.

Type of vehicle	Morning	Afternoon
Cars	60%	46%
Vans	26%	19%
Lorries	14%	35%
Total	100%	100%

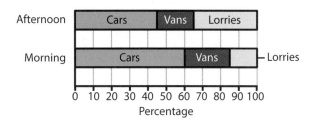

Asa then counts the number of cars every morning for the rest of the week.

Here are the results.

Day	Monday	Tuesday	Wednesday	Thursday	Friday	Saturday	Sunday
Cars	55	43	61	58	70	29	15

And here is a chart to show the results.

The chart shows how the number of cars vary from one day to the next.

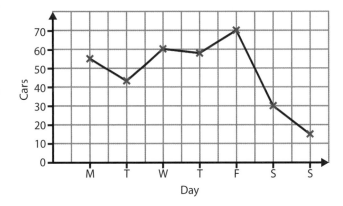

> **Quick Test**

These questions are about the charts and tables in this topic.

1   Look at the bar chart and the pie chart at the beginning of this topic.
    Give one advantage of each.
2   Look at the pie chart. Estimate the angle at the centre of the sector labelled Vans.
3   Look at the table that shows the numbers of vehicles in the morning and in the afternoon.
    Work out the percentage of all the vans that were seen in the morning.
4   Look at the final chart. Describe how the number of cars seen in the morning varies during the week.
5   Asa says, "The average number of cars in the morning during the week was 47.3". How many mornings
    was the number of cars above average?

Averages

Learning aims:

Syllabus links:
C9.3; E9.3

- Calculate averages and measures of spread
- **E** Estimate a mean or a modal class from grouped data

Averages and range

Here are the results of spinning a six-digit spinner eight times: 2, 4, 5, 4, 6, 3, 4, 1.

The **range** of the results is largest – smallest = 6 – 1 = 5

The most common result is 4.

The mode, mean and median are all averages.

Here are the masses of five books: 179 g, 277 g, 453 g, 187 g, 150 g.

Mean mass = $\dfrac{179 + 277 + 453 + 187 + 150}{5} = \dfrac{1246}{5} = 249.2$ g

To find the **median**, write the masses in order: 150, 179, 187, 277, 453.

The median is the middle data value, the third, which is 187 g.

Three more books are added. Their masses are 120 g, 224 g and 341 g.

Now the eight masses in order are: 120, 150, 179, 187, 224, 277, 341, 453.

The median is between the fourth and fifth values: median mass

$= \dfrac{187 + 224}{2} = 205.5$ g

> **Key Point**
>
> range = largest – smallest,
> mode = the most
> common value

> **Key Point**
>
> mean = sum ÷ number
> of values

> **Key Point**
>
> The median is the
> middle value of ordered
> data. The median of
> n data values is at
> position $\dfrac{n+1}{2}$.

Frequency tables

If there is a large set of numbers, the data can be displayed in a table.

162 people are shown five photographs of famous people and asked to identify them.

The number they get right is recorded. Here are the results.

Number correct	0	1	2	3	4	5
Frequency	12	17	43	53	29	8

The mean is $\dfrac{0 \times 12 + 1 \times 17 + 2 \times 43 + 3 \times 53 + 4 \times 29 + 5 \times 8}{162} = \dfrac{418}{162}$

= 2.58 to 2 d.p.

$\dfrac{162 + 1}{2} = 81.5$, so the median is between the 81st and 82nd values.

1st	12th 13th	29th 30th	72nd 73rd	125th
0	0 1	1 2	2 3	3.....

The median is 3.

The mode is the most common number of correct answers. The mode is 3.

The range is 5 – 0 = 5

> **Key Point**
>
> For a data set
> with n values, the
> lower quartile is at
> position $\dfrac{n+1}{4}$ and the
> upper quartile is at
> position $3 \times \dfrac{n+1}{4}$.

E Quartiles

The median divides a set of values in half. The **quartiles** divide it into quarters.

For the data in the last example there were 162 values.

The **lower quartile** is the $\dfrac{162+1}{4} = \dfrac{163}{4} = 40.75$th value. The lower quartile is 2.

The **upper quartile** is the $3 \times 40.75 = 122.25$ value. The upper quartile is 3.

The **interquartile range** = upper quartile – lower quartile = $3 - 2 = 1$

E Grouped data

The data in large data sets can be grouped into classes.

Here are the masses of 71 books.

Mass, m (g)	$0 < m \leq 100$	$100 < m \leq 200$	$200 < m \leq 300$	$300 < m \leq 400$	$400 < m \leq 500$
Frequency	3	27	19	14	8

The modal class is the class with the highest frequency. It is $100 < m \leq 200$.

You do not know the exact masses, but you can find an estimate by using the midpoint of each class.

Mass, m (g)	Frequency	Midpoint	Frequency × Midpoint
$0 < m \leq 100$	3	50	150
$100 < m \leq 200$	27	150	4050
$200 < m \leq 300$	19	250	4750
$300 < m \leq 400$	14	350	4900
$400 < m \leq 500$	8	450	3600
Total	71		17 450

Estimate of the mean $= = \dfrac{17\,450}{71} = 246$ g to 3 s.f.

> ### Quick Test

1. Here are ten test marks: 20, 17, 17, 15, 18, 9, 15, 17, 10, 11.
   Work out:
   a) the mean mark   **b)** the median mark   **c)** the mode   **d)** the range.
2. The mean mass of 35 parcels is 1.42 kg. Calculate the total mass.
3. Here are the number of letters in 45 words in a book for young children.

Letters	1	2	3	4	5	6	7	8
Frequency	4	7	10	9	6	5	3	1

   Work out:
   a) the mean number of letters   **b)** the mode   **c)** the median.

E 4. This table has the times of 103 runners in a race.

Time, x (min)	$30 < x \leq 40$	$40 < x \leq 50$	$50 < x \leq 60$	$60 < x \leq 70$
Frequency	12	32	41	18

   a) Write down the modal class.
   b) Estimate the mean time to the nearest minute.

Charts and diagrams

Syllabus links:
C9.4; E9.4

Learning aims:

- Draw and interpret bar charts and pie charts
- Draw and interpret pictograms, stem-and-leaf diagrams

Charts

The members of a running club vote on the colour of a new club vest. Here are the results.

Colour	Red	Blue	Orange	Green	Black	Total
Votes	6	17	14	4	19	60

You can show this information in different ways.

Pictogram

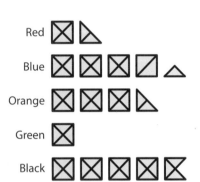

Bar chart

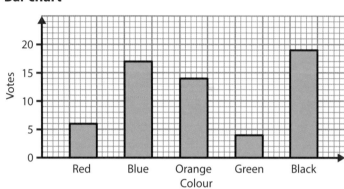

Pie chart

The angles are fractions of 360°. For example Red $= \dfrac{6}{60} \times 360 = 36°$.

Colour	Red	Blue	Orange	Green	Black
Votes	6	17	14	4	19
Angle	36°	182°	84°	24°	114°

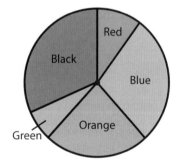

Stem-and-leaf table

Here are the ages of 25 people:

17, 22, 35, 20, 47

39, 40, 15, 17, 53

28, 37, 37, 31, 18

44, 51, 26, 23, 33

44, 33, 20, 31, 42

Here are the ages in a **stem-and-leaf table**.

```
1 | 5  7  7  8
2 | 0  0  2  3  6  8
3 | 1  1  3  3  5  7  7  9
4 | 0  2  4  4  7
5 | 1  3
```

Key: 2 | 3 = 23

From the table:

range is 53 − 15 = 38

median is the 13th age which is 33

> **Key Point**
>
> In a stem-and-leaf table write the numbers in order and include a key.

Analysing charts

50 girls and 50 boys are given a test. There is a maximum of 10 marks.

This chart shows the results.

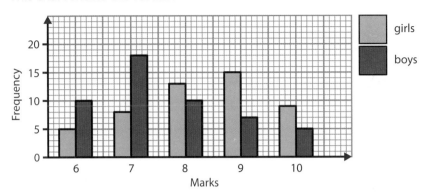

You can use averages to compare the marks of the girls and boys.

The mode is the highest column.

The mode for the girls is 9. The mode for the boys is 7.

Add successive frequencies to find the median. It is between the 25th and 26th values.

The median for the girls is 8: $5 + 8 = 13 < 25$; $5 + 8 + 13 = 26$ so the 25th and 26th values are 8.

The median for the boys is 7: $10 + 18 = 28$ so the 25th and 26th values are 7.

The mean for the boys is $\dfrac{6 \times 10 + 7 \times 18 + 8 \times 10 + 9 \times 7 + 10 \times 5}{50} = 7.58$

The mean for the girls is $\dfrac{6 \times 5 + 7 \times 8 + 8 \times 13 + 9 \times 15 + 10 \times 9}{50} = 8.3$

All three averages show the girls scoring better than the boys.

Quick Test

1. 40 people are asked when they were born. Here are the results.

Season	Spring	Summer	Autumn	Winter
Frequency	14	11	8	7

   Draw a pie chart to show these results.

2. 30 people are asked to translate some writing. These are the times taken, in minutes.

   24, 27, 35, 41, 50, 36, 17, 25, 19, 40

   31, 36, 27, 28, 53, 47, 22, 29, 36, 32

   19, 26, 25, 45, 38, 24, 16, 33, 20, 40

   a) Draw a stem-and-leaf diagram to show this data.
   b) Find: i) the range ii) the median.

3. Look at the data in the last example about the test marks of girls and boys.
   Copy and complete this composite bar chart.

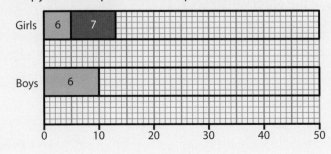

Scatter diagrams

Learning aims:

- Using scatter diagrams
- Identify positive and negative correlation
- Draw and use a line of best fit

Syllabus links: C9.5; E9.5

Linked pairs of values of two variables can be shown on a scatter diagram.

Here are two examples:

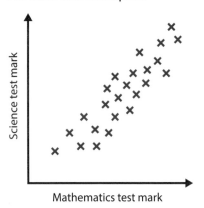 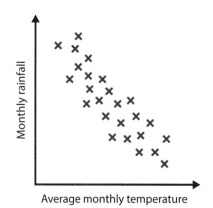

Correlation

Correlation is a connection between the values of two variables.

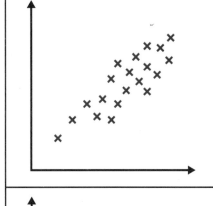

Positive correlation:

Large values of one variable are paired with large values of the other variable.

Small values of one variable are paired with small values of the other variable.

Negative correlation:

Large values of one variable are paired with small values of the other variable.

Small values of one variable are paired with large values of the other variable.

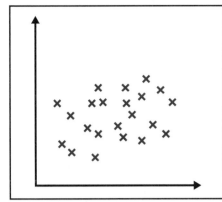

No correlation:

There is no connection between pairs of values.

Line of best fit

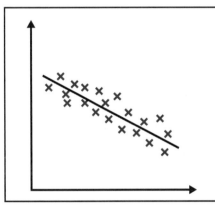

If there is positive or negative correlation you can draw a **line of best fit** through the data points:

use a ruler to draw one straight line

it should extend through all the points

it should have points on both sides over the whole length of the line.

If there is correlation between two variables and you know a value of one of the variables, you can use a line of best fit to estimate the value of the other variable.

> **Quick Test**
>
> 1. a) Name the type of correlation in the scatter diagram of test marks in the first example in this topic.
>   b) Describe what this tells you about students' marks for mathematics and science.
> 2. a) Name the type of correlation in the scatter diagram of temperature and rainfall in the second example in this topic.
>   b) Describe what this tells you about average monthly temperature and monthly rainfall.

E Cumulative frequency

Syllabus links:
E9.6

Learning aims:

- E Draw cumulative frequency diagrams
- E Estimate median, quartiles, interquartile range and percentiles

Cumulative frequency tables

458 people take part in a half marathon race.

This grouped frequency table shows their times.

Time, t (min)	Frequency
$70 < t \leq 80$	3
$80 < t \leq 90$	20
$90 < t \leq 100$	35
$100 < t \leq 110$	75
$110 < t \leq 120$	90
$120 < t \leq 130$	82
$130 < t \leq 140$	72
$140 < t \leq 150$	41
$150 < t \leq 160$	22
$160 < t \leq 170$	12
$170 < t \leq 180$	6

These results can be put in a **cumulative frequency** table by adding the successive frequencies.

Time, t (min)	Cumulative frequency	
$t \leq 70$	0	
$t \leq 80$	3	$3 + 20 = 23$
$t \leq 90$	23	$23 + 35 = 58$
$t \leq 100$	58	and so on.
$t \leq 110$	133	
$t \leq 120$	223	
$t \leq 130$	305	
$t \leq 140$	377	
$t \leq 150$	418	
$t \leq 160$	440	
$t \leq 170$	452	
$t \leq 180$	458	

Cumulative frequency graphs

Use the cumulative frequency table above to draw a cumulative frequency graph.

Mark the points $(70, 0)$, $(80, 3)$, $(90, 23)$, … with crosses and join them with a smooth curve.

> **Key Point**
>
> To draw a cumulative frequency curve: mark the points with small crosses and join them with a smooth curve.

To estimate the median:

- find half of 458 = 229
- go across from 229 and down to find a time of 121 minutes. This is the median.

To estimate the lower quartile:

- find a quarter of 458 = 114.5
- go across from 114.5 and down to find a time of 108 minutes. This is the lower quartile.

To estimate the upper quartile:

- find three-quarters of 458 = 343.5
- go across from 343.5 and down to find a time of 135 minutes. This is the upper quartile.

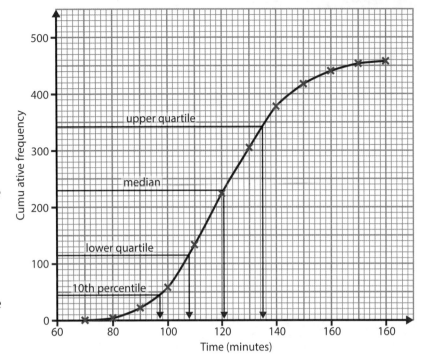

An estimate of the interquartile range is 135 – 108 = 27 minutes

The median is also called the 50th **percentile**. The lower quartile is the 25th percentile and the upper quartile is the 75th percentile.

You can find other percentiles from the cumulative frequency graph.

For example, to find the 10th percentile:

- 10% of 458 = 0.1 × 458 = 45.8
- Go across from 45.8 and down to find the time 97 minutes.

The 10th percentile is 97 minutes. 10% of the runners have a time of 97 minutes or less.

> **Quick Test**

1. Use the cumulative frequency graph above to estimate the 85th percentile of the runners' times.
2. The median of a set of ages is 42.5 years.
   The upper quartile is 56.2 years.
   The interquartile range is 20.8 years.
   Find the lower quartile.
3. The median of a set of lengths is 257 mm.
   The lower quartile is 183 mm, and the upper quartile is 312 mm.
   What can you say about the value of:
   a) the 60th percentile
   b) the 10th percentile?

E Histograms

Syllabus links:
E9.7

Learning aims:

- E Calculate frequency density

- E Draw and interpret a histogram

Frequency density

A **histogram** is a graph where area represents frequency.

The graph has a scale on both axes.

The scale on the vertical axis is **frequency density**.

This histogram shows the distribution of the masses of 150 parcels.

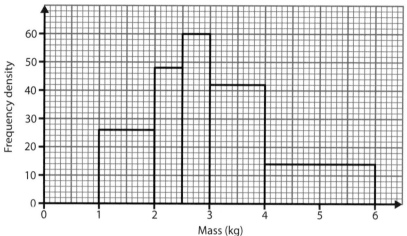

> **Key Point**
>
> $$\text{frequency density} = \frac{\text{frequency}}{\text{class width}}$$

The frequency for any class is the class width × frequency density

This table shows the frequencies for the classes.

Notice that the sum of the frequencies in the last column is 50.

Mass, m (kg)	Class width	Frequency density	Frequency
$1 < m \leq 2$	$2 - 1 = 1$	26	$1 \times 26 = 26$
$2 < m \leq 2.5$	$2.5 - 2.0 = 0.5$	48	$0.5 \times 48 = 24$
$2.5 < m \leq 3$	$3 - 2.5 = 0.5$	60	$0.5 \times 60 = 30$
$3 < m \leq 4$	$4 - 3 = 1$	42	$1 \times 42 = 42$
$4 < m \leq 6$	$6 - 4 = 2$	14	$2 \times 14 = 28$

Drawing histograms

Given a grouped frequency table, you can draw a histogram by first calculating the frequency density for each class.

The table shows the blood pressure of 86 people.

Blood pressure, b	$110 < b \leq 140$	$140 < b \leq 150$	$150 < b \leq 155$	$155 < b \leq 160$	$160 < b \leq 170$	$170 < b \leq 190$
Frequency	12	8	10	14	24	18

To draw a histogram, first put the data in a table and work out the frequency densities.

Blood pressure, b	Frequency	Class width	Frequency density
$110 < b \leq 140$	12	30	0.4
$140 < b \leq 150$	8	10	0.8
$150 < b \leq 155$	10	5	2.0
$155 < b \leq 160$	14	5	2.8
$160 < b \leq 170$	24	10	2.4
$170 < b \leq 190$	18	20	0.9

In the histogram the vertical scale must go up to 2.8. Label the axes.

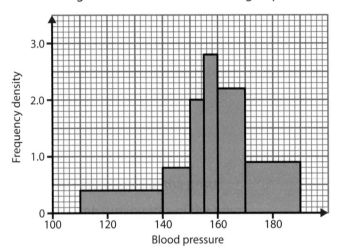

Quick Test

1. Here is a frequency table.

Time, t (min)	$30 < t \leq 40$	$40 < t \leq 60$	$60 < t \leq 100$
Frequency	80	150	420

Calculate the frequency density for each class.

2. This is part of a histogram. It represents a frequency of 40. Find the value of k.

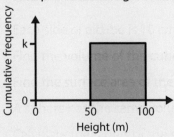

3. Look back at the blood pressure data from the worked example.
   If the $150 < b \leq 155$ and $155 < b \leq 160$ classes were combined into a single $150 < b \leq 160$ class, find the frequency density for the $150 < b \leq 160$ class.

Statistical data

1 This chart shows the ages of 60 children.

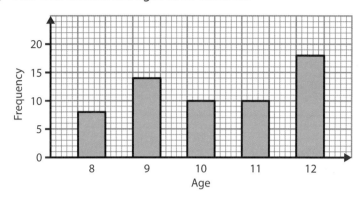

a Write down the most common age. [1]

b How many children are 10 years old or less? [2]

c What percentage of the children are 9 years old? [2]

2 This chart shows the percentage of the votes for four parties, A, B, C and D, in elections in 2020 and 2024.

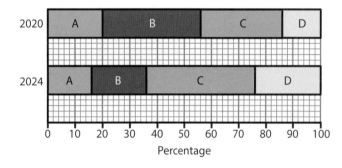

a Find the party that had most votes in 2020. [1]

b Find the percentage that voted for party C in 2024. [2]

c There were 15000 voters in 2024. Work out how many voted for party D. [2]

3 This chart shows the midday temperature on ten consecutive days.

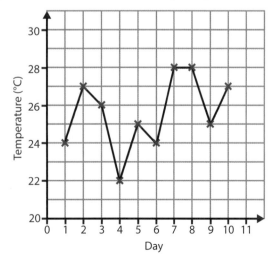

a Find the highest midday temperature. [1]

b Find the largest decrease in temperature form one day to the next. [2]

c Can you predict the temperature on day 11 from the data in the chart? Give a reason for your answer. [2]

4 A survey asked people to name their favourite sport. The pie chart shows the results.

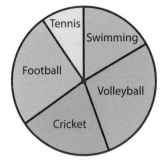

a Name the most popular sport. [1]

b One sport had about 10% of the votes. Name the sport. [1]

c 75 people voted for football. Estimate the total number of people in the survey. [2]

Averages

1 Here are five times: 13 s, 17 s, 19 s, 27 s, 16 s.

a Find the median time. [1]

For the **median**, put the numbers in order before you find the middle one

b Find the mean time. [1]

c A sixth time is added to the list. The range is now 18 s.

Find two possible values of the sixth time. [2]

2 The mean of 12 test scores is 38.

The mean of another 8 test scores is 30.

Find the mean of all 20 test scores. [3]

3 70 students are taking exams. This table shows the numbers of subjects they are studying.

Subject	5	6	7	8	9	10
Number of students	12	7	12	13	17	9

a Find the median number of subjects. [2]

b Find the mode. [1]

c Calculate the mean number of subjects. [3]

4 The goals scored in 10 football matches are: 0, 4, 1, 3, 0, 0, 2, 1, 5, 0.

a Find the mode. [1]

b Find the median. [2]

c Find the mean. [2]

d After two more matches the mean is 1.5.

What can you say about the goals scored in the last two matches? [2]

E **5** This table shows the speeds of cars passing a speed check.

Speed, x (km/h)	$40 < x \leq 50$	$50 < x \leq 60$	$60 < x \leq 70$	$70 < x \leq 80$	$80 < x \leq 90$
Frequency	4	17	20	35	38

a Find the modal class. [1]

b Estimate the mean speed. [4]

> **Show me**

Mid-points of classes are 45, 55, ..., ..., ...

Total number of car = 4 + 17 + ... = ...

Estimate of mean = {(45 × 4) + (55 × ...) + ... } ÷ .... = ...

Charts and diagrams

1 This table shows how 34 people travel to work.

Travel	Car	Bus	Cycle	Walk
Frequency	10	7	4	13

Copy and complete this pictogram. [3]

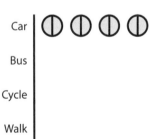

Car 〇〇〇〇

Key
〇 = 2 people

Bus

Cycle

Walk

2 This table shows the number of brothers that 72 children have.

Number of brothers	0	1	2	3
Frequency	31	23	11	7

a Show this information in a pie chart. [4]

b Find the mode. [1]

c Find the median. [1]

3 This composite bar chart shows the ages of people in a town.

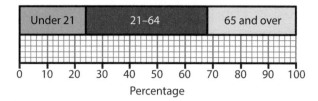

a What percentage are aged 21–64? [1]

Here are the figures for a different town.

Age	Under 21	21–64	65 and over
Percentage	34%		28%

b Find the missing percentage. [1]

c Show this town in a composite bar chart. [3]

Scatter diagrams

1 Here are the masses and heights of 12 young children.

Mass (kg)	14.4	14.8	15.4	15.7	16.2	16.5	17.0	17.5	17.8	18.3	18.5	19.0
Height (cm)	95	100	99	102	100	105	109	107	111	110	115	112

a Draw a scatter diagram. Use axes like these. [4]

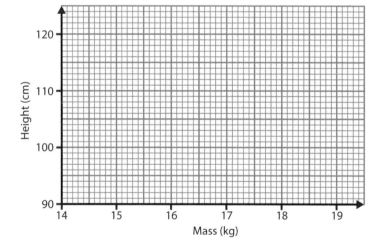

b State the type of correlation. [1]

c Draw a line of best fit. [2]

Correlation can be positive or negative

d Estimate the height of a child with a mass of 16.8 kg. [1]

2 This table shows the midday temperature and the number of visitors to an indoor pool on 14 days.

Temperature (°C)	5	8	13	13	15	15	17	20	23	25	27	30	30	32
Visitors	240	180	180	210	120	150	180	100	150	170	110	70	100	20

a Draw a scatter diagram. Use axes like these. [4]

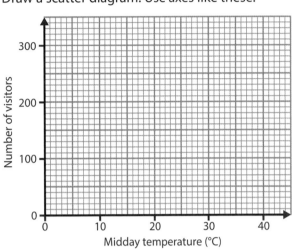

b What type of correlation does this show? [1]

c Draw a line of best fit on the scatter diagram. [2]

d Use the diagram to estimate the number of visitors on a day when the midday temperature is 10 °C. [1]

E Cumulative frequency

1 This cumulative frequency curves shows the heights of 160 trees.

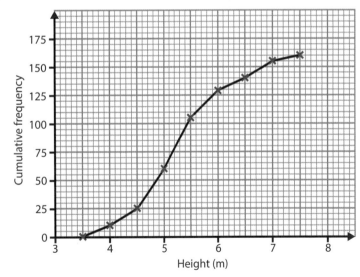

Use the graph to estimate:

a the median tree height [2]

b the interquartile range [2]

c the 90th percentile. [2]

2 This table shows the heights of 72 people.

Height, h (cm)	$155 < h \leq 160$	$160 < h \leq 165$	$165 < h \leq 170$	$170 < h \leq 175$	$175 < h \leq 180$	$180 < h \leq 185$	$185 < h \leq 190$	$190 < h \leq 195$
Frequency	2	4	14	18	14	8	6	6

a Draw a cumulative frequency curve to show the distribution of heights. **[5]**

> **Show me**
>
> Complete a cumulative frequency table:
>
> | Height | 155 | 160 | .... | 195 |
> |---|---|---|---|---|
> | Cumulative frequency | 0 | 2 | .... | ….. |
>
> Draw axes on graph paper and plot the points. Join them with a smooth curve.

b Use your graph to estimate:

   i) the median height **[2]**

   ii) the interquartile range **[2]**

   iii) the 35th percentile. **[2]**

E Histograms

1 This histogram shows the results of a survey of how long patients had to wait to see a doctor.

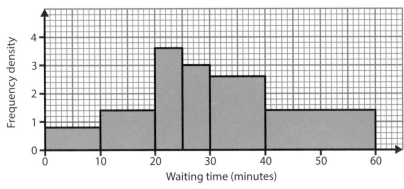

Frequency = frequency density x class width

a Find the number of people waited more than 40 minutes. **[2]**

b Find the number of people in the survey. **[3]**

2 ▶ This table shows the masses of 75 people.

Mass, m (kg)	$40 < m \leq 50$	$50 < m \leq 60$	$60 < m \leq 65$	$65 < m \leq 70$	$70 < m \leq 90$
Frequency	13	17	10	13	22

a Find the frequency density for the class $40 < m \leq 50$. [1]

Here is the start of a histogram to show the masses.

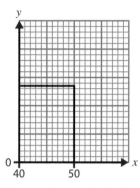

b Copy and complete the histogram. [5]

Mixed exam-style questions: Core

1 A number 3A bus leaves a station every 8 minutes.

A number 3B bus leaves the station every 10 minutes.

A 3A and a 3B both leave the station at 10 15

Find the next time when two buses leave the station simultaneously. **[2]**

2 **a** Find three different prime numbers with a sum of 21. **[1]**

b Write 200 as a product of prime factors. **[2]**

c Find the highest common factor of 126 and 198. **[3]**

3

a What fraction of this rectangle is shaded? Write your answer as simply as possible. **[2]**

b What percentage of the rectangle is **not** shaded? **[1]**

c Write down the ratio of shaded squares : unshaded squares. Write your answer as simply as possible. **[2]**

4 There are 300 men, women and children at a concert.

a There are 186 women. What percentage are women? **[2]**

b There are 45 children. What percentage are **not** children? **[2]**

5 This table shows the number of spectators in a sports stadium for three matches.

Date	2 April	9 April	16 April
Number of spectators	13 812	19 844	16 204

a Calculate the percentage change from 2 April to 9 April. **[2]**

b Calculate the percentage change from 9 April to 16 April. **[2]**

6 This table shows the population, in millions, of Germany and Japan in 2020.

Country	Total	Aged 0–19	65 and over
Germany	83.1	15.7	18.0
Japan	127.2	21.6	36.1

Compare the percentage of the population of each country aged 65 and over. **[4]**

7 The fuel tank of a car can hold 51 litres.

There are 15 litres of fuel in the tank.

Fuel costs $1.50 per litre.

How much will it cost to fill the tank? **[2]**

NC 8 ▸ Some glasses each hold $\frac{1}{5}$ of a litre of water.

A bottle of water holds 1 litre.

a How many glasses can you fill from 4 bottles of water? [1]

b How many bottles do you need to fill 55 glasses? [1]

NC 9 ▸ Work out $(-2 + x)^2$ when:

a $x = 5$ [1]

b $x = -5$ [1]

NC 10 ▸ A and B are two sets.

$n(A) = 10, n(B) = 7, n(A \cap B) = 2$

Work out $n(A \cup B)$. [2]

NC 11 ▸ The capacity of one bottle is 2 litres.

The capacity of another bottle is 750 ml.

Work out the ratio of their capacities. [2]

NC 12 ▸ The ratio of easy questions to hard questions in an examination is 5 : 3.

There are 40 questions in the examination.

Work out the number of easy questions. [2]

NC 13 ▸ The density of silver is 10.5 g/cm^3.

a Calculate the mass of 18 cm^3 of silver. [2]

b Calculate the volume of 500 g of silver. [2]

NC 14 ▸ A photocopier takes 3 minutes to print 20 copies.

Calculate the time to print 150 copies. Give your answer in minutes and seconds. [2]

NC 15 ▸ A car travels 90 km at an average speed of 60 km/h.

It travels a further 100 km at an average speed of 40 km/h.

Calculate the average speed for the whole journey. [3]

NC 16 ▸ An athlete runs 100 metres in 10.0 s.

Find the average speed of the athlete in km/h. [3]

NC 17 ▸ The area of the United States is 9 831 510 km^2.

a Round the area to the nearest thousand km^2. [1]

b Round the area to one significant figure. [1]

NC 18 ▸ $N = 8.93154$

Estimate:

a N^2 [1]

b $\sqrt{N}$. [1]

19 Here is an exchange rate: 1 euro = 90.56 Indian rupees.

A coat costs 145 euros. A shirt costs 45.50 euros. Trousers cost 93.90 euros.

Calculate the total cost of the three items in rupees. Give your answer to the nearest rupee. **[2]**

20 $y = x - 2z$

a Rearrange the formula to make x the subject. **[1]**

b Rearrange the formula to make z the subject. **[2]**

21

This shape is made from 5 identical squares.

The length of the side of a square is x.

a Write down a formula for the area A of the shape in terms of x. **[1]**

b Rearrange your formula to make x the subject. **[2]**

22 **a** Expand and simplify $2(e - 4) - 6(e - 1) + 2(2e + 5)$. **[3]**

b Factorise $12ab^2 - 18a^2b$ as much as possible. **[2]**

23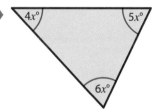

The sum of the angles of this triangle is 180°.

a Write down an equation to show this. **[1]**

b Work out the largest of the triangle. **[2]**

24 Asher has x dollars. Bella has y dollars.

a Bella has 16 dollars more than Asher. Write an equation to show this. **[1]**

b Bella has 3 times what Asher has. Write an equation to show this. **[1]**

c Work out how much Asher has. **[2]**

25 c is an integer and $-13.5 \leq c \leq 0$.

Write down:

a the greatest possible value of c **[1]**

b the least possible value of c. **[1]**

26 Temperature is measured in degrees Celsius (°C) or degrees Fahrenheit (°F).

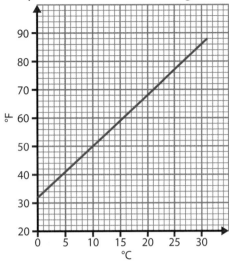

Use this conversion graph to convert:

a 30 °C to °F [1]

b 68 °F to °C [1]

If x °C $= y$ °F, then $y = 1.8x + 32$.

c Use this formula to convert −50 °C to °F. [2]

27 Paula and Sami cycle the same route. The graph shows their journeys.

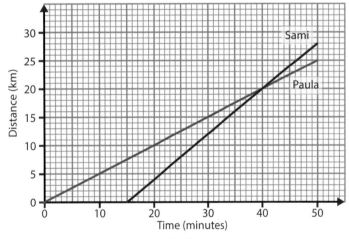

a How far did Paula travel in the first 30 minutes? [1]

b Work out Paula's average speed in km/h. [2]

c Sami started later than Paula. How many minutes later? [1]

d Work out Sami's average speed in km/h. [2]

28

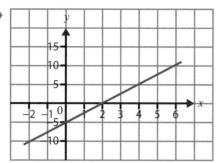

(a) Work out the gradient of this straight line. [2]

(b) Find the equation of the straight line. [1]

29 Fill in the missing numbers in this sequence.

93, ___, 79, 72, 65, ___, 51 [2]

30 Here are the first four terms of a sequence.

15, 20, 25, 30

(a) Find the 7th term. [1]

(b) Find the nth term. [2]

31

1   2   3   4

The length of the side of each small triangle is 1 cm.

(a) The perimeter of the 3rd pattern is 9 cm.

Find the perimeter of the nth pattern. [2]

(b) There are nine small triangles in the 3rd pattern.

Find the number of small triangles in the nth pattern. [2]

32 (a) Write 5^{-2} as a decimal. [2]

(b) Write 0.25 as a power of 4. [2]

33 Simplify $\dfrac{c^6 \times c^5}{c^{-2} \times c^{-4}}$. [3]

34 17 mathematics books cost $269.45.

Find the cost of 27 mathematics books. [2]

35

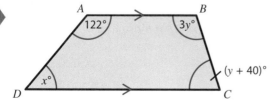

ABCD is a trapezium.

(a) Find the value of x. [1]

(b) Find the value of y. [3]

36

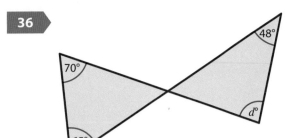

Find the value of d.

[3]

37

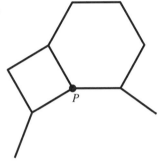

A square, a regular hexagon and another regular polygon meet at point P.

Work out the number of sides the third polygon has.

[3]

38

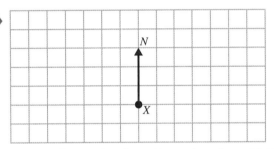

A plane flies 35 km from X on a bearing of 310° to reach Y.

Then it flies 76 km from Y on a bearing of 098° to reach Z.

a   Make a scale drawing of the journey. Use a scale of 1 cm to 10 km.   [4]

b   Find the distance from X to Z.   [1]

c   Find the bearing of X from Z.   [1]

39

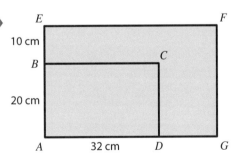

Rectangle AEFG is an enlargement of rectangle ABCD.

a   Find the scale factor of the enlargement.   [2]

b   Find the length of DG.   [2]

40 The diagram shows a sketch of a sheet of metal.

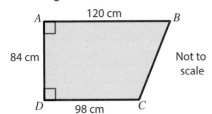

a Make an accurate scale drawing of the sheet. Use a scale of 1 mm to 2 cm. [3]

b Work out the length of the diagonal AC. [1]

41 The diagram shows a right-angled triangle.

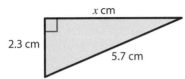

a Calculate the value of x. [2]

b Calculate the smallest angle of the triangle [2]

42

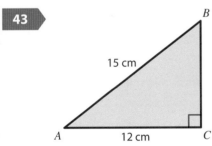

Calculate the area of this isosceles triangle. [3]

43

a Calculate angle BAC. [2]

b Calculate the length of BC. [2]

44

PR is a diameter of the circle.

a Explain why angle $PQR = 90°$. [1]

b The radius of the circle is 12.5 cm. Calculate the length of PQ. [2]

45

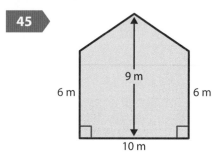

This diagram shows the end of a building.

Work out the area. [3]

46

The hexagon is made from 6 equilateral triangles with sides of 12 cm.

a Find the perimeter of the hexagon. [1]

b Find the circumference of the circle. [2]

c Find the area of the circle. [2]

47

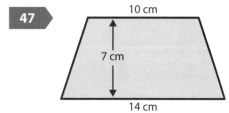

The cross-section of a prism is the trapezium shown here.

The volume of the prism 2100 cm^3.

Work out the length of the prism. [3]

48

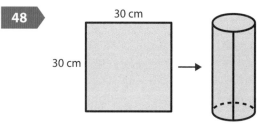

Each side of a square of card is 30 cm.

Two edges of the card are joined to make a hollow cylinder.

Show that the volume of the cylinder is 2150 cm^3 to 3 significant figures. [3]

49 This shape is made from two semi-circles.

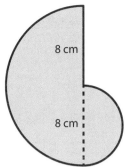

8 cm

8 cm

a Find the area of the shape. Give your answer as a multiple of π. [2]

b Find the perimeter of the shape. Give your answer in terms of π. [2]

50 This shape is made from a cone and a half a sphere.

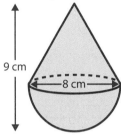

9 cm

8 cm

Show that the volume is 218 cm^3 to 3 significant figures.

Volume of a cone: $V = \frac{1}{3}\pi r^2 h$

Volume of a sphere: $V = \frac{4}{3}\pi r^3$ [3]

51

For this shape write down:

a the number of lines of symmetry [1]

b the order of rotational symmetry. [1]

52

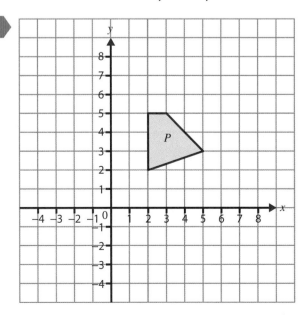

a   Copy the diagram. Translate P by $\begin{pmatrix} 3 \\ 2 \end{pmatrix}$ and label the image Q.   **[2]**

b   Translate P by $\begin{pmatrix} -5 \\ 0 \end{pmatrix}$ and label the image R.   **[2]**

c   Translate P by $\begin{pmatrix} 2 \\ -4 \end{pmatrix}$ and label the image S.   **[2]**

d   Write down the vector for the translation from S to P.   **[1]**

53

Monday

Tuesday

Wednesday

Key = ... hours

a   On Monday there were 5 hours of sunshine.

Copy the pictogram and complete the key.   **[1]**

b   Find the number of hours of sunshine on Tuesday.   **[1]**

c   There were 3 hours of sunshine on Wednesday. Show this on the pictogram.   **[1]**

54   Here are the ages of the audience in a cinema.

Age	10–19	20–29	30–39	40–49	50–59
Number of people	4	8	13	11	7

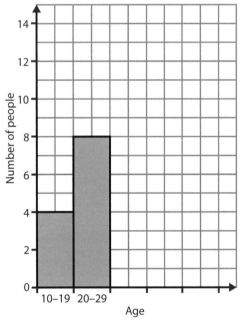

a   Copy and complete the bar chart.   **[2]**

b   Work out how many people were under 40.   **[2]**

c   State one fact about the age of the oldest person.   **[1]**

55 This table shows the favourite sport of 60 people.

Sport	Number of people	Angle on pie chart
Football	25	
Rugby	16	
Cricket	19	

a Work out the angle on a pie chart for each sport and put it in a copy of the table. [2]

b Draw the pie chart. [2]

56 Here are the masses and heights of seven candles.

Mass (g)	23	11	80	95	62	108	42
Height (cm)	16	10	21	27	18	23	15

a Find the range of the masses. [1]

b Find the median height. [2]

c Find the mean mass. [2]

57 Here are six pulse rates: 56, 58, 90, 73, 61, 67.

a Find the median pulse rate. [2]

b Find the mean pulse rate. [2]

c Find the range. [1]

58 In five matches the mean number of goals scored by a football team is 1.6 goals.

After a 6th game the mean is 2.0 goals.

Work out the number of goals scored in the 6th match. [3]

59 This frequency table shows the number of people living in each of 40 apartments.

Number of people	Frequency
1	6
2	12
3	9
4	8
5	5

a Write down the modal number of people. [1]

b Find the median number of people. [2]

c Show that the mean number of people in each apartment is 2.85 [3]

60 The diagram shows a fair five-sided spinner.

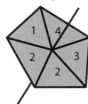

a Find the probability that when it is spun it shows:

i) 4 [1]

ii) 2 or 3 [1]

iii) 5. [1]

b The spinner is spun 80 times.

How many times would you expect to see an odd number? [2]

61 Two boxes, A and B, contain black and white balls.

 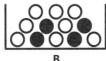

a A ball is chosen at random from box A. Find the probability that it is black. [1]

b A ball is chosen at random from box B. Show that the probability that it is black is $\frac{1}{3}$. [1]

Three balls are added to box B. Each ball is either black or white. The probability of choosing a black ball from either box is now the same.

c Work out the colours of the three added balls. [2]

62

One of these cards is chosen at random.

a Find the probability that the letter chosen is:

i) A or B [1]

ii) not I [1]

iii) in the word PRIME. [1]

b Five cards that spell the word TRAIL are removed.

One card is chosen at random from those that are left.

Find the probability that B is chosen. [1]

63 One card is chosen at random from each set. The numbers are added.

| 1 | 2 | 3 | 4 | 5 | | 1 | 2 | 3 |
Set A   Set B

a Copy and complete this diagram to show the totals.

Set B	3		5			
	2	3	4			
	1					
		1	2	3	4	5
		Set A				

[2]

b Find the probability that the total is:

i) 4 [1]

ii) more than 4 [2]

iii) an even number. [2]

E Mixed exam-style questions: Extended

64 **a** Write $\frac{7}{11}$ as a decimal. [2]

b Write $0.08\dot{3}$ as a fraction. [3]

65 Sheena has a loan on her credit card of $500.

Each month 2% compound interest is added to the loan.

Show that after 12 months the cost of the loan has increased by 26.8%. [3]

66 The price of a concert ticket is $40.04.

This includes a booking fee of 4%.

Calculate the booking fee. [2]

67 The population of a country in 2020 is 84.0 million. The population increases by 4% every ten years.

Calculate the population in 2070. [3]

68 **a** The circumference of the Earth round the equator is 40 100 km, to the nearest hundred km.

Find an upper bound for this length. [1]

b The side of a cube is 12 cm to 2 significant figures.

Find a lower bound for the volume of the cube. [2]

69 The mass of a molecule of water is 3×10^{-26} kg.

The mass of 1 litre of water is 1 kg.

Work out the number of molecules of water in 1 litre. [2]

70 Expand and simplify $(2x + 1)^3$. [4]

71 **a** Factorise $4x^2 - 20x + 25$. [3]

b Solve the equation $4x^2 + 25 = 20x$. [2]

72 **a** Simplify $\frac{x}{3} - \frac{x}{5}$. [2]

b Factorise and simplify $\frac{x^2 + 3x + 2}{x^2 - 1}$. [3]

73 **a** Solve the equation $(x + 4)(x - 5) = 0$. [2]

b Solve the equation $2x^2 + 4x = 1$. Round your answer to 3 significant figures. [4]

NC **74** Here is an equation: $x^2 = 2x + 1$.

a Show that one solution is $x = 1 + \sqrt{2}$. [3]

b Find another exact solution. [2]

75 Solve the equation $\frac{x}{2} + \frac{6}{x} = 4$. [4]

76 Solve this pair of simultaneous equations:

$y = x^2 \quad y = 5x - 4$ [4]

77 A car is travelling at 5 m/s.

It accelerates from 5 m/s at 2 m/s^2.

a How long will it take to reach a speed of 25 m/s? [2]

b Show the acceleration on a graph. Show speed on the vertical axis with a scale of 1 cm to 5 m/s. [4]

c Work out the distance travelled while accelerating from 5 m/s to 25 m/s. [3]

78

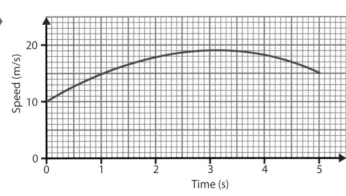

The graph shows the speed of a vehicle over a 5-second interval.

a Find the speed after 1 second. [1]

b Estimate the acceleration after 1 second. [2]

79 **a** Write $x^2 + 3x - 4$ in complete square form. [2]

b Find the turning point of the graph of $y = x^2 - 3x - 4$. [2]

c Solve the equation $x^2 + 3x - 4 = 0$. [3]

d Sketch a graph of $y = x^2 + 3x - 4$. [3]

80 **a** Copy and complete this table.

x	–2	–1	0	1	2	3	4
$x^3 - 3x^2 + 4$	–16					4	

[2]

b Copy these axes and draw a graph of $y = x^3 - 3x^2 + 4$.

[3]

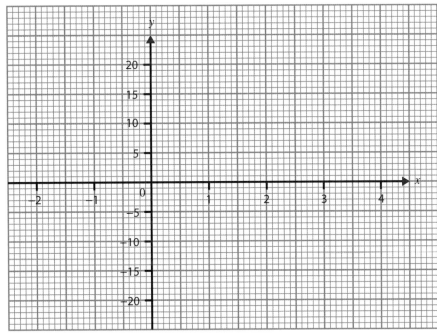

c Solve the equation $x^3 - 3x^2 + 4 = 0$. [2]

d Draw a straight line to solve the equation $x^2(x - 3) = 4(x - 1)$. [5]

81 Find the value of:

a $100^{\frac{5}{2}}$ [2]

b $100^{-\frac{3}{2}}$. [2]

82 Solve these equations.

a $5^x = 125$ [2]

b $25^x = 125$ [2]

83 Find three inequalities to show the shaded triangle. [5]

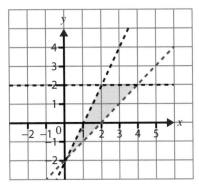

84 $p(x) = 5^x$. The domain of p is $\{-1, 0, 1, 2\}$.

Find the range of p. [2]

85 $h(x) = \dfrac{12}{x+1}$

a Work out $h(5)$. [1]

b Find $hh(11)$. [2]

c Solve the equation $h(x) = 6$. [2]

d Find $h^{-1}(x)$. [3]

e Solve the equation $h(x) = x$. [5]

86 The equation of a curve is $y = x^3 - 6x^2 + 10x$.

a Find $\dfrac{dy}{dx}$. [2]

b Find the coordinates of the two points on the graph where the gradient is 1. [5]

87

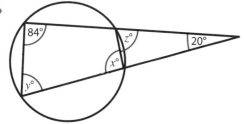

a Find the value of x. [1]

b Find the value of y. [1]

c Find the value of z. [1]

88

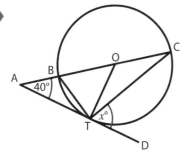

O is the centre of the circle. $ABOC$ is a straight line.

AT is a tangent to the circle at T.

Show that $x = 65$. Give a geometrical reason for each step of your answer. [3]

89 The length of a cuboid is 25 cm and its volume is 2000 cm³.

a Work out the volume of a similar cuboid with a length of 1 metre. [2]

b Find the length of a similar cuboid with a volume of 250 cm³. [2]

90

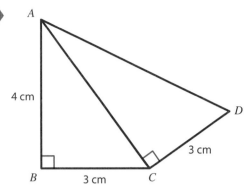

a   Calculate the length of AD.   [3]

b   Calculate angle BAD.   [3]

91   Show that the length of XZ is $12(1 + \sqrt{3})$.   [2]

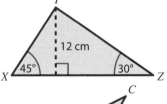

92

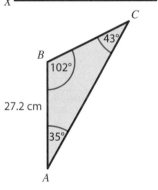

The diagram shows a triangular field ABC.

Calculate the shortest distance from B to side AC.   [2]

93

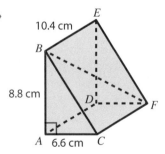

The diagram shows a prism.

The cross-section is a right-angled triangle ABC.

a   Calculate the area of face CBEF.   [3]

b   Calculate the angle between BF and the base ACFD.   [3]

94

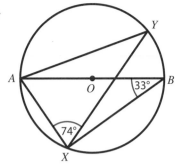

O is the centre of the circle. The length of the diameter AOB is 25 cm.

Angle $AXY = 74°$ and angle $ABY = 33°$.

a   Show that $AX = 13.6$ cm to 3 significant figures.   **[2]**

b   Show that $AY = 24.0$ cm to 3 significant figures.   **[4]**

c   Calculate the area of triangle AXY.   **[3]**

95

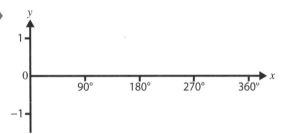

a   Copy the axes and sketch a graph of $y = \tan x$ for $0° \le x \le 360°$.   **[2]**

b   On the graph draw the line $y = -1$.   **[1]**

c   Solve the equation $\tan x = -1$ for $0° \le x \le 360°$.   **[2]**

d   Solve the equation $2 \tan x = 3$ for $0° \le x \le 360°$.   **[2]**

96

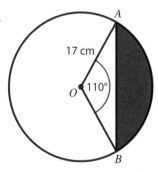

O is the centre of a circle of radius 17 cm.

AB is a chord and angle $AOB = 110°$.

Calculate the area of the shaded segment.   **[5]**

97

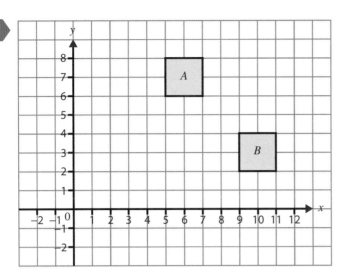

a Find the equation of the mirror line for a reflection mapping A onto B. [2]

b Find the coordinates of the centre of a 180° rotation mapping A onto B. [2]

c Find the coordinates of the centre of a 90° clockwise rotation mapping A onto B. [2]

d Find the coordinates of the centre of a 90° anticlockwise rotation mapping A onto B. [2]

98 $x = \begin{pmatrix} 6 \\ -1 \end{pmatrix}$ and $y = \begin{pmatrix} -3 \\ 4 \end{pmatrix}$

a Find $3x + 2y$. [2]

b Find the magnitude of $3x + 2y$. [2]

99

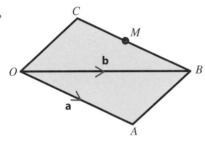

O is the origin and OABC is a parallelogram.

The position vector of A is **a**.

The position vector of B is **b**.

M is the midpoint of CB.

Find in terms of **a** and **b**, as simply as possible:

a the position vector of C [2]

b the position vector of M [2]

c $\overrightarrow{MA}$. [2]

100 A bag contains three black counters and seven white counters.

One counter is taken out at random.

Then a second counter is taken out.

Find the probability that:

a both counters are white [2]

b one counter is black and the other is white. [3]

101 This table shows the time 158 students spent doing homework.

Time, t (min)	$10 < t \leq 30$	$30 < t \leq 40$	$40 < t \leq 60$	$60 < t \leq 100$
Frequency	60	42	32	24

This is part of a histogram.

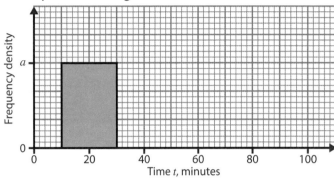

a Find the value of a. [1]

b Copy and complete the histogram. [3]

c Estimate the mean time spent doing homework. [4]

Practice Paper 1: Non-calculator (Core)

Instructions

- Answer **all** questions.
- You must **not** use a calculator.
- You may use tracing paper.
- You may refer to the formulas list on page 224.
- Show all necessary working clearly.
- The total mark for the paper is 80. The time allowed is 1 hour 30 minutes.

1 Write the number **forty-two thousand and seven** in figures.

.... [1]

2 These are the hours spent completing homework in one week for nine students.

3   2   9   5   6   4   3   9   3

a Write down the mode.

.... [1]

b Find the range.

.... [1]

3 Carlos competes in a long jump competition, jumping 7.85 m.

a Change 7.85 metres into centimetres.

....cm   [1]

b Write 7.85 correct to one decimal place.

.... [1]

4 Write down a square number that is also a cube number.

.... [1]

5

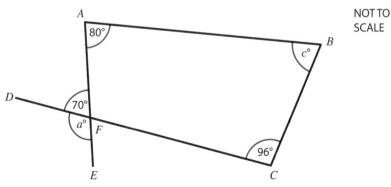

NOT TO SCALE

CD and AE are straight lines.

a Find the value of a.

Give a geometric reason for your answer.

$a =$ .... because ....

....

....   [2]

b Find the value of c.

$c =$ .... **[1]**

6 Solve

a $\dfrac{x}{6} = 5$

$x =$ .... **[1]**

b $3x + 7 = 31$

$x =$ .... **[2]**

c $5(x - 4) = -15$

$x =$ .... **[2]**

7

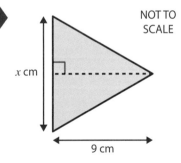

NOT TO SCALE   The area of this triangle is 45 cm^2.

Calculate the value of x.

x cm

9 cm

.... cm   **[2]**

8 Three people share some money.

Aja receives \$200.

Bob receives \$250.

Charlie receives \$175.

a Write down the ratio of Aja : Bob : Charlie.

Give your answer in its simplest form.

.... : .... : ....   **[2]**

b Write down the ratio of Aja : Bob in the form 1 : n.

1 : .... [2]

9 Calculate the value of $4x^2 - 2y$ when $x = 5$ and $y = -3$.

.... [2]

10 Estimate, by rounding each number correct to 1 significant figure.

$$\frac{9.91^2 - \sqrt{407}}{95}$$

You must show all your working.

.... [2]

11 Work out.

a $-11 + (-7)$

.... [1]

b $-6 - (-8)$

.... [1]

c $-33 \div (-3)$

.... [1]

12 These are the first five terms in a sequence.

7   10   13   16   19

a Find the next term in the sequence.

.... [1]

b Find an expression for the nth term of the sequence.

.... [2]

c Find the first term greater than 50.

.... **[2]**

13 Write 4 million in standard form.

.... **[2]**

14 ξ = {1, 2, 3, 5, 8, 13, 21, 34, 55}

$A = \{x: x$ is an odd number$\}$

$B = \{x: x$ is a prime number$\}$

a Complete the Venn diagram. **[2]**

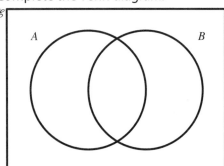

b Find $n(A)$.

.... **[1]**

c List the elements of A'.

.... **[1]**

d List the elements of A ∩ B.

.... **[1]**

15 Marshall starts the week with $72.

On Wednesday, Marshall gives $18 to his brother.

On Friday, Marshall buys 7 books at $3.99 each.

On Sunday, Marshall is given an allowance of $25.50.

How much money does Marshall have in total at the end of Sunday?

$.. **[3]**

16 **a** Simplify.

$7x - 4y - x - 2y$

.... **[2]**

b Make y the subject of the formula $x = \dfrac{y + z}{5}$.

.... **[2]**

c Factorise completely $15x^2y - 25xy^2$.

.... **[2]**

17 Find the highest common factor (**HCF**) of 64 and 96.

.... **[2]**

18 Four sports teams, Red United, Blue City, Green Rovers and Yellow Town, play 15 games in a season.

The bar chart shows the results.

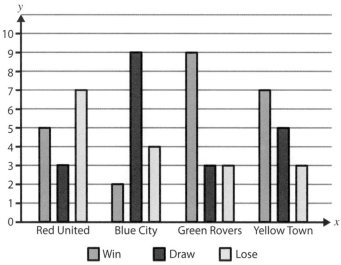

a Which team won the fewest matches?

.... **[1]**

b How many matches did Red United lose?

.... **[1]**

A win is worth 3 points.

A draw is worth 1 point.

A loss is worth 0 points.

c How many points did Green Rovers finish the season with?

.... [2]

d The table shows the number of games won by Red United during the last 10 seasons.

Number of games won	3	4	5	6	7
Frequency	2	3	4	0	1

Calculate the mean number of games won.

.... [3]

19 Jack pays a total rent of $1525 for 5 months.

Calculate Jack's rent for 1 year.

$.. [3]

20 The diagram shows a cuboid.

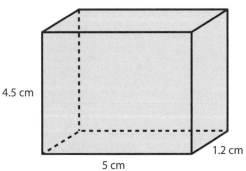

a Find the total surface area of the cuboid.

.... cm^2 [3]

a Show that the volume of the cuboid is 27 cm^3.

[2]

21 Work out $3\frac{2}{3} - 2\frac{1}{7}$.

You must show all your working and give your answer as a mixed number in its simplest form.

.... **[4]**

22 An isosceles triangle has sides 6 cm and 8 cm.

a **Using a ruler and compasses only**, construct a possible isosceles triangle, stating clearly the length of each side.

The 6 cm line has been drawn for you.

Show all your construction arcs.

6 cm

[2]

b **Using a ruler and compasses only**, construct a **different** possible isosceles triangle, stating clearly the length of each side.

The 6 cm line has been drawn for you.

Show all your construction arcs.

_____
6 cm

[2]

23 Simplify $\left(3x^4y\right)^3$.

.... [3]

24 Find the equation of the line parallel to $y = \dfrac{1}{2}x + 5$ that passes through $(-6, 9)$.

.... [3]

Total: 80 marks

Practice Paper 2: Non-calculator (Extended)

Instructions

- Answer **all** questions.
- You must **not** use a calculator.
- You may use tracing paper.
- You may refer to the formulas list on page 225.
- Show all necessary working clearly.
- The total mark for the paper is 100. The time allowed is 2 hours.

1 Write 101.9968 correct to 4 significant figures.

.... **[1]**

2 Write down the reciprocal of $3\frac{1}{2}$.

.... **[1]**

3 Convert 4 m^3 into cm^3.

.... cm^3 **[1]**

4 $72 = 2^3 \times 3^2$

Given that $1512 = 72 \times 21$, write 1512 as a product of its prime factors.

.... **[1]**

5 **a** Expand.

$3x(x^2 - 7)$

.... **[2]**

b Simplify.

$2x - 4y - 7x + 6y$

.... **[2]**

6 Jack and Sarah share some sweets in the ratio 4 : 7.

a What fraction of the sweets does Jack have?

.... **[1]**

Sarah has 21 more sweets than Jack.

b How many sweets do Jack and Sarah have in total?

.... **[2]**

7 **a** $\mathbf{a} = \begin{pmatrix} -6 \\ 4 \end{pmatrix}$, $\mathbf{b} = \begin{pmatrix} 4 \\ -1 \end{pmatrix}$

Find $\mathbf{a} - 3\mathbf{b}$.

.... [2]

b $\overrightarrow{PQ} = \begin{pmatrix} -2 \\ p \end{pmatrix}$ and $|\overrightarrow{PQ}| = \sqrt{13}$

Calculate the two possible values of p.

$p =$ .... and $p =$ .... [3]

8 The table shows the time spent revising for 92 students.

Time, t (h)	$0 \leq t < 4$	$4 \leq t < 8$	$8 \leq t < 12$	$12 \leq t < 16$	$16 \leq t < 20$
Frequency	15	21	33	17	6

a State the modal class interval.

.... [1]

Tom says the median time spent revising is 12.2 hours.

b Explain why Tom is wrong. [2]

9 Solve the inequality.

$-5 \leq 4x + 7 < 12$

.... [2]

10 In a bag there are only red, blue, yellow and green counters.

A counter is taken at random from the bag.

The probability that the counter will be blue is three times the probability that the counter will be green.

The table shows the probability of choosing a red or yellow counter.

Complete the table. [2]

Colour	Red	Blue	Yellow	Green
Probability	0.15		0.45	

11 **a** Write 64×16^x as a single power of 2 in terms of x.

.... **[2]**

b Simplify $\left(\dfrac{27}{1000}\right)^{-\frac{2}{3}}$.

Give your answer as a mixed number.

.... **[3]**

12

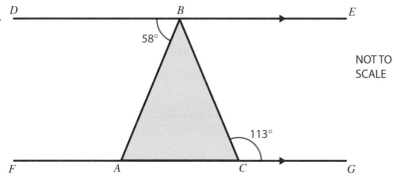

The diagram shows triangle *ABC*.

DE is parallel to *FG*.

Show that triangle *ABC* is scalene. **[3]**

13 36% of *r* is 720.

Find 124% of *r*.

.... **[2]**

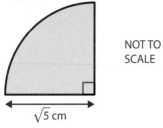

14

NOT TO SCALE

$\sqrt{5}$ cm

The diagram shows a quarter-circle with radius $\sqrt{5}$ cm.

Calculate the area of the quarter-circle.

Give your answer in exact form.

.... cm^2　[3]

15 Solve $\dfrac{3(2x - 4)}{5} = \dfrac{7 - 3x}{3}$.

You must show all your working.

$x =$ ....　[3]

16

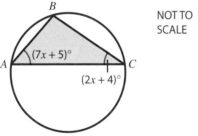

NOT TO SCALE

B

$(7x + 5)°$

A

C

$(2x + 4)°$

The diagram shows triangle ABC inside a circle.

AC is the diameter of the circle.

Find the value of x.

$x =$ ....　[4]

17 **a** A is directly proportional to b^3.

When $b = 5$, $A = 25$.

Find a formula for A in terms of b.

$A =$ .... **[3]**

b Calculate the value of b when $A = 2$.

Give your answer in the form $\sqrt[3]{p}$, where p is an integer.

$b =$ .... **[2]**

18 **a** Write $y = x^2 - 6x - 2$ in the form $(x + a)^2 + b$ where a and b are integers.

.... **[2]**

b Hence or otherwise, solve $x^2 - 6x - 2 = 0$.

Give your answer in exact surd form.

$x =$ .... and $x =$ .... **[2]**

19 **a** Write $2.3\dot{6}$ as an improper fraction in its simplest form.

Show all your working.

.... **[3]**

b Write $23.\dot{6}\dot{3}$ as an improper fraction in its simplest form.

.... **[1]**

20 **a** Write as a single fraction in its simplest form.

$$\frac{2x^2 - 3x}{x^2 + 2x - 8} \div \frac{2x - 3}{x + 4}$$

.... **[4]**

b Write as a single fraction in its simplest form.

$$\frac{2x - 1}{x + 2} + \frac{x - 2}{x}$$

.... **[3]**

21 A is the point $(-2, 5)$ and B is the point $(6, 9)$.

a Show that the length of AB is $\sqrt{80}$.

You must show all your working.

[3]

b Find the coordinate of the midpoint of AB.

(.................................... , ...) [2]

c Find the equation of the perpendicular bisector of AB.

Give your answer in the form $y = mx + c$.

.... [4]

22 **a** On the axes, sketch the graph of $y = \cos x$ for $0° \leq x \leq 360°$.

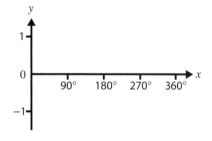

[2]

b Solve $4\cos x + 1 = 3$ for $0° \leq x \leq 360°$.

$x =$ .... and $x =$ .... [3]

23 **a** Show that $(2 - \sqrt{20})(5 - \sqrt{5}) = 20 - 12\sqrt{5}$

Show each stage of your working.

[2]

b Rationalise the denominator.

Give your answer in its simplest form.

$$\frac{6}{\sqrt{8} - \sqrt{2}}$$

.... [3]

24 The diagram shows triangle ABC.

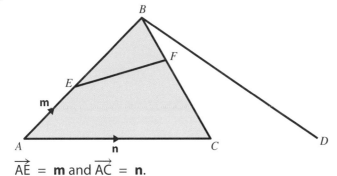

$\overrightarrow{AE} = \mathbf{m}$ and $\overrightarrow{AC} = \mathbf{n}$.

E is the midpoint of AB.

BF : FC = 1 : 2.

a Find, in terms of **m** and **n**, in simplest form:

i) $\overrightarrow{BC}$

.... [2]

ii) $\overrightarrow{EF}$.

.... [2]

$\overrightarrow{BD} = a\mathbf{m} + b\mathbf{n}$

b Given that ACD are collinear, state the value of a.

$a =$ .... [1]

25 The diagram shows a frustum.

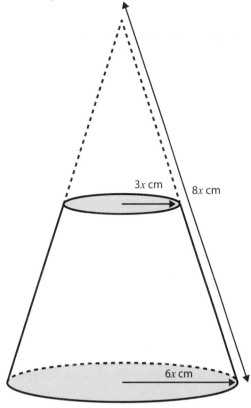

3x cm

8x cm

6x cm

A frustum is made by removing a small cone from a large cone.

The slant height of the large cone is $8x$ cm.

The radius of the base of the large cone is $6x$ cm. The radius of the base of the small cone is $3x$ cm.

a Show that the total surface area of the frustum is $81x^2\pi$ cm^2.

.... [5]

b The frustum has the same surface area as a sphere with radius 9 cm.

Find the value of x.

$x =$ .... [2]

26 ▶ A curve has the equation $y = \frac{2}{3}x^3 - 2x^2 + 3$.

Find the coordinates of its two stationary points and state whether they are maxima or minima.

[6]

Total: 100 marks

Practice Paper 3: Calculator (Core)

Instructions

- Answer **all** questions.

- You may use a scientific calculator.

- You may use tracing paper.

- You may refer to the formulas list on page 224.

- Show all necessary working clearly.

- Unless specified differently in the question, give non-exact answers to 3 significant figures, or 1 decimal place for angles in figures.

- For π, use either your calculator value or 3.142.

- The total mark for the paper is 80. The time allowed is 1 hour 30 minutes.

1 **a** Draw all the lines of symmetry on the regular pentagon below. [1]

b Write down the order of rotational symmetry of a regular pentagon.

.... [1]

c Draw two lines on the diagram below to split the regular pentagon into three isosceles triangles.

.... [1]

d State the number of lines of symmetry on an isosceles triangle.

.... [1]

2 Write these numbers in ascending order.

a 404   4.4   40.04   4.04   4.404

.... , ... , ... , ... , ... [1]

b −5 −2 −12   −1.8   −1$\frac{1}{4}$

.... , ... , ... , ... , ... [2]

3 Insert brackets into this statement to make it correct. [1]

6 + 5 × 5 − 2 = 33

4 Simplify.

a $5x^0$

.... [1]

b $3x^4 \times 7x^5$

.... [2]

c $15x^{17}y^{12} \div 5x^6y^4$

.... [3]

5 **a** Complete the table of values for $y = 4 - 3x$. [2]

x	−2	−1	0	1	2	3
y		7			−2	−5

b On the grid, draw the graph of $y = 4 - 3x$ for $-2 \leq x \leq 3$. [3]

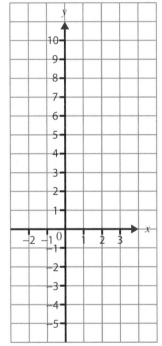

6 A bag contains cards which are numbered from 1 to 9.

Four cards are randomly selected from the bag. Three are shown here. | 5 | 3 | 6 | |

a Write down the probability that the next card selected is the number 7.

.... [1]

b Find the probability that the next card selected is an even number.

Give your answer as a fraction in simplest form.

.... [2]

c Calculate the probability that the total of the four cards is at least 21.

.... [3]

7 **a** Calculate

$$\frac{\sqrt[3]{463} - 0.35^2}{0.283}$$

Write down all the figures on your calculator display.

.... [1]

b Round your answer to part **(a)** to two significant figures.

.... [1]

8 **a** Write down the inequality, in terms of x, shown by the number line.

.... [2]

b Solve

$4k + 6 \leq 5$

.... [2]

c Write down the integer values of n that satisfy the inequality $-3 < n \leq 1$.

.... [2]

9 The price of a book is $4.50.

In a sale, this price is reduced by 28%.

Find the sale price of the book.

$.. [2]

10 Expand and simplify

$(x + 4)(x + 5)$

.... **[2]**

11 Write 52 as a product of its prime factors.

.... **[2]**

12 Solve the simultaneous equations.

You must show all your working.

$3x + 5y = 1$

$2x - 3y = 7$

$x =$.., $y =$.. **[4]**

13 Terry is travelling from New York to Paris.

He changes $500 into euros.

The exchange rate is $1 = 0.88 euros.

Terry spends $\frac{3}{4}$ of his euros.

Calculate the number of euros Terry has remaining.

 ....euros **[3]**

14 The bearing of B from C is 050°.

Calculate the bearing of C from B.

....° [2]

15 The number of text messages received by each of 25 students in a given day are shown below.

64	52	33	28	11
5	15	47	53	7
17	44	26	29	8
9	19	24	30	48
35	11	27	12	36

a Draw an ordered stem-and-leaf diagram for this data. [2]

0	
1	
2	
3	
4	
5	
6	

Key: 3 | 4 represents 34 text messages

b Find the median for this data.

.... [1]

c Calculate the percentage of students who received less than 20 text messages.

....% [2]

16 A biased, four-colour spinner has a red, a blue, a green and a yellow segment.

The probability that the spinner will land on red or blue is given in the table.

The probability that the spinner will land on yellow is twice the probability that it will land on green.

Colour	Red	Blue	Green	Yellow
Probability	0.1	0.21		

a Find the probability that the spinner will land on yellow.

.... [3]

b The spinner is spun 300 times.

Work out the expected number of times the spinner lands on blue.

.... [1]

17 **a** Calculate the area of a circle with diameter 8 cm.

....cm^2 [2]

b A different circle has an area of 45 cm^2.

Calculate the circumference of this circle.

....cm [4]

18 Shape A is drawn on the grid.

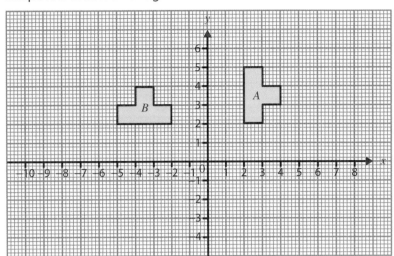

a On the grid, draw the image of

i) shape A after a reflection in the line $y = 1$. [2]

ii) shape B after a translation by the vector $\begin{pmatrix} -3 \\ -6 \end{pmatrix}$. [2]

b Describe fully the **single** transformation that maps shape A onto shape B.

....

.... [3]

19 Seven students record the time, in minutes, spent on their mathematics homework and their percentage grade on the assignment. The scatter diagram shows the data.

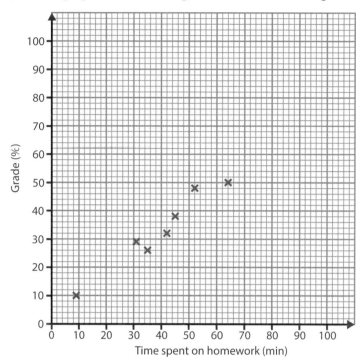

The table shows the time spent on their mathematics homework and the percentage grade for a further three students.

Time spent on homework (min)	69	72	90
Grade (%)	61	85	100

a Plot the data for the three further students on the scatter diagram. [2]

b What type of the correlation is shown in the scatter diagram?

.... [1]

c On the grid, draw a line of best fit. [1]

d Use your line of best fit to find an estimate for the percentage grade for a student who spent 58 minutes on their homework.

....% [1]

20 The diagram shows a shape made from two different right-angled triangles.

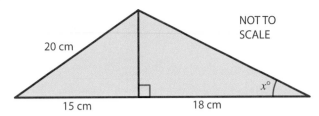

NOT TO SCALE

20 cm

15 cm

18 cm

$x°$

Find the value of x.

$x =$.. [4]

Total: 80 marks

Practice Paper 4: Calculator (Extended)

Instructions

- Answer **all** questions.
- You may use a scientific calculator.
- You may use tracing paper.
- You may refer to the formulas list on page 225.
- Show all necessary working clearly.
- Unless specified differently in the question, give non-exact answers to 3 significant figures, or 1 decimal place for angles in figures.
- For π, use either your calculator value or 3.142.
- The total mark for the paper is 100. The time allowed is 2 hours.

1   ξ = (1, 2, 3, 4, 5, 6, 7, 8, 9, 10)

A = {2, 3, 5, 7}

B = {x:x is an odd number}

List the elements in $A \cap B'$.

.... [1]

2   A film starts at 6.20 pm. The film lasts 205 minutes.

What time does the film finish?

.... [1]

3

Triangle XYZ is equilateral of side 9 cm.

Using a ruler and compasses only, construct triangle XYZ.

The line XY has been drawn for you.

[2]

4 A regular n-sided polygon has interior angles greater than 160°.

Write an inequality to show the possible values of n.

.... **[2]**

5 **a** Work out $2.75 as a percentage of $62.50.

....% **[1]**

b Guz buys a coat in a sale for $54.60.

This sale price is after a reduction of 35%.

Calculate the original price of the coat.

$.. **[3]**

6

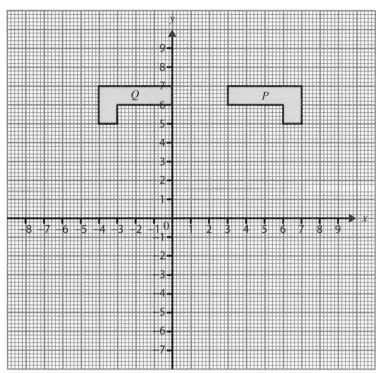

a Describe fully the single transformation that maps shape P onto shape Q.

....

.... [2]

b On the grid, draw the image of:

i) shape P after a rotation about the point (1, 4) through 180° [2]

ii) shape P after an enlargement by scale factor −2, centre (3, 3). [2]

7 Ayville is on a bearing of 240° from Beetown.

Find the bearing of Beetown from Ayville.

.... [2]

8 It takes 8 machines take 5 hours to make 2000 bricks.

All machines work at the same rate.

Work out how many hours it would take 16 machines to make 8000 bricks.

.... hours [2]

9 The probability that a biased spinner will land on six is 0.24.

The spinner is spun 250 times.

Find the number of times that the spinner is expected to land on six.

.... [1]

10 Show that $4\frac{1}{3} \div 2\frac{5}{6} = 1\frac{9}{17}$.

You must show all your working.

.... [3]

11 Yusef is making tofu sandwiches consisting of a tofu burger and a bread bun.

Tofu burgers are sold in packs of 8.

Bread buns are sold in packs of 6.

Yusef wants to make at least 100 tofu sandwiches and wants to have no tofu burgers or bread buns left over.

a Find the smallest number of tofu sandwiches Yusef can make.

.... [2]

Packs of tofu burgers cost $2.47.

Packs of bread buns cost $1.97.

Yusef sells all of the tofu sandwiches, making a profit of $175.55.

b How much does Yusef sell each tofu sandwich for?

$.. [3]

12 The table shows some values for $y = 5 - \dfrac{3}{(x-2)^2}$.

x	−2	−1	0	1		3	4	5
y	4.81		4.25	2		2	4.25	

a **i)** Complete the table. [2]

ii) On the grid, draw the graph of $y = 5 - \dfrac{3}{(x-2)^2}$ for $-2 \le x \le 5$.

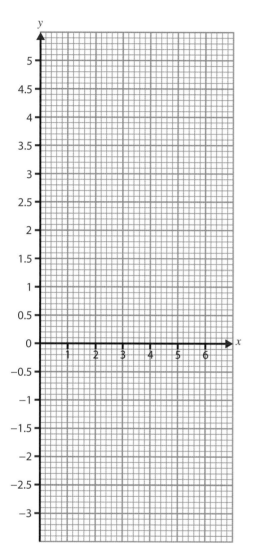

[4]

b By drawing a suitable straight line, solve the equation $3 - \dfrac{1}{2}x - \dfrac{3}{(x-2)^2} = 0$ for $-2 \le x \le 5$.

$x =$ .... [3]

13 $\dfrac{p(m-n)}{5} = mn$

Make n the subject of the formula.

.... [4]

14 Two solids are mathematically similar.

The surface area of the smaller solid is 26 cm^2 and the volume of the smaller solid is 103 cm^3.

The surface area of the larger solid is 162.5 cm^2.

Find the volume of the larger solid.

..............................cm^3 [3]

15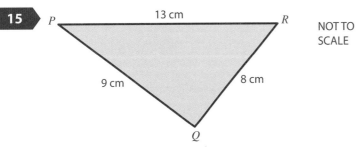

Calculate the area of triangle PQR.

..............................cm^2 [4]

16 Evaluate

$(2x + 3)^2(x - 4)$

.... [3]

17 The population of Singapore in 1974 was 2.23×10^6.

The population of Singapore in 2024 is 5.64×10^6.

Calculate the percentage increase in the population of Singapore from 1974 to 2024.

....% [3]

18 Samuel invests $5500 for five years in an account paying **compound interest**.

For the first two years, Samuel's investment **grows** at a rate of 5.6%.

In years three and four, Samuel's investment **grows** at a rate of 2.49%.

In the fifth year, the value of Samuel investment **shrinks** at a rate of 3.95%.

a Show that at the end of the five-year period, the value of Samuel's investment is $6188.01. [3]

b What rate of interest is required in the next five years for Samuel to double his initial investment?

....% [3]

19 ▷ These are the first five terms of a sequence.

25   49   81   121   169

Find the nth term of the sequence.

Give your answer in the form $(an + b)^2$ where a and b are integers.

.... **[4]**

20 ▷ A train travels 70 km, correct to nearest 5 km.

The train's average speed is 53.5 km/h, correct to 3 significant figures.

Calculate the upper bound of the time taken to complete this journey.

Give your answer in hours.

.... hours   **[4]**

21 The diagram shows a right-angled triangle.

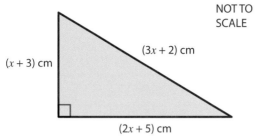

NOT TO SCALE

$(3x + 2)$ cm

$(x + 3)$ cm

$(2x + 5)$ cm

a Show that $2x^2 - 7x - 15 = 0$. [4]

b By factorising and solving $2x^2 - 7x - 15 = 0$, find the perimeter of the triangle.

.... cm   [5]

22 $f(x) = 6x + 5$, $g(x) = \dfrac{x - 2}{3}$

a **i)** Find f(7).

.... [1]

ii) Find gg(−2).

.... [1]

b Solve.

$fg(x) = g^{-1}(x)$

$x =$ .... [4]

23 Solve

$$y - x = 5$$

$$y^2 + x^2 = 15$$

Give your answers correct to 2 decimal places.

$x =$ .... , ...

$y =$ .... , ... **[6]**

24 Jack has a bag containing n counters.

8 of the counters are red, the rest are yellow.

Jack selects two counters from the bag.

Show that the probability of choosing two red counters is $\dfrac{56}{n(n-1)}$. **[2]**

25 The histogram shows the time, in hours, spent on homework by 22 students.

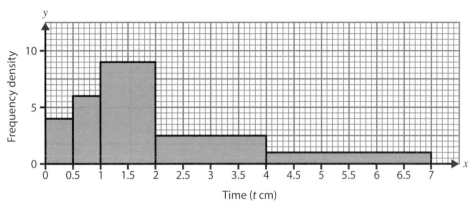

a Complete the frequency table.

Time, t (cm)	$0 < t \leq 0.5$	$0.5 < t \leq 1$	$1 < t \leq 2$	$2 < t \leq 4$	$4 < t \leq 7$
Frequency					

[3]

b What fraction of students spent longer than 2 hours on their homework?

Give your answer in simplest form.

.... [1]

c Calculate an estimate of the mean.

Give your answer in hours and minutes, to the nearest minute.

You must show your working.

.... hours and .... minutes [4]

Total: 100 marks

List of formulas (Core)

Area, A, of triangle, base b, height h. $\qquad\qquad\qquad\qquad\qquad\qquad\qquad A=\dfrac{1}{2}bh$

Area, A, of circle of radius r. $\qquad\qquad\qquad\qquad\qquad\qquad\qquad\qquad A=\pi r^2$

Circumference, C, of circle of radius r. $\qquad\qquad\qquad\qquad\qquad\qquad C=2\pi r$

Curved surface area, A, of cylinder of radius r, height h. $\qquad\qquad A=2\pi rh$

Curved surface area, A, of cone of radius r, sloping edge l. $\qquad\qquad A=\pi rl$

Surface area, A, of sphere of radius r. $\qquad\qquad\qquad\qquad\qquad\qquad A=4\pi r^2$

Volume, V, of prism, cross-sectional area A, length l. $\qquad\qquad\qquad V=Al$

Volume, V, of pyramid, base area A, height h. $\qquad\qquad\qquad\qquad V=\dfrac{1}{3}Ah$

Volume, V, of cylinder of radius r, height h. $\qquad\qquad\qquad\qquad V=\pi r^2h$

Volume, V, of cone of radius r, height h. $\qquad\qquad\qquad\qquad\qquad V=\dfrac{1}{3}\pi r^2h$

Volume, V, of sphere of radius r. $\qquad\qquad\qquad\qquad\qquad\qquad V=\dfrac{4}{3}\pi r^3$

List of formulas (Extended)

Area, A, of triangle, base b, height h. $A=\frac{1}{2}bh$

Area, A, of circle of radius r. $A=\pi r^2$

Circumference, C, of circle of radius r. $C=2\pi r$

Curved surface area, A, of cylinder of radius r, height h. $A=2\pi rh$

Curved surface area, A, of cone of radius r, sloping edge l. $A=\pi rl$

Surface area, A, of sphere of radius r. $A=4\pi r^2$

Volume, V, of prism, cross-sectional area A, length l. $V=Al$

Volume, V, of pyramid, base area A, height h. $V=\frac{1}{3}Ah$

Volume, V, of cylinder of radius r, height h. $V=\pi r^2h$

Volume, V, of cone of radius r, height h. $V=\frac{1}{3}\pi r^2h$

Volume, V, of sphere of radius r. $V=\frac{4}{3}\pi r^3$

For the equation $\quad ax^2+bx+c=0$, where $a\neq0$, $\qquad x=\dfrac{-b\pm\sqrt{b^2-4ac}}{2a}$

For the triangle shown,

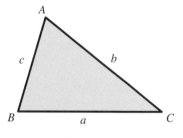

$$\frac{a}{\sin A}=\frac{b}{\sin B}=\frac{c}{\sin C}$$

$$a^2=b^2+c^2-2bc\cos A$$

$$\text{Area}=\frac{1}{2}ab\sin C$$

Pages 6-31: Section 1 Revise Questions

Page 7 Types of number
1   a)   35
      b)   32
      c)   31 and 37
2    $150 = 2 \times 3 \times 5^2$
3   a)   6
      b)   90

Page 9 Sets
1   a) $\mathscr{E}$

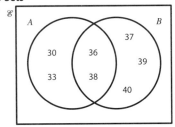

      b)   {30, 33, 36, 37, 38, 39, 40}
2   a)   odd numbers
      b)   multiples of 10
3   a)   2
      b)   False
4   15

Page 11 Powers and roots
1   14
2   7
3   5
4   2
5   8

Page 13 Fractions, decimals and percentages
1    $6\frac{2}{3}$
2   a)   0.08
      b) $\frac{2}{25}$
3   a)   12.5%
      b) $\frac{1}{8}$
4    $\frac{5}{6}$

Page 15 Ordering and the four operations
1    $-14 < -7 < -2 < 3 < 8$
2   a)   1
      b)   −10
3   a) $1\frac{7}{12}$
      b) $\frac{5}{8}$
      c) $\frac{9}{10}$
4   a)   0.08
      b)   50
5   9.25

Page 17 Indices and standard form
1   3^{-4}
2   8
3   5.2×10^7
4   125
5   5×10^{11}

Page 19 Estimation and limits of accuracy
1   25 000
2   3.142
3   0.0508
4    $40 \times 50 = 2000$
5   5.602 cm to 3 d.p.

Page 21 Ratio and proportion
1   5 : 3
2   40 kg
3   42
4    $57.50

Page 23 Rates
1   28 hours [1]
2   4.6 km/h
3   135 litres
4   0.952 g/cm^3 to 3 d.p.
5   700 people/km^2

Page 25 Percentages
1   56.4% to 1 d.p.
2    $212.80
3    $616
4    $11 013.10
5   7.5 kg

Page 27 Using a calculator
1   2.32
2   42 minutes
3   38 hours 40 minutes
4    $1 = 55.4069 pesos
5    $520.78

Page 29 Exponential growth and decay
1   89 057
2    $450 \times 0.9^4 = 295 < 300$
3   17%

Page 31 Surds
1    $9\sqrt{2}$
2    $\sqrt{7}$
3    $-1 + 2\sqrt{2}$
4    $\frac{1}{2}\sqrt{10}$
5    $3(3 + \sqrt{5})$

Pages 32-41: Section 1 Practise Questions

Page 32 Types of number
1   a)   81 [1] and 100 [1]
      b)   64 [1]
2   a)   91 [1]
      b)   99 [1]
      c)   97 [1]
3   31 [1] and 37 [1]
4   a) $264 = 2^3 \times 3 \times 11$ [3]
      b)   33 (Use the answer to part a)) [2]
5   a)   195 [2]
      b)   13 [2]
6   8 [2]

Page 32 Sets
1   a) $\mathscr{E}$ [2]

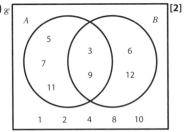

      b)   {3, 9} [1]
      c)   {1, 2, 4, 6, 8, 10, 12} [1]
2   a) $\mathscr{E}$ [2]

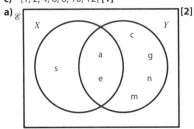

      b)   {a, c, e, g, m, n, s} [1]
3   a)   8 [1]
      b)   {8, 9, 11, 12, 13, 14, 16} [2]
      c)   23 [1]

Page 33 Powers and roots
1   a)   11 [1]
      b)   5 [1]
2   The sum is $1 + 8 + 27 = 36 = 6^2$ [2]
3   1 [1] and 49 [1]
4   a) 8^2 [1]
      b) 4^3 [1]
      c) 2^6 [1]
5   12 (36 ÷ 3) [2]
6   a) $243 \times 3 = 729$ [2]
      b) $243 \div 3 = 81$ [2]
7    $7 \times 5 = 35$ [2]
8   a) $25 + 125 = 150$ [2]
      b) $100 + 1000 = 1100$ [2]

Page 34 Fractions, decimals and percentages
1   a) $\frac{3}{5}$
      b)   40% [2]
2   a)   85% [2]
      b)   0.025 [1]
3   162.5% [2]
4    $\frac{3}{4} + \frac{2}{5} = 1\frac{3}{20}$ [3]
5   a)   2.25 [1]
      b)   0.444… [2]
6   Either write them as decimals: 0.6 and 0.666… or find equivalent fractions with the same denominator such as $\frac{9}{15}$ and $\frac{10}{15}$ [2]
7    $1\frac{17}{33}$ [3]
8    $\frac{29}{45}$ [3]

Page 34 Ordering and the four operations
1   3 °C [1]
2    $\frac{13}{20} < \frac{7}{10} < \frac{3}{4}$ [2]
3   a)   23 [1]
      b)   12 [1]
      c)   −13 [1]
4   a)   0.42 [1]
      b)   0.036 [2]
5   a) $\frac{1}{4}$ [2]
      b) $3\frac{5}{12}$ [1]
6   a) $\frac{2}{5}$ [1]
      b) $1\frac{4}{5}$ [2]
7    $3\frac{1}{4}$ [3]
8    $1\frac{3}{5}$ [3]
9   0.2 [2]
10   a)   0.04 [1]
      b)   25 [1]
11   One half [2]

Page 35 Indices and standard form
1   a)   0.000 036 2 [1]
      b) 7.21×10^8 [1]
2   a) 3^{-3} [2]
      b)   81 [2]
      c)   0.2 [2]
3   a) 7^{-15} [1]
      b) 2^{12} [2]
4   a) 1.26×10^{-8} [2]
      b) 2.58×10^{-4} [2]
5   a)   32 [2]
      b)   9 [2]
      c) $2\frac{8}{3}$ [2]

4   a) $\notin$ [1]
      b) $\in$ [1]
      c) $\subseteq$ [1]

Page 36 Estimation and limits of accuracy
1. 26 000 **[1]**
2. a) 58.824 **[1]**
   b) 58.8 **[1]**
3. 0.0081 **[1]**
4. a) 30 **[1]**
   b) $8 \times 10 \div 4 = 20$ **[2]**
5. 15.75 cm **[1]**
6. $(6 \times 6) \div (3 \times 4) = 36 \div 12 = 3$ **[2]**
7. 119.5 kg **[1]**
8. a) 296 mm **[2]**
   b) 5385.75 mm^2 **[2]**
9. 7.551 g/cm^3 **[3]**

Page 36 Ratio and proportion
1. $3:4:5$ **[1]**
2. $1:8$ **[1]**
3. a) $3:4$ **[1]**
   b) $4:5$ **[2]**
   c) $1:2$ **[2]**
4. $180 **[2]**
5. a) $5:2$ **[1]**
   b) 75 mm **[2]**
6. a) $54.40 **[2]**
   b) 20 litres **[2]**
7. 625 g **[2]**
8. 1 kg bag: $0.85 for 100 g; 600 g bag: $0.83 for 100 g; smaller bag is better value. **[3]**

Page 37 Rates
1. 7711.88 Baht **[1]**
2. a) 2.5 hours **[1]**
   b) 22.1 km/litre **[1]**
3. 5.56 g/cm^3 **[2]**
4. a) $223.20 **[1]**
   b) 6.5 m **[2]**
5. a) $37 440 **[1]**
   b) 8 months **[2]**
6. $196.06 **[2]**
7. a) 1217.50 Reals **[1]**
   b) $51.33 **[1]**
8. a) 772 g **[1]**
   b) 51.8 cm^3 **[2]**
   c) $1250.64 **[2]**
9. Spain 92.3; Slovenia 101.4 **[2]**

Page 38 Percentages
1. 56.0% **[2]**
2. a) 40% **[2]**
   b) $518 **[2]**
3. $6110 **[2]**
4. a) 15.6% **[2]**
   b) 56 ml **[2]**
5. 21.6% **[1]**
6. a) $4520 **[2]**
   b) $4545.90 2]**
7. 2.4%
8. $6500 \times 1.043^6 = 8367.95...$ **[2]**
9. $327.25 **[2]**
10. $5200 **[2]**

Page 39 Using a calculator
1. a) 06 15 on Saturday **[2]**
   b) 5721.23 dirhams **[1]**
   c) 765 km/h **[2]**
2. a) 5.01 **[2]**
   b) 4.06 **[2]**
3. a) 10 080 **[1]**
   b) 16 minutes and 40 seconds **[2]**
4. 120 days If it's an analogue clock then it'll be correct again after 60 days **[2]**
5. a) 16 45 **[1]**
   b) 21 15 **[2]**
6. a) 23 minutes **[1]**
   b) 16 minutes **[2]**

Page 39 Exponential growth and decay
1. 4.05 million **[2]**
2. a) $9098 **[2]**
   b) 6 years **[2]**
3. a) $75 514 **[2]**
   b) $345 597 **[2]**
4. 6.15% **[3]**
5. 18.92% **[3]**
6. 0.8% **[3]**

Page 41 Surds
1. $11\sqrt{3}$ **[2]**
2. $3\sqrt{2}$ **[2]**
3. $8\sqrt{5}$ **[2]**
4. a) 60 **[2]**
   b) 15 **[2]**
5. $1 + \sqrt{3}$ **[2]**
6. $9 + 4\sqrt{5}$ **[2]**
7. a) $3 + 2\sqrt{2}$ **[2]**
   b) $7 + 5\sqrt{2}$ **[2]**
8. $2\sqrt{5} - 1$ **[2]**
9. $\frac{1}{2}\sqrt{2}$ **[3]**
10. $8 + 3\sqrt{5}$ **[3]**

Pages 42-67: Section 2 Revise Questions

Page 43 Introduction to algebra
1. 2
2. 19
3. 11
4. 63
5. −202.5

Page 45 Algebraic manipulation
1. $-2ab + 6a \quad 3$
2. $15x^2 - 10xy$
3. $4ab(3c + 2ab)$
4. $3(3a + b)(3a - b)$
5. $3x^3 - 12x^2 + 12x$

Page 47 Algebraic fractions
1. $\frac{x + 10}{6}$
2. $4x$
3. $\frac{2a^2 + 4a - 2}{(a + 3)(a + 2)}$
4. $\frac{2a}{a + 3}$

Page 49 Further indices
1. -2
2. $49x^8$
3. $3a^{-2}$
4. $12a^5$
5. $\frac{32}{9}a^{\frac{1}{2}}$

Page 51 Equations
1. $x = 9.5$
2. $b = \frac{1}{2}p - a$
3. $x = 6$ and $y = 2$
4. $x = 6$ or -3

Page 53 Inequalities
1.
2. $-10, -9, -8, -7, -6$
3. $x \geq 14.5$
4.

5.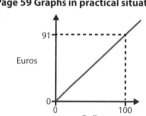

Page 55 Sequences
1. 35, 43, 51
2. 48
3. $27 - 2n$
4. 135
5. $n^2 + 4$

Page 57 Proportion
1. 405
2. 7.5
3. a) 1600
   b) 6
4. 125
5. 3.06 to 3 s.f.

Page 59 Graphs in practical situations
1.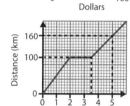
2.
3. a)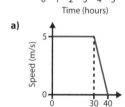
   b) 175 m

Page 61 Graphs of functions

1.

x	−2	−1	0	1	2	3
$x^2 + 2x - 4$	−4	−5	−4	−1	4	11

2.

x	−6	−3	3	6	9
$\frac{36}{x}$	−6	−12	12	6	4

3.

x	−2	−1	0	1	2	3
2^x	0.25	0.5	1	2	4	8

4.

x	−2	−1	0	1	2	3
$x^3 + 2x^2 - 4$	−4	−3	−4	−1	12	41

Page 63 Sketching graphs

1

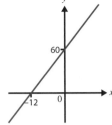

2

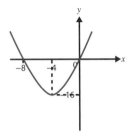

3

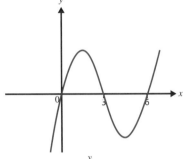

4

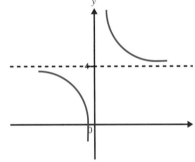

Page 65 Differentiation

1 $\dfrac{dy}{dx} = 4x^3 + 6x$

2 $a = 4$ and $n = 5$

3 $(2, -16)$ and $(-2, 16)$

4 $\dfrac{dy}{dx} = 4x^3 - 36x$. When $x = 3$, $\dfrac{dy}{dx} = 0$.
It is a minimum.

Page 67 Functions

1 $\{y: -6 \leq y \leq 10\}$

2 $g^{-1}(x) = \dfrac{4x + 1}{3}$

3 $fg(12) = 28$ and $gf(2) = 4$

4 $gh(x) = 7 - 12x$

Page 68-79 Section 2 Practise Questions

Page 68 Introduction to algebra

1 **a)** 10 **[1]**
  b) 28 **[2]**

2 **a)** 98 **[2]**
  b) 8 **[2]**

3 $2.37\dot{5}$ **[2]**

4 3.75 **[2]**

5 57.9 cm^3 **[2]**

6 62 cm^2 **[2]**

---

7 **[2]**

x	−2	0	2	5
y	−21	−5	11	35

8 **[3]**

x	−4	−2	0	2	4
y	2	−4	−2	8	26

Page 69 Algebraic manipulation

1 $5x - x^2 + 3$ **[2]**

2 **a)** $8a^2 + 12ab$ **[2]**
  b) $4x^2 - 4xy - 3y^2$ **[2]**

3 $3a^2 + 2ab + 3b^2$ **[2]**

4 **a)** $2x(2x + 3)$ **[2]**
  b) $3y(4x - 3y + 1)$ **[2]**

5 $x^2 - 11x + 30$ **[2]**

6 $7x^2$ **[2]**

7 5 **[3]**

8 $(x - 4)^2 + 5$ **[2]**

9 **a)** $(x + 16)(x - 1)$ **[2]**
  b) $(x - 4)^2$ **[2]**

10 $x(x - 6)(x + 3)$ **[2]**

11 $x^3 + 4x^2 + x - 6$ **[3]**

Page 70 Algebraic fractions

1 $\dfrac{11x + 3}{15}$ **[2]**

2 $\dfrac{2a}{(a + 3)(a + 1)}$ **[2]**

3 $\dfrac{a + 1}{4a}$ **[3]**

4 $\dfrac{4x^2 - 12x}{x^2 - 1}$ **[3]**

5 $\dfrac{2}{a(a + 2)}$ **[3]**

6 $\dfrac{x + 5}{x + 1}$ **[3]**

7 $\dfrac{x + 2}{x - 1}$ **[4]**

8 $\dfrac{10x}{(x - 1)(x + 4)}$ **[4]**

Page 70 Further indices

1 **a)** 9^{-2} **[1]**
  b) 3^{-4} **[1]**

2 **a)** 0.04 **[2]**
  b) 1 **[2]**

3 c^9 **[2]**

4 $12x^2$ **[2]**

5 $\dfrac{1}{9}a^{-8}$ **[2]**

6 $20xy^5$ **[2]**

7 $x = 4$

8 $x = \dfrac{3}{2}$ **[1]**

9 $10x^{\frac{1}{2}}$ **[2]**

10 $\dfrac{1}{2}$ **[3]**

11 $\dfrac{3}{2x}$ **[2]**

Page 71 Equations

1 $x = 19$ **[2]**

2 $x = 6$ **[2]**

3 $x = \dfrac{y + 3z}{2}$ **[2]**

4 **a)** $y = x + 16$ **[1]**
  b) $y = 3x$ **[1]**
  c) \$8 **[2]**

5 $x = 5$ and $y = 6$ **[4]**

6 $x = 3.85$ or -2.85 **[4]**

7 **a)** $(x - 2)^2 = 5$ **[2]**
  b) $x = 2 \pm \sqrt{5}$ **[2]**

8 $x = 2$ or 6 **[4]**

9 4 and −1 **[6]**

10 $g = \dfrac{4l}{t^2}$ **[2]**

Page 72 Inequalities

1 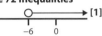 **[1]**

2 $-40 \leq x < 20$ **[1]**

3 22, 24, 26, 28 **[2]**

4 $0 \leq x^2 \leq 9$ **[2]**

5 $x \geq 6$ **[2]**

6 $-1.5 < x \leq 5$ **[3]**

7 $3 <= x <= 7$ **[2]**

8

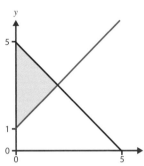

9 $3 < x < 8$ and $4 < y < 7$ **[3]**

Page 72 Sequences

1 **a)** 18 and 22 **[1]**
  b) $4n + 2$ **[2]**
  c) 24 **[2]**

2 **a)** 3 rows with 5, 4, 5 dots **[1]**
  b) 5, 8, 11, 14 **[2]**
  c) 17 **[1]**
  d) $3n + 2$ **[2]**
  e) 16th **[2]**

3 **a)** 36 **[1]**
  b) 108 **[1]**
  c) $3n^2$ **[2]**
  d) $3n^2 + 2$ **[1]**

4 **a)** 17, 23, 30 **[2]**
  b) 107 **[1]**
  c) 68 **[1]**

5 **a)** four rows of five crosses **[1]**
  b) 2, 6, 12 and 20 **[1]**
  c) $n(n + 1)$ **[2]**
  d) 10th **[2]**

6 **a)** −7, −12, −15 **[2]**
  b) 9 **[2]**
  c) −16 **[2]**

7 **a)** 46, 59 **[2]**
  b) $n^2 + 10$ **[2]**

Page 75 Proportion

1 6 g **[3]**

2 100 **[3]**

3 $a = 1875, b = 8$ **[5]**

4 **a)** 0.625 **[3]**
  b) 0.5 or −0.5 **[2]**

5 $1\dfrac{2}{3}$ **[2]**

6 $3\sqrt{2}$ **[3]**

Page 75 Graphs in practical situations

1 **a)** 15 m/s **[1]**
  b) 36 m/s **[1]**
  c) 216 km/h **[2]**

2 **a)** 08 00 **[1]**
  b) 12 km/h **[2]**
  c) 30 minutes **[1]**
  d) 10 km/h **[3]**
  e) 9.8 km/h to 1 d.p. **[3]**

3 **a)** 3.2 m/s^2 **[2]**
  b) 0.8 m/s **[2]**
  c) 240 m **[4]**

Page 76 Graphs of function

1 a)

x	−4	−3	−2	−1	0	1	2	3	4
y	−8	−1	4	7	8	7	4	−1	−8

b) [3], c) [2]

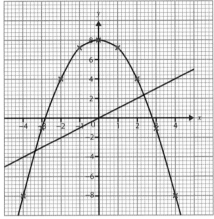

d) $x = -3.4$ or 2.4 **[2]**

2 a) [2]

x	1	2	3	4	5	6	7	8	9	10
y	10	5	3.33	2.5	2	1.67	1.43	1.25	1.11	1

b) [3], c) [2]

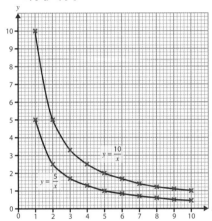

3 a) [3]

x	−3	−2	−1	0	1	2	3	4
y	−18	0	4	0	−6	−8	0	24

b) [3], c) [3]

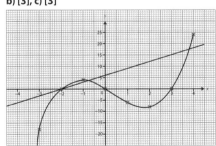

d) $x = -2, -0.8$ or 3.8 **[3]**

4 a) [3]

x	0	1	2	3	4	5
y	0	3	4.83	6.46	8	9.47

b) [3]

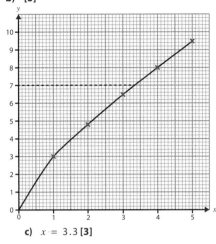

c) $x = 3.3$ **[3]**

Page 77 Sketching graphs

1 a) [2]

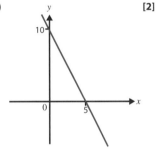

b) $y = x + 3$ **[2]**

2 a) $x = 3$ or −5 **[3]**

b) $(x + 1)^2 - 16$ **[2]**

c) **[3]**

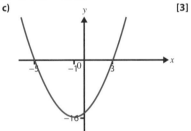

3 A(0, 7), B(1, 0), C(7, 0), D(4, −9) **[6]**

4 a) $x(x + 2)(x - 2)$ **[2]**

b) [3]

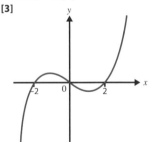

5 a) $a = 3.4$ and $b = 3.2$ **[2]**

b) $x = 0, y = 3$ **[2]**

c) [3]

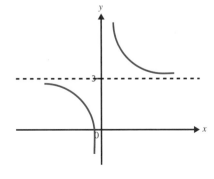

6 **[3]**

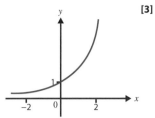

Page 78 Differentiation

1 a) [3], b) [2]

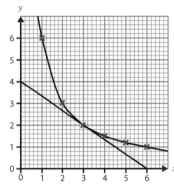

c) an answer between 0.65 and 0.7 **[2]**

2 a) $3x^2 - 4x + 4$ **[2]**

b) 4 **[2]**

3 $y = 25 - 5x$ **[5]**

4 a) $3x^2 - 12x + 10$ **[2]**

b) (1, 5) and (3, 3) **[5]**

5 a) $3x^2 - 6x$ **[2]**

b) −3 **[1]**

c), d) (0, 3) is a maximum and (2, −1) is a minimum. **[4]**

Page 79 Functions

1 a) 5 **[1]**

b) 4 **[2]**

c) $f^{-1}(x) = \dfrac{12}{x - 2}$ **[2]**

d) $\{f(x): 2 < f(x) \le 14\}$ **[2]**

2 a) 4 **[1]**

b) −8 **[2]**

c) $f^{-1}(x) = \dfrac{10 - x}{2}$

d) $x = 1$ or 5 **[2]**

3 a) 38 **[2]**

b) $15x - 2$ **[2]**

c) $30x + 16$ **[2]**

d) 13 **[2]**

4 a) −1 **[1]**

b) $\dfrac{10}{x} + 3$ **[2]**

c) 5 or −2 **[4]**

5 a) 25 **[2]**

b) $x = 3$ or −3 **[2]**

c) $x = 4$ or −2 **[4]**

Pages 80-83: Section 3 Revise Questions

Page 81 Linear graphs 1

1 6

2 a)

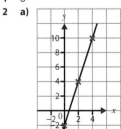

b) 3

3 $y = -x + 6$

ANSWERS

Page 83 Linear graphs 2
1 1.5
2 −1.2
3 $y = 0.5x − 3$
4 a) 13
   b) (−1.5, 8)

Pages 84-85: Section 3 Practise Questions

Page 84 Linear graphs 1
1 a) $\frac{1}{2}$ [2]
   b) $y = \frac{1}{2}x + 1$ [2]
   c) $y = \frac{1}{2}x + 4$ [2]
2 a) [3]
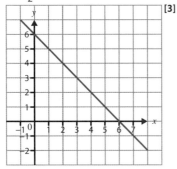
   b) −1 [2]
   c) 6 [1]
   d) $y = −x + 6$ [1]
3 a) 4 [1]
   b) (0, 10) [1]
   c) $y = 4x$ [1]
   d) $y = 4x − 8$ [2]
4 a) $y = −2x + 8$ [2]
   b) $y = −2x − 4$ [1]
   c) $y = −2x + 4$ [2]
5 a) 6
   b) −3
   c) −24

Page 85 Linear graphs 2
1 a) $\frac{4}{3}$ [2]
   b) 15 [2]
   c) (−5.5, 8) [2]
2 a) 0.8 [2]
   b) $y = 0.8x + 1.4$ [2]
   c) $y = −1.25x + 5.5$ [3]
3 a) −4.5 [2]
   b) $2x + 3y = 24$ [3]
   c) $y = 1.5x − 7$ [3]
4 a) A is (6, 0) and B is (0, 4.5) [2]
   b) 7.5 [2]
   c) −0.75
   d) $y = \frac{4}{3}x + 4.5$ [3]
5 a) (4.5, 1)
   b) $y = 4x − 17$
6 $y = \frac{3}{2}x − \frac{9}{2}$

Pages 86-97: Section 4 Revise Questions

Page 87 Geometric terms and constructions
1 8
2 square
3 8
4

a possible answer

Page 89 Scale drawings
1 24.8 km
2 6.4 cm and 3.6 cm
3 080°
4 135°

Page 91 Similarity
1 133 mm
2 456 cm^2
3 21 600 cm^3

Page 93 Symmetry
1 6
2 8
3 4

Page 95 Angles
1 120°. The sum of the angles is 360°.
2 $a = 53°$, vertically opposite angles,
   $b = 127°$, co-interior angles
3 140°
4 1800°

Page 97 Circle theorems
1 54°
2 135° and 67°

Pages 98-104: Section 4 Practise Questions

Page 98 Geometric terms and constructions
1 a) decagon [1]
   b) trapezium [1]
   c) equilateral triangle [1]
2 a) diameter [1]
   b) chord [1]
   c) tangent [1]
3 a) 62 cm^2 [2]
   b) 40 cm [2]
   c) 30 cm^3 [1]
4 a) 74° or 75° shows an accurate drawing [1]

Page 99 Scale drawings
1 a) 050° [1]
   b) 110° [2]
   c) 170° [2]
2 a) drawing [4]
   b) An answer of 2.8 m shows that the
       drawing is accurate. [2]
3 a) drawing
   b) An answer of 57 m shows that the
       drawing is accurate.
4 a) drawing [4]
   b) 95 km [2]
   c) 258° [2]

Page 100 Similarity
1 45 cm [2]
2 41.5 cm [4]
3 490 cm^2 [3]
4 a) 1850 cm^3 [3]
   b) 100 cm^2 [3]

Page 102 Symmetry
1 a) D and F [2]
   b) 3 [2]
2 a) [1] and b) [1] in either order
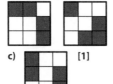
   c)   [1]
3 a) 5 [2]
   b) through the centre of each of the
       square faces [2]

4 a) through the centre of two
       opposite edges [2]
   b) through two opposite vertices [2]

Page 103 Angles
1 a) 65°, vertically opposite angles [2]
   b) 72°, alternate angles [2]
   c) 43°, angle sum of a triangle [2]
   d) 137°, angles on a straight line [2]
2 a) $180 − (63 + 54) = 63$ so two angles are
       equal [2]
   b) They are both 34°. [2]
3 a) 60° [2]
   b) 144° [3]
4 a) 15 sides [2]
   b) 88° [3]

Page 104 Circle theorems
1 a) 28°; diameter is perpendicular to the
       tangent [2]
   b) 62°; C is the angle in a semicircle which
       is 90° [2]
2 a) $x = 65$ [2]
   b) $y = 20$ [2]
3 a) $x = 46°$; angles at the circumference are
       equal [2]
   b) $y = 51°$; angles in the same segment [2]
4 $DAB = DBA = 90°$; radius perpendicular
   to tangent. $ADB = 360 − 90 − 90 − 110 =$
   70°; sum of the angle of a quadrilateral is
   360°. $a = 35°$; half the angle at the centre.
   [3]

Pages 106-115: Section 5 Revise Questions

Page 109 Units of measure
1 80 kg
2 4.52 m
3 6 200 litres
4 0.09 km

Page 109 Perimeter and area
1 36 cm
2 $x = 7$
3 a) 28 cm
   b) 36 cm^2
4 a) 32 cm
   b) 44 cm^2

Page 111 Circles, arcs and sectors
1 79.6 cm
2 5.64 cm
3 25π cm^2
4 724.6 cm^2

Page 113 Surface area and volume
1 $x = 4$
2 15 m^2
3 a) 4520 cm^3
   b) 1220 cm^2
4 2.82 cm

Page 115 Compound shapes and solids
1 a) 510 cm^2
   b) 130 cm
2 24π
3 838 cm^3

Page 116-121: Section 5 Practise Questions

Page 116 Units of measure
1 8 km [2]
2 320 g [2]
3 a) 15 cm [2]
   b) 12.5 cm^2 [2]
4 a) 4200 [1]
   b) 0.42 [1]

5 a) 50 000 **[1]**
   b) 50 **[1]**
6 8.7 m **[2]**
7 a) 360 000 **[1]**
   b) 0.36 **[1]**

Page 117 Perimeter and area
1 234 cm^2 **[3]**
2 $h = 16$ **[3]**
3 a) 72 cm^2 **[3]**
   b) 32 cm **[2]**
4 a) 54 cm **[2]**
   b) 114 cm^2 **[2]**

Page 118 Circles, arcs and sectors
1 a) 72.3 cm **[2]**
   b) 415 cm^2 **[2]**
2 a) 77.1 cm **[3]**
   b) 353 cm^2 **[2]**
3 a) 50.3 cm^2
   b) 13.7 cm^2 **[2]**
4 29 cm **[4]**

Page 119 Surface area and volume
1 a) 120 cm^3 **[1]**
   b) 148 cm^2 **[3]**
2 a) 288 cm^3 **[3]**
   b) 336 cm^2 **[4]**
3 24π **[4]**
4 a) 1000 cm^3 **[2]**
   b) 600 cm^2 **[2]**
   c) 6.20 cm **[3]**
   d) 484 cm^2 **[2]**

Page 120 Compound shapes and solids
1 110 m^2 **[3]**
2 a) 144 cm **[2]**
   b) 864 cm^2 **[3]**
3 218 cm^3 **[4]**
4 a) 2650 cm^3 **[3]**
   b) 225 cm^2 **[1]**
   c) 755 cm^2 **[3]**

Pages 122-129: Section 6 Revise Questions

Page 123 Right-angled triangles
1 23.8 cm
2 65.0°
3 6.48
4 6.22 cm

Page 125 Trigonometric functions
1 1
2 $x = 45°$ or 135°
3 52.4° or 232.4°
4 $k = 3$

Page 127 Non right-angled triangles
1 104.5°
2 72.6 cm^2
3 3.63 m

Page 129 Trigonometry in three dimensions
1 13.9 cm
2 a) 10.8 cm
   b) 68.2°

Pages 130-133: Section 6 Practise Questions

Page 130 Right-angled triangles
1 a) 8.18 m **[2]**
   b) 38.6° **[3]**
2 052.1° **[3]**
3 60 cm^2 **[4]**
4 a) 22.9° **[3]**
   b) 113.5 m **[3]**

Page 131 Trigonometric functions
1 $10\sqrt{3}$ **[2]**
2 a) sketch should show 90°, 180°, 270°, 360°
      on the x-axis and 1 and –1 on the y-axis **[2]**
   b) 210° and 330° **[2]**
3 $x = 45°$ or 225° **[3]**
4 a) sketch should show 90°, 180°, 270°, 360°
      on the x-axis and 1 and –1 on the y-axis **[2]**
   b) 51.3° or 308.7° **[3]**
5 110.6° and 290.6° **[3]**
6 $x = 10\sqrt{2}$ **[4]**

Page 131 Non right-angled triangles
1 129° **[4]**
2 a) 6.26 cm **[3]**
   b) 89.7° **[3]**
   c) 12.2 cm^2 **[3]**
3 a) 2210 m^2 **[3]**
   b) 116 m **[3]**
   c) 102.2° **[4]**

Page 132 Trigonometry in three dimensions
1 a) 29.0 cm **[3]**
   b) 20.2° **[3]**
2 a) 4.75 m **[3]**
   b) 59.6° **[3]**
3 12.6° **[5]**

Pages 134-137: Section 7 Revise Questions

Page 135 Transformations
1 reflection in $y = 4$
2 rotation 90° anticlockwise about $(4, 3)$
3 translation $\begin{pmatrix} 6 \\ -4 \end{pmatrix}$
4 enlargement, centre $(-2, 5)$, scale factor 2
5 rotation 90° clockwise about $(5, 4)$

Page 137 Vectors
1 $\begin{pmatrix} 9 \\ -16 \end{pmatrix}$
2 17
3 $\frac{1}{2}\mathbf{s} + \frac{1}{2}\mathbf{t}$

Pages 138-139: Section 7 Practise Questions

Page 138 Transformations
1 a) reflection in $x = 1$ **[2]**
   b) translation $\begin{pmatrix} 4 \\ -3 \end{pmatrix}$ **[2]**
   c) rotation 90° anticlockwise centre $(5, 4)$ **[3]**
2 a) **[2]**, b) **[3]**, c) **[3]**

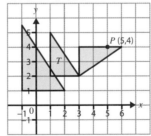

3 a) enlargement, scale factor –0.5, centre
      $(2, 1.5)$ **[3]**
   b) rotation 90° clockwise centre $(0, 1)$ **[3]**

Page 139 Vectors
1 a) i) $\begin{pmatrix} 3 \\ -1 \end{pmatrix}$ **[1]**
      ii) $\begin{pmatrix} -12 \\ -20 \end{pmatrix}$ **[1]**
      iii) $\sqrt{53}$ **[1]**
   b) $\begin{pmatrix} -8 \\ 3 \end{pmatrix}$ **[2]**
2 a) $\frac{1}{5}\mathbf{a} + \frac{4}{5}\mathbf{b}$ **[2]**
   b) $\frac{1}{5}\mathbf{a} + \frac{3}{10}\mathbf{b}$ **[2]**

3 A, B and C are in a straight line. B divides AC
   in the ratio 2 : 1 or AB is $\frac{2}{3}$ of AC. **[2]**
4 a) i) $\mathbf{b} - \mathbf{a}$ **[2]**
      ii) $\frac{1}{2}\mathbf{b} - \frac{1}{4}\mathbf{a}$ **[2]**
   b) $\overrightarrow{XB} = \overrightarrow{XO} + \overrightarrow{OB} = \mathbf{b} - \frac{1}{2}\mathbf{a} = \frac{1}{2}\overrightarrow{YZ}$ **[2]**

Pages 140-143: Section 8 Revise Questions

Page 141 Introduction to probability
1 a) $\frac{1}{9}$
   b) $\frac{2}{9}$
   c) 0
2 95%
3 0.4
4 36
5 $\frac{5}{12}$

Page 143 Probability of combined events
1 $\frac{1}{4}$
2 a) diagram
   b) $\frac{7}{20}$
3 $\frac{9}{10}$

Pages 144-147: Section 8 Practise Questions

Page 144 Introduction to probability
1 a) $\frac{1}{3}$ **[1]**
   b) $\frac{1}{2}$ **[1]**
   c) $\frac{5}{6}$ **[1]**
   d) 0 **[1]**
2 a) $\frac{7}{15}$ **[1]**
   b) $\frac{1}{5}$ **[1]**
   c) $\frac{2}{5}$ **[1]**
   d) 1 **[1]**
3 a) i) $\frac{7}{20}$ **[1]**
      ii) $\frac{3}{5}$ **[1]**
      iii) $\frac{3}{4}$ **[1]**
   b) 4 **[1]**
4 a) 84 **[2]**
   b) 46% or 0.46 **[2]**
   c) 55% or 0.55 **[2]**
5 a) $\frac{2}{3}$ **[1]**
   b) 32 **[2]**

Page 145 Probability of combined events
1 a) **[2]**

×	1	2	3	4
1	1	2	3	4
2	2	4	6	8
3	3	6	9	12

   b) i) $\frac{1}{6}$ **[1]**
      ii) $\frac{2}{3}$ **[1]**
      iii) $\frac{7}{12}$ **[1]**
2 a) 0.48 **[1]**
   b) 0.4 **[1]**
   c) 0.08 **[2]**
3 a) $\frac{6}{24} = \frac{1}{4}$ **[1]**
   b)

First counter   Second counter **[2]**

$\frac{1}{4}$ black — $\frac{1}{4}$ → black
                     — $\frac{3}{4}$ → white

231

c) i) $\frac{1}{16}$ **[1]**

ii) $\frac{9}{16}$ **[1]**

iii) $\frac{3}{8}$ **[2]**

4 a) $\frac{1}{28}$ **[2]**

b) $\frac{5}{14}$ **[2]**

c) $\frac{1}{4}$ **[2]**

Pages 148-159: Section 9 Revise Questions

Page 149 Statistical data

1 The bar chart shows the number for each type of vehicle. The bar chart illustrates the proportion for each type of vehicle.
2 90°
3 60%
4 The largest number was on Friday. There were fewer on Saturday and Sunday.
5 4

Page 151 Averages

1 a) 14.9
   b) 16
   c) 17
   d) 11
2 49.7 kg
3 a) 3.84 to 2 d.p.
   b) 3
   c) 4
4 a) $50 < x \le 60$
   b) 51 minutes

Page 153 Charts and diagrams

1 Angles: spring 126°, summer 99°, autumn 72°, winter 63°

2 a)
```
1 | 6  7  9  9
2 | 0  2  4  4  5  5  6  7  7  8  9
3 | 1  2  3  5  6  6  6  8
4 | 0  0  1  5  7
5 | 0  3
```
Key: 3 | 5 = 35

   b) 37
   c) 30

3

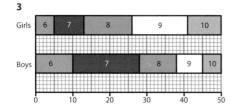

Page 155 Scatter diagrams

1 a) positive correlation
   b) Students who get a high mark in one subject are likely to get a high mark in the other. Similarly, students who get a low mark in one subjects are likely to get a low mark in the other.
2 a) negative correlation
   b) The higher the average temp in a month, the lower the rainfall and the lower the average temp in a month, the higher the rainfall.

Page 157 Cumulative frequency

1 142 minutes
2 35.4 years
3 a) It is between 257 mm and 312 mm
   b) It is less than 183 mm.

Page 159 Histograms

1 8, 7.5, 10.5
2 0.8
3 2.4

Pages 160-166: Section 9 Practise Questions

Page 160 Statistical data

1 a) 12 **[1]**
   b) 32 **[2]**
   c) 23.3% **[2]**
2 a) B **[1]**
   b) 40% **[2]**
   c) 3600 **[2]**
3 a) 28 °C **[1]**
   b) 4 °C **[2]**
   c) No. There is no pattern in the temperatures. **[2]**
4 a) volleyball **[1]**
   b) tennis **[1]**
   c) 300 **[2]**

Page 161 Averages

1 a) 17 s **[1]**
   b) 18.4 s **[1]**
   c) 9 s or 31 s **[2]**
2 34.8 **[3]**
3 a) 8 **[2]**
   b) 9 **[1]**
   c) 7.61 to 2 d.p. **[3]**
4 a) 0 **[1]**
   b) 1 **[2]**
   c) 1.6 **[2]**
   d) The total is 2 so it is either 2 and 0, or 1 goal in each match. **[2]**
5 a) $80 < x \le 90$ **[1]**
   b) 72.5 km/h to 1 d.p. **[4]**

Page 162 Charts and diagrams

1 **[3]**

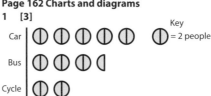

2 a)

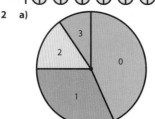

Angles are 0: 155°; 1: 115°; 2: 55°; 3: 35° **[4]**

   b) 0 **[1]**
   c) 1 **[1]**
3 a) 44% **[1]**
   b) 38% **[1]**
   c) **[3]**

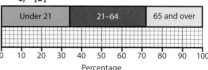

Page 163 Scatter diagrams

1 a) **[4]**, c) **[2]**

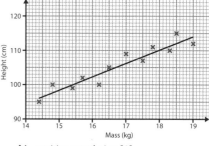

   b) positive correlation **[1]**
   d) about 105 or 106 cm **[1]**
2 a) **[4]**, c) **[1]**

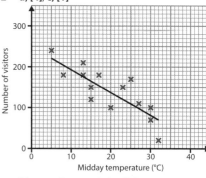

   b) negative correlation **[2]**
   d) about 200 people **[1]**

Page 164 Cumulative frequency

1 a) 5.2 m
   b) 1.1 m
   c) 6.7 m
2 a)

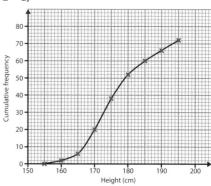

   b) 174 cm **[2]**
   c) 12 cm **[2]**
   d) 171 cm **[2]**

Page 165 Histograms

1 a) 28 **[2]**
   b) 109 **[3]**

2 a) 1.3 **[1]**
b) **[5]**

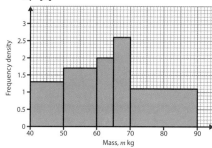

frequency densities of 1.3, 1.7, 2, 2.6, 1.1

Pages 167-179: Mixed Exam-Style Questions: Core

1 The LCM of 8 and 10 is 40. So 40 mins after 10 15 is 10 55 **[M1 A1]**

2 a) $3 + 5 + 13$ or $3 + 7 + 11$ **[1]**
b) $200 = 8 \times 25 = 2^3 \times 5^2$ **[M1 A1]**
c) $126 = 2 \times 3^2 \times 7; 198 = 2 \times 3^2 \times 11$
HCF $= 2 \times 3^2 = 18$ **[M1 M1 A1]**

3 a) $\frac{8}{20} = \frac{2}{5}$ **[M1 A1]**
b) 60% **[1]**
c) $8 : 12 = 2 : 3$ **[M1 A1]**

4 a) $186 \div 300 = 0.62 = 62\%$ **[M1 A1]**
b) $300 - 45 = 255 ; 255 \div 300 = 0.85 = 85\%$ **[M1 A1]**

5 a) $19\,844 \div 13\,812 = 1.4367...; 43.7\%$ increase **[M1 A1 — must say increase or equivalent]**
b) $16\,204 \div 19\,844 = 0.8165...; 1 - 0.8165... = 0.1834...; 18.3\%$ decrease **[M1 A1 — must say decrease or equivalent]**

6 Germany $18.0 \div 83.1 = 21.7\%$ **[M1 A1]**
Japan 28.4% **[A1]**
A greater proportion of Japan's population is 65 or over **[A1 for any equivalent statement]**

7 $(51 - 15) \times 1.5 = 36 \times 1.5 = \$54$ **[M1 A1]**

8 a) 20 **[1]**
b) 11 **[1]**

9 a) 9 **[1]**
b) 49 **[1]**

10 $10 + 7 - 2 = 15$ **[M1 A1]**

11 2 litres = 2000 ml **[M1]**
$8 : 3$ or $3 : 8$ **[A1]**

12 $40 \div 8 = 5$ **[M1]**
$5 \times 5 = 25$ **[A1]**

13 a) $18 \times 10.5 = 189\,g$ **[M1 A1]**
b) $500 \div 10.5 = 47.619... = 47.6\,cm^3$ (to 1 d.p.) **[M1 A1]**

14 $150 \div 20 \times 3 = 22.5 = 22\,min\,30\,s$ **[M1 A1]**

15 $90 \div 60 = 1.5\,h; 100 \div 40 = 2.5\,h$ **[M1]**
$190 \div 4 = 47.5\,km/h$ **[M1 A1]**

16 There are $60 \times 60 = 3600$ seconds in one hour, so 10 m/s $= 10 \times 3600 = 36\,000$ m/h **[M1]**
$36\,000 \div 1000 = 36\,km/h$ **[M1 A1]**
or any alternative method

17 a) 9 832 000 **[1]**
b) 10 000 000 **[1]**

18 a) 81 or 80 **[1]**
b) 3 **[1]**

19 $(145 + 45.5 + 93.9) \times 90.56 = 25\,755.264$
25 755 to nearest rupee **[M1 A1]**

20 a) $x = y + 2z$ **[1]**
b) $z = \frac{1}{2}(x - y)$ or an equivalent formula **[M1 A1]**

21 a) $A = 5x^2$ **[1]**
b) $x^2 = \frac{A}{5}$ therefore $x = \sqrt{\frac{A}{5}}$ **[M1 A1]**

22 a) $2e - 8 - 6e + 6 + 4e + 10 = 8$ **[M1 A1 A1]**
b) $6ab(b - a)$ **[A2; A1 for incomplete factorisation]**

23 a) $15x = 180$ **[1]**
b) $x = 12; 6 \times 12 = 72°$ **[M1 A1]**

24 a) $y = x + 16$ **[1]**
b) $y = 3x$ **[1]**
c) $3x = x + 16$ **[1]**
$2x = 16$ and $x = 8$ **[1]**

25 a) 0 **[1]**
b) −13 **[1]**

26 a) 86 **[1]**
b) 20 **[1]**
c) $1.8 \times -50 + 32 = -58$ **[M1 A1]**

27 a) 15 km **[1]**
b) If she travels 15 km in half an hour, then in a full hour she travels $15 \times 2 = 30$ **[M1 A1]**
c) 15 **[1]**
d) e.g. $(28 - 4) \times 2$ or $8 \times 6 = 48\,km/h$ **[M1 A1]**

28 a) $10 \div 4 = 2.5$ **[M1 A1]**
b) $y = 2.5x - 5$ **[1]**

29 86 and 58 **[2]**

30 a) 45 **[1]**
b) $5n + 10$ **[1]**

31 a) Perimeters are: 3, 6, 9, 12, ... So $3n$ **[M1 A1]**
b) 1, 4, 9, 16, ... So n^2 **[M1 A1]**

32 a) $\frac{1}{25} = 0.04$ **[M1 A1]**
b) $\frac{1}{4} = 4^{-1}$ **[M1 A1]**

33 $\frac{c^{11}}{c^{-6}} = c^{17}$ **[M1 A2]**

34 $269.45 \div 17 \times 27 = \$427.95$ **[M1 A1]**

35 a) 58 **[1]**
b) $3y + y + 40 = 180$ **[M1]**
$4y = 140$ **[M1]**
$y = 35$ **[A1]**

36 $180 - (70 + 65) = 45$ **[M1]**
$180 - (45 + 48) = 87$ **[M1 A1]**

37 Angle $= 360 - (90 + 120) = 150$ **[M1]**
Exterior angle $= 180 - 150 = 30$.
$360 \div 30 = 12$ sides **[M1 A1]**

38 a)

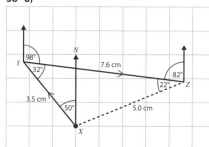

Values have been added to aid marking
b) 50 ± 0.1 (f.t. from diagram)
c) 256 ± 1 (f.t. from diagram)

39 a) $(20 + 10) \div 20 = 1.5$
b) $AG = 32 \times 1.5 = 48\,cm$ **[M1]**
$DG = 48 - 32 = 16\,cm$ **[A1]**

40 a) $AB = 6.0\,cm$ **[1]**
$AD = 4.2\,cm$ **[1]**
$DC = 4.9\,cm$ **[1]**
b) 128 or 130 cm (measured 6.4 or 6.5 cm) **[1]**

41 a) $\sqrt{5.7^2 + 18.4 - 2.3^2} = 5.22\,cm$ **[M1 A1]**
b) $\sin^{-1}\left(\frac{2.3}{5.7}\right) = 23.8°$ **[M1 A1]**

42 Height $= \sqrt{7^2 - 6^2} = 3.605...$ **[M1]**
Area $= 6\frac{1}{2} \times 12 \times 3.605... = 21.6\,cm^2$ to 3 s.f. **[M1 A1]**

43 a) $\cos^{-1}(12 \div 15) = 36.9°$ **[M1 A1]**
b) $\sqrt{15^2 - 12^2} = 9\,cm$ **[M1 A1]**

44 a) Angle in a semicircle **[1]**
b) Length PR is $12.5 \times 2 = 25$
$25 \cos 29° = 21.9\,cm$ **[M1 A1]**

45 Rectangle $6 \times 10 = 60$ **[1]**
Triangle $\frac{1}{2} \times 10 \times 3 (9 - 6) = 15$ **[1]**
$60 + 15 = 75\,m^2$ **[1]**

46 a) 72 cm **[1]**
b) $24\pi = 75.4\,cm$ **[M1 A1]**
c) $\pi \times 12^2 = 452.4\,cm^2$ **[M1 A1]**

47 Area $= 12\frac{1}{2} \times (10 + 14) \times 7 = 84\,cm^2$ **[M1]**
$2100 \div 84 = 25\,cm$ **[M1 A1]**

48 Diameter $= 30 \div \pi = 9.549...$ **[1]**
Radius $= 4.774...$
Volume $= \pi \times 4.774...^2 \times 30 = 2148.59...$ **[1]**
$= 2150$ to 3 s.f. **[1]**

49 a) $\pi \times 8^2 \div 2 + \pi \times 4^2 \div 2 = 40\pi\,cm^2$ **[M1 A1]**
b) $\pi \times 16 \div 2 + \pi \times 8 \div 2 + 8 = (12\pi + 8)\,cm$ **[M1 A1]**

50 Half the sphere $= \frac{2}{3}\pi \times 4^3 = 134.04...\,cm^3$ **[1]**
Cone $= \frac{1}{3}\pi \times 4^2 \times 5 = 83.77...\,cm^3$ **[1]**
Total $= 217.81 = 218\,cm^3$ to 3 s.f. **[1]**

51 a) 12 **[1]**
b) 12 **[1]**

52 a), b), c) [2 for each correct Q, R and S. Allow 1 mark if one part of the translation is correct]

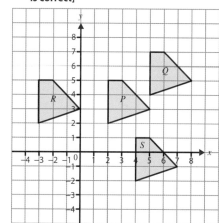

d) $\begin{pmatrix} -2 \\ 4 \end{pmatrix}$ **[1]**

53 a) Put 2 in key **[1]**
b) $1\frac{1}{2}$ **[1]**
c) One and a half squares drawn on Wednesday **[1]**

54 a) [1 mark for correct bars, 1 mark for correct labels]

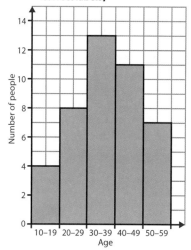

b) $13 + 8 + 4 = 25$ **[M1 A1]**
c) The person is less than 60 **[1]**

55 a) Angles are 150°, 96°, 114° **[2-1 mark if 1 correct and total is 360°]**

b)

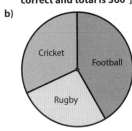

56 a) 97 g **[1]**

b) 18 cm **[M1 A1]**

c) 421 ÷ 7 = 60.1 g **[M1 A1]**

57 a) Median is halfway between 61 and 67: 64 **[M1 A1]**

b) 405 ÷ 6 = 67.5 **[M1 A1]**

c) 34 **[1]**

58 1.6 × 5 = 8 and 2.0 × 6 = 12 **[M1 A1]**
12 – 8 = 4 goals **[A1]**

59 a) 2 **[1]**

b) 20th and 21st both 3 **[M1 A1]**

c) (6 + 24 + 27 + 32 + 25) ÷ 40 **[M1]**
= 114 ÷ 40 = 2.85 **[M1 A1]**

60 a) i) $\frac{1}{5}$ **[1]**

ii) $\frac{3}{5}$ **[1]**

iii) 0 **[1]**

b) $\frac{2}{5} \times 80 = 32$ **[M1 A1]**

61 a) $\frac{2}{5}$ **[1]**

b) $\frac{4}{12} = \frac{1}{3}$

c) Probability $\frac{6}{15}$ so 2 black and 1 white **[M1 A1]**

62 a) i) $\frac{3}{11}$ **[1]**

ii) $\frac{9}{11}$ **[1]**

iii) $\frac{4}{11}$ **[1]**

b) $\frac{2}{6} = \frac{1}{3}$ **[1]**

63 a) **[2 — lose 1 mark for each error, up to 2 errors]**

4	5	6	7	8
3	4	5	6	7
2	3	4	5	6

b) i) $\frac{3}{15} = \frac{1}{5}$

ii) $\frac{9}{15} = \frac{3}{5}$ **[M1 A1]**

iii) By counting, there are 8 even numbers: $\frac{8}{15}$ **[M1 A1]**

Pages 179-186: Mixed Exam-Style Questions: Extended

64 a) 0.6363… or 0.6̇3̇ **[M1A1]**

b) So if $f = 0.8333…10f = 0.8333…$ so $9f = 0.75$ **[1]**

So $f = \frac{3}{4} \div 9 = \frac{3}{36}\frac{1}{12}$ **[M1 A1]**

65 $500 \times 1.02^{12} = 634.12$ **[1]**
$634.12 \div 500 = 1.268$ **[1]**
That is the multiplier for 26.8% increase **[1]**

66 $40.04 \div 1.04 = 38.50$ **[M1]**
$40.04 - 38.50 = \$1.54$ **[A1]**

67 $84.0 \times 1.04^5 = 102.2$ **[M1 A1]**
So population is 102.2 million **[A1]**

68 a) 40 150 **[1]**

b) lower = $11.5^3 = 1520.875$ cm³ **[M1 A1]**

69 $1 \div (3 \times 10^{-26}) 3.333… \times 10^{25}$ **[M1 A1]**

70 $(2x + 1)(4x^2 + 4x + 1)$ **[M1 A1]**
$= 8x^3 + 8x^2 + 2x + 4x^2 + 4x + 1$ **[A1]**
$= 8x^3 + 12x^2 + 6x + 1$ **[A1]**

71 a) $(2x - 5)(2x - 5)$ or $(2x - 5)^2$ **[M2 A1]**

b) $2x - 5 = 0$ so $x = 2.5$ **[M1 A1]**

72 a) $\frac{5x - 3x}{15} = \frac{2x}{15}$ **[M1 A1]**

b) $\frac{(x + 1)(x + 2)}{(x + 1)(x - 1)} = \frac{x + 2}{x - 1}$
[M1 A2 — allow A1 if only one of numerator or denominator is correct]

73 a) –4 and 5 **[2]**

b) $2x^2 + 4x - 1 = 0$
$a = 2, b = 4, c = -1$ **[M1]**
$x = \frac{-4 \pm \sqrt{16 + 8}}{4} = \frac{-4 \pm \sqrt{24}}{4}$ **[M1]**
$x = 0.225$ or -2.225 **[A1 A1]**

74 a) **Either** complete the square:
$x^2 - 2x = 1$ therefore $(x - 1)^2 - 1 = 1$ **[1]**
$(x - 1)^2 = 2$ therefore $x - 1 = \pm\sqrt{2}$ **[1]**
and $1 + \sqrt{2}$ is a solution **[1]**
Or substitution:
If $x = 1 + \sqrt{2}$
then $x^2 = (1 + \sqrt{2})^2 = 1 + 2\sqrt{2} + 2$ **[2]**
$= 2(1 + \sqrt{2}) + 1 = 2x + 1$ **[1]**

b) $1 - \sqrt{2}$ **[2]**

75 $\frac{x^2 + 12}{2x} = 4$ **[M1]**
$x^2 + 12 = 8x$
$x^2 - 8x - 12 = 0$ **[M1]**
$(x - 6)(x - 2) = 0$ **[M1]**
$x = 2$ or 6 **[A1]**

76 $x^2 - 5x + 4 = 0$
$(x - 4)(x - 1) = 0$ **[M1]**
$x = 4$ or 1 **[M1]**
Either $x = 4$ and $y = 16$ **[A1]**
or $x = 1$ and $y = 1$ **[A1]**

77 a) $(25 - 5) \div 2 = 10$ s **[M1 A1]**

b)

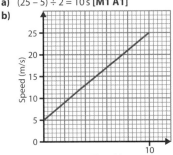

[1 mark for Any horizontal scale showing 10
2 marks for End points
1 mark for Straight line]

c) $\frac{5 + 25}{2} \times 100$ or an equivalent method **[M1 A1]**
= 150 m **[A1]**

78 a) 15 m/s **[1]**

b) The gradient shows acceleration - at time 1 s, the gradient is approximately 4 m/s² **[M1 A1]**

79 a) $(x + 1.5)^2 - 6.25$ **[M1 A1]**

b) (–1.5, –6.25) **[2]**

c) $(x + 4)(x - 1) = 0$ **[M1]**
$x = -4$ and 1 **[A2]**

d) **[1 mark for intercepts, 1 mark for minimum, 1 mark for parabola shape]**

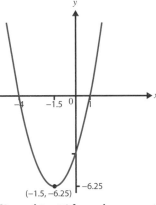

80 a) **[2 — subtract 1 for each error, up to 2 errors]**

x	–2	–1	0	1	2	3	4
$x^3 - 3x^2 + 4$	–16	0	4	2	0	4	20

b) **[2 marks for passing through points, 1 mark for correct shape]**

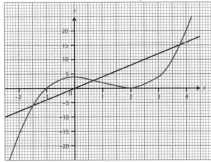

c) $= -1$ and 2

d) Rearrange as $x^3 - 3x^2 + 4 = 4x$ **[M1 A1]**
Draw $y = 4x$ **[M1]**
$x = -1.5$ and 0.7 and 3.8 **[A2 — allow A1 for two correct from graph]**

81 a) $100^{\frac{1}{2}} = 10, 10^5 = 100\,000$ **[M1 A1]**

b) $100^{\frac{1}{2}} = 10, 10^{-3}, \frac{1}{10^3} = \frac{1}{1000}$ or 0.001 **[M1 A1]**

82 a) $x = 3$ **[M1 A1]**

b) $2x = 3$ therefore $x = 1.5$ **[M1 A1]**

83 $y < 2$ **[1]**
$y < 2x - 2$ **[2]**
$y > x - 2$ **[2]**

84 {0.2, 1, 5, 25} **[2 — 1 mark for 3 correct]**

85 a) 2 **[1]**

b) h(11) = 1, and h(1) = 6 **[M1 A1]**

c) $\frac{12}{x + 1} = 6$ so $x = 1$ **[M1 A1]**

d) $y = \frac{12}{x + 1}$ **[M1]**
$x = \frac{12}{y} - 1$ **[A1]**
$h^{-1}(x) = \frac{12}{x} - 1$ **[A1]**

e) $\frac{12}{x + 1} = x$ **[M1]**
$12 = x^2 + x$ **[M1]**
$x^2 + x - 12 = 0$ **[A1]**
$(x + 4)(x - 3) = 0$ **[M1]**
$x = 3$ or –4 **[A2]**

86 a) $\frac{dy}{dx} = 3x^2 - 12x + 10$ **[A2 — 1 mark for two terms correctly differentiated]**

$3x^2 - 12x + 10 = 1$ **[M1]**
$3x^2 - 12x + 9 = 0$

$x^2 - 4x + 3 = 0$
$(x - 1)(x - 3) = 0$
So $x = 1$ or 3 **[M1]** $(1, 5)$ and $(3, 3)$ **[A2]**

87 a) 96 **[1]**
   b) 76 **[1]**
   c) 76 **[1]**

88 Angle $ATO = 90°$ (radius perpendicular to tangent) so angle $AOT = 180 - 90 - 40 = 50°$ **[1]**
Triangle OBT is isosceles so angle $OBT = (180 - 50) \div 2 = 65°$ **[1]**
Angle DTC = angle OBT (alternate segment theorem) so $x = 65$ **[1]**

89 a) Scale factor = 4
   $2000 \times 4^3 = 128\ 000$ cm^3 **[M1 A1]**
   b) $250 \div 2000 = 0.125$ **[M1 A1]**
   $25 \times \sqrt[3]{0.125} = 25 \times 0.5 = 12.5$ cm

90 a) $AC = \sqrt{4^2 + 3^2} = 5$ **[M1]**
   $AD = \sqrt{5^2 + 3^2} = 5.83$ cm **[M1 A1]**
   b) $\tan^{-1}\left(\frac{3}{4}\right) + \tan^{-1}\left(\frac{3}{5}\right) = 67.8°$ **[M2 A1]**

91 $XZ = 12\cos 45° \frac{12}{\tan 45°} + \frac{12}{\tan 30°}$
   $= 12 + 12\sqrt{3} = 12(1 + \sqrt{3})$ **[M1 A1]**

92 $27.2\sin 35° = 15.6$ cm **[M1 A1]**

93 a) $BC = \sqrt{6.6^2 + 8.8^2} = 11$ **[M1 A1]**
   Area = $11 \times 10.4 = 114.4$ cm^2 **[A1]**
   b) $AF = \sqrt{6.6^2 + 10.4^2} = 12.3$ **[M1]**
   $\tan^{-1}\left(\frac{8.8}{12.3}\right) = 35.6°$ **[M1 A1]**

94 a) Angle $AXB = 90°$
   So $AX = 25\sin 33° = 13.6$ cm **[M1 A1]**
   b) Angle AYX = 33° (using angles in same segment theorem) **[M1]**
   $\frac{AY}{\sin 74°} = \frac{13.6}{\sin 33°}$ **[M1]**
   $AY = \frac{13.6\sin 74°}{\sin 33°} = 24.0$ cm **[M1 A1]**
   c) Angle XAY = 73° **[M1]**
   Area = $\frac{1}{2} \times 13.6 \times 24.0 \sin 73° = 156$ cm^3 to 3 s.f. **[M1 A1]**

95 a) Check that zeros and discontinuities are correct
   Straight horizontal line
   c) 135° and 315° **[A2]**
   d) $\tan x = 1.5$
   $x = 56.3°$ and $236.3°$ **[A2]**

96 Triangle = $\frac{1}{2} \times 17^2 \times \sin 110° = 135.8$ **[M1 A1]**
Sector = $\frac{110}{360} \times \pi \times 17^2 = 277.4$ **[M1 A1]**
Segment = $277.4 - 135.8 = 142$ cm^2 to 3 s.f. **[A1]**

97 a) $y = x - 3$ **[2]**
   b) $(8, 5)$ **[2]**
   c) $(6, 3)$ **[2]**
   d) $(10, 7)$ **[2]**

98 a) $\begin{pmatrix} 18 \\ -3 \end{pmatrix} + \begin{pmatrix} -6 \\ 8 \end{pmatrix} = \begin{pmatrix} 12 \\ 5 \end{pmatrix}$ **[M1 A1]**
   b) $\sqrt{12^2 + 5^2} = 13$ **[M1 A1]**

99 a) OA and CB are parallel, so CB(arrow) = OA(arrow) = **a**. Then position of C is **b** − **a** **[M1 A1]**
   b) **b** − **a** + $\frac{1}{2}$**a** = **b** − $\frac{1}{2}$**a** **[M1 A1]**
   c) $\overrightarrow{MO} + \overrightarrow{OA} = -\mathbf{b} + \frac{3}{2}\mathbf{a}$ **[M1 A1]**

100 a) $\frac{7}{10} \times \frac{6}{9} = \frac{7}{15}$ **[M1 A1]**
   b) $\frac{3}{10} \times \frac{7}{9} + \frac{7}{10} \times \frac{3}{9} = \frac{7}{15}$ **[M1 M1 A1]**

101 a) $a = 3$ **[1]**
   b) [1 mark for each correct column]

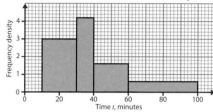

   c) $\frac{60 \times 20 + 42 \times 35 + 32 \times 50 + 24 \times 80}{158}$ **[M1 A1]**
   $= \frac{6190}{158} = 39.2$ minutes **[M1 A1]**

Pages 187-194: Practice Paper 1

1 42 007 **[1]**

2 a) 3 **[1]**
   b) $9 - 2 = 7$ **[1]**

3 a) 785 cm **[1]**
   b) 7.9 **[1]**

4 Any square number that is also a cube number e.g. 64 **[1]**

5 a) 110° **[A1]**
   Angles on a straight line sum to 180° **[B1]**
   b) Angle $AFC = 110°$ **[M1]**
   $80 + 96 + 110 = 286, 360 - 286 = 74°$ **[A1]**

6 a) $x = 30$ **[For 1-markers, mostly just put [1] instead of [A1]1]**
   b) $3x = 24, x = \frac{24}{3} = 8$ **[M1 A1]**
   c) $x - 4 = -3, x = 1$ **[M1 A1]**

7 $45 \times 2 = 90, 90 \div 9 = 10$ **[M1 A1]**

8 a) $200 : 250 : 175 = 8 : 10 : 7$ **[M1 A1]**
   b) $200 : 250 = 1 : 1.25, n = 1.25$ **[M1 A1]**

9 $4(5)^2 - 2(-3) = 100 + 6 = 106$ **[M1 A1]**

10 $\frac{10^2 - \sqrt{400}}{100}, \frac{100 - 20}{100}, \frac{80}{100} = 0.8$ **[M1 A1]**

11 a) -18 **[1]**
   b) 2 **[1]**
   c) 11 **[1]**

12 a) 22 **[1]**
   b) $3n + 4$ **[M1 A1]**
   c) $3n + 4 > 50. n > 15\frac{1}{3}$ **[M1]**
   $n = 16$
   $3 \times 16 + 4 = 52$ **[A1]**

13 4 000 000 **[M1]**
   4×10^6 **[A1]**

14 a)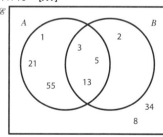
   [B1] for 3, 5, 13 **[A1]** for all correct
   b) 6 **[1]**
   c) 2, 8, 34 **[1]**
   d) 3, 5, 13 **[1]**

15 $72 - 18 = 54$ **[M1]**
   $7 \times 3.99 = 27.93$ **[M1]**
   $54 - 27.93 + 25.50 = 51.57$ **[A1]**

16 a) $6x - 6y$ **[M1 A1]**
   b) $5x = y + z, y = 5x - z$ **[M1 A1]**
   c) $5xy(3x - 5y)$ **[M1 A1]**

17 64: 1, 2, 4, 8, 16, 32, 64
   96: 1, 2, 3, 4, 6, 8, 12, 16, 24, 32, 48, 96 **[M1]**
   HCF = 32 **[A1]**

18 a) Blue City **[1]**
   b) 7 **[1]**
   c) $3 \times 9 + 3 = 30$ **[M1 A1]**
   d) $3 \times 2 + 4 \times 3 + 5 \times 4 + 6 \times 0 + 7 \times 1$
   $= 6 + 12 + 20 + 0 + 7 = 45$**[M1]**
   Mean $= \frac{6 + 12 + 20 + 0 + 7}{10} = \frac{45}{10} = 4.5$ **[M1 A1]**

19 1 month = $305 **[M1]**
   1 year = 12 months = 12×305 = $3660 **[M1 A1]**

20 a) $2 \times 5 \times 4.5 + 2 \times 5 \times 1.2 + 2 \times 4.5 \times 1.2$ **[M1]**
   $45 + 12 + 10.8 = 67.8$ cm^2 **[M1 A1]**
   b) $1.2 \times 5 \times 4.5 = 27$ **[1]**

21 $3 - 2 = 1$ **[M1]**
   $\frac{2}{3} - \frac{1}{7} = \frac{14}{21} - \frac{3}{21} = \frac{11}{21}$ **[M1 A1]**
   Anwer is $1\frac{11}{21}$ **[A1]**

22 a) Correct triangle (6,6,8 or 6,8,8) with construction arcs **[M1 A1]**
   b) Correct triangle (6,6,8 or 6,8,8 depending on **a**)) with construction arcs **[M1 A1]**

23 $27x^{12}y^3$ **[M1 M1 A1]**

24 $y = \frac{1}{2}x + c$ **[M1]**
   $(9) = \frac{1}{2}(-6) + c,$
   $9 = -3 + c, c = 12, y = \frac{1}{2}x + 12$ **[M1 A1]**

Pages 195-203: Practice Paper 2

1 102.0 **[1]**

2 $\frac{2}{7}$ **[1]**

3 4 000 000 cm^3 **[1]**

4 $2^3 \times 3^2 \times 3 \times 7 = 2^3 \times 3^3 \times 7$ **[1]**

5 a) $3x^3 - 21x$ **[M1 A1]**
   b) $2y - 5x$ **[Method not shown A1]**

6 a) $\frac{4}{11}$ **[1]**
   b) $21 \div 3 = 7, 4 \times 7 + 7 \times 7$
   $= 28 + 49 = 77$ **[No method shown A1]**

7 a) $\begin{pmatrix} -6 \\ 4 \end{pmatrix} - 3\begin{pmatrix} 4 \\ -1 \end{pmatrix} = \begin{pmatrix} -6 \\ 4 \end{pmatrix} - \begin{pmatrix} 12 \\ -3 \end{pmatrix} = \begin{pmatrix} -18 \\ 7 \end{pmatrix}$ **[M1 A1]**
   b) $(-2)^2 + p^2 = 13, 4 + p^2 = 13, p^2 = 9, p = \pm 3$ **[M1 M1 A1]**

8 a) $8 \leq t < 12$ **[1]**
   b) Median must lie in $8 \leq t < 12$ as that is where the 46.5th piece of data lies. **[M1 A1]**

9 $-3 \leq x < 1.25$ **[M1 A1]**

10 $1 - (0.15 + 0.45) = 0.4, 0.4 \div 4 = 0.1,$
   P(Blue) = 0.3, P(Green) = 0.1 **[M1 A1]**

11 a) $64 \times 16^x = 2^6 \times (2^4)^x = 2^{6+4x}$ **[M1 A1]**
   b) $\left(\frac{1000}{27}\right)^{\frac{2}{3}} = \left(\sqrt[3]{\frac{1000}{27}}\right)^2 = \left(\frac{10}{3}\right)^2$
   $= \frac{100}{9} = 11\frac{1}{9}$ **[M1 M1 A1]**

12 Angle $ACB = 67°$ [angles on a straight-line sum to 180°] **[M1]**
   Angle $BAC = 58°$ [alternate angles are equal] **[M1]**
   Angle $ABC = 55°$ [angles in a triangle sum to 180°]
   Scalene as all three angles are different **[A1]**

13 $720 \div 36 = 20, r = 20 \times 124 = 2480$ **[M1 A1]**

14 $\frac{\pi \times (\sqrt{5})^2}{4} = \frac{5\pi}{4}$ **[M1 M1 A1]**

15 $\dfrac{6x-12}{5} = \dfrac{7-3x}{3}$ **[M1]**

$18x - 36 = 35 - 15x$ **[M1]**

$33x = 71$, $x = \dfrac{71}{33}$ **[A1]**

16 Angle $ABC = 90°$, so $7x + 5 + 2x + 4 = 90$

[M1 M1]

$9x + 9 = 90$, $9x = 81$, $x = 9$ **[M1 A1]**

17 a) $A \propto b^3$, $A = kb^3$, $25 = k(5)^3$,

$k = \dfrac{25}{125} = \dfrac{1}{5}$, $A = \dfrac{1}{5}b^3$ **[M1 M1 A1]**

b) $2 = \dfrac{1}{5}b^3$, $b^3 = 10$, $b = \sqrt[3]{10}$ **[M1 A1]**

18 a) $(x-3)^2 - 11$ **[M1 A1]**

b) $x = 3 \pm \sqrt{11}$ **[M1 A1]**

19 a) $x = 2.3\dot{6}$, $100x = 236.3\dot{6}$, $99x = 234$,

$x = \dfrac{234}{99} = \dfrac{78}{33} = \dfrac{26}{11}$ **[M1 M1 A1]**

b) $23.6\dot{3} = \dfrac{260}{11}$ **[1]**

20 a) $\dfrac{x(2x-3)}{(x+4)(x-2)} \times \dfrac{x+4}{2x-3} = \dfrac{x}{x-2}$

[M1 M1 M1 A1]

b) $\dfrac{x(2x-1) + (x-2)(x+2)}{x(x+2)}$

$= \dfrac{2x^2 - x + x^2 - 4}{x(x+2)}$

$= \dfrac{3x^2 - x - 4}{x^2 + 2x}$ **[M1 M1 A1]**

21 a) $\sqrt{(6--2)^2 + (9-5)^2} = \sqrt{8^2 + 4^2}$

$= \sqrt{80}$ **[M1 M1 A1]**

b) $(2,7)$ **[A1 A1]**

c) Gradient of AB $= \dfrac{9-5}{6-(-2)} = \dfrac{4}{8} = \dfrac{1}{2}$

[M1]

Gradient of perpendicular bisector

$= -2$, **[M1]** $y = -2x + c$,

$(7) = -2(2) + c$, $c = 11$ **[A1]**

$y = -2x + 11$ **[A1]**

22 a)

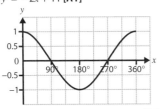

[A1 A1]

b) $\cos x = \dfrac{1}{2}$ **[M1]**

$x = 60$ and $x = 360 - 60 = 300$

[A1 A1]

23 a) $(2 - 2\sqrt{5})(5 - \sqrt{5})$

$= 10 - 2\sqrt{5} - 10\sqrt{5} + 10 = 20 - 12\sqrt{5}$

[M1 A1]

b) $\dfrac{6}{2\sqrt{2} - \sqrt{2}} = \dfrac{6}{\sqrt{2}} = \dfrac{6\sqrt{2}}{2} = 3\sqrt{2}$

[M1 M1 A1]

24 a) i) $\mathbf{n} - 2\mathbf{m}$ **[M1 A1]**

ii) $\overrightarrow{EB} + \overrightarrow{BF} = \mathbf{m} + \dfrac{1}{3}(\mathbf{n} - 2\mathbf{m})$

$= \mathbf{m} + \dfrac{1}{3}\mathbf{n} - \dfrac{2}{3}\mathbf{m}$

$= \dfrac{1}{3}\mathbf{m} + \dfrac{1}{3}\mathbf{n}$ **[M1 A1]**

b) -2 **[1]**

25 a) Slant height of small cone $= 4x$

Curved surface area of frustum $=$

$(\pi \times 6x \times 8x) - (\pi \times 3x \times 4x)$ **[M1 A1]**

$= 48x^2\pi - 12x^2\pi = 36x^2\pi$

Area of base $= \pi \times (6x)^2 = 36x^2\pi$

[A1]

Area of top $= \pi \times (3x)^2 = 9x^2\pi$ **[A1]**

Total area $= 36x^2\pi + 36x^2\pi + 9x^2\pi$

$= 81x^2\pi$ **[A1]**

b) $81x^2\pi = 4\pi \times 9^2$, $x^2 = 4$, $x = 2$

[M1 A1]

26 $\dfrac{dy}{dx} = 2x^2 - 4x = 0$, $2x(x-2) = 0$

[M1]

$x = 0, 2$, $y = 3$, $\dfrac{1}{3}$ Stationary points $(0, 3)$

and $\left(2, \dfrac{1}{3}\right)$ **[A1 A1]**

$\dfrac{d^2y}{dx^2} = 4x - 4$ **[M1]**

$x = 0$, $\dfrac{d^2y}{dx^2} = -4$ (maximum), **[A1]**

$x = 2$, $\dfrac{d^2y}{dx^2} = 4$ (minimum) **[A1]**

Pages 204–212: Practice Paper 3

1 a) Five lines of symmetry correctly drawn.
[1]

b) 5 **[1]**

c) Two lines drawn creating three isosceles triangles. **[1]**

d) 1 **[1]**

2 a) 4.04, 4.4, 4.404, 40.04, 404 **[1]**

b) $-12, -5, -2, -1.8, -1\dfrac{1}{4}$ **[M1 A1]**

3 $(6 + 5) \times (5 - 2) = 33$ **[1]**

4 a) 5 **[1]**

b) $21x^9$ **[M1 A1]**

c) $3x^{11}y^8$ **[M1 M1]**

5 a)

x	-2	-1	0	1	2	3
y	10	7	4	1	-2	-5

[A1]

b) Correct line. **[M1 M1]**

6 a) $\dfrac{1}{6}$ **[1]**

b) 2, 4 or 8, $\dfrac{3}{6} = \dfrac{1}{2}$ **[M1 A1]**

c) $5 + 3 + 6 = 14$, $21 - 14 = 7$ **[M1]**
7, 8 or 9 **[A1]**

$\dfrac{3}{6}$ or equivalent **[A1]**

7 a) 26.90349002 **[1]**

b) 27 **[1]**

8 a) $-4 < x \le 1$ **[M1 A1]**

b) $4k \le -1$ **[M1]**

$k \le -\dfrac{1}{4}$ **[A1]**

c) $-2, -1, 0, 1$ **[A2]**
B1 if one error

9 $3.24 **[M1 A1]**

10 $x^2 + 5x + 4x + 20$ **[M1]**
$x^2 + 9x + 20$ **[A1]**

11 $2 \times 2 \times 13$ **[M1 A1]**

12 $6x + 10y = 2$, $6x - 9y = 21$ **[M1]**
$19y = -19$, $y = -1$ **[A1]**
$2x + 3 = 7$, $2x = 4$ **[M1]**
$x = 2$ **[A1]**

13 $500 \times 0.88 = 440$ **[M1]**
$440 \div 4 \times 3 = 330$ **[M1]**
$440 - 330 = 110$ **[A1]**

14 $180 - 50 = 130$ **[M1]**
$360 - 130 = 230$ **[A1]**

15 a)

0	5 7 8 9	**[2]**
1	1 1 2 5 7 9	
2	4 6 7 8 9	
3	0 3 5 6	
4	4 7 8	
5	2 3	
6	4	

Key: 3 | 4 represents 34 text messages

b) 27 **[1]**

c) $\dfrac{10}{25} = 40\%$ **[M1 A1]**

16 a) $1 - (0.1 + 0.21) = 0.69$,
$0.69 \div 3 = 0.23$, $0.23 \times 2 = 0.46$
[M1 M1 A1]

b) $300 \times 0.21 = 63$ **[1]**

17 a) $8 \div 2 = 4$, $\pi \times 4^2 = 50.3$ **[M1 A1]**

b) $\sqrt{45 \div \pi} = 3.78...$,
$2 \times \pi \times 3.78... = 23.8$ **[M1 M1 A1]**

18 a) i) Correct reflection.
Vertices at $(2,0)$, $(3,0)$, $(3,-1)$, $(4,-1)$, $(4,-2)$, $(3,-2)$, $(3,-3)$, $(2,-3)$ **[2]**

ii) Correct translation.
Vertices at $(-8,-4)$, $(-5,-4)$, $(-5,-3)$, $(-6,-3)$, $(-6,-2)$, $(-7,-2)$, $(-7,-3)$, $(-8,-3)$ **[2]**

b) Rotation **[M1]**
90° anti-clockwise [270° clockwise] **[M1]**
centre $(0,0)$ **[A1]**

19 a) Points plotted at $(69, 61)$, $(72, 85)$, $(90, 100)$ **[M1 A1]**

b) Positive. **[1]**

c) Correct ruled line of best fit drawn. **[A1]**

d) 54–56% **[A1]**

20 $\sqrt{20^2 - 15^2} = 13.228...$ **[M1 M1]**

$\tan^{-1}\left(\dfrac{13.228...}{18}\right) = 36.3°$ **[M1 A1]**

Pages 213–223: Practice Paper 4

1 2 **[1]**

2 9:45 pm **[1]**

3 Correct triangle with sides of 9 cm and with construction arcs **[M1 A1]**

4 $\dfrac{360}{180 - 160} = 18$, $n > 18$ **[M1 A1]**

5 a) $\dfrac{2.75}{62.50} \times 100\% = 4.4\%$ **[1]**

b) 35% reduction $= 65\%$ of original **[M1]**

$\dfrac{54.60}{0.65} = \$84$ **[M1 A1]**

6 a) Reflection, $x = 1.5$ **[M1 A1]**

b) i) Correct rotation.
Vertices at $(-1, 1)$, $(-1, 2)$, $(-4, 2)$, $(-4, 3)$, $(-5, 3)$, $(-5, 1)$. **[2]**

b) ii) Correct enlargement.
Vertices at $(3, -5)$, $(3, -3)$, $(-3, -3)$, $(-3, -1)$, $(-5, -1)$, $(-5, -5)$. **[2]**

7 Alternate angles are equal, $240° - 180° = 060°$ **[M1 A1]**

8 16 machines $= 5$ hours $= 4000$ bricks.
16 machines $= 10$ hours $= 8000$ bricks.
10 hours **[2]**

9 $0.24 \times 250 = 60$ **[M1 A1]**

10 $4\dfrac{1}{3} \div 2\dfrac{5}{6} = \dfrac{13}{3} \div \dfrac{17}{6} = \dfrac{13}{3} \times \dfrac{6}{17}$

$= \dfrac{26}{17} = 1\dfrac{9}{17}$ **[M1 M1 A1]**

11 a) Common multiples of 6 and 8 $= 24, 48, 72, 96, 120$. **[M1]**
120 **[A1]**

b) $15 \times 2.47 + 20 \times 1.97 = 76.45$ **[M1]**

$\dfrac{76.45 + 175.55}{120} = 2.1$ **[M1]**

$2.10 **[A1]**

12 a) i)

x	-2	-1	0	1	3	4	5
y	4.81	**4.67**	4.25	2	2	4.25	**4.67**

ii) Correct graph.
Points plotted at $(-2, 4.81)$, $(-1, 4.67)$, $(0, 4.25)$, $(1, 2)$, $(3, 2)$, $(4, 4.25)$, $(5, 4.67)$ [1 mm error interval allowed] **[M1 M1 M1]**

Smooth curves between points. Asymptotes at $y = 5$ and $x = 2$ [not labelled but clear from curves]. **[A1]**

b) $y = \frac{1}{2}x + 2$ derived and plotted.

[M1 M1]

$x = [0.7, 1], [3.5, 3.8]$ **[A1]**

13 $pm - pn = 5mn, pm = 5mn + pn,$
$pm = n(5m + p)$ **[M1 M1 M1]**

$\frac{pm}{5m + p} = n$ **[A1]**

14 $\left(\sqrt{\frac{162.5}{26}}\right)^3 \times 103 = 1609.375$ cm^3

[M1 M1 A1]

15 Angle $PQR = \cos^{-1}\left(\frac{8^2 + 9^2 - 13^2}{2 \times 8 \times 9}\right)$

$= 99.5...°$ **[M1 M1]**

Area of $PQR =$

$\frac{1}{2} \times 9 \times 8 \times \sin\ (99.6...) = 35.5$ cm^2

[M1 A1]

16 $(4x^2 + 12x + 9)(x - 4)$ **[M1]**
$4x^3 - 16x^2 + 12x^2 - 48x + 9x - 36$
$= 4x^3 - 4x^2 - 39x - 36$ **[M1 A1]**

17 $\frac{5.64 \times 10^6 - 2.23 \times 10^6}{2.23 \times 10^6} \times 100$

$= 152.91...\%$ **[M1 M1 A1]**

18 a) 5500×1.056^2
$\times 1.0249^2 \times 0.9605 = \$6188.01$

[M1 M1 A1]

b) $6188.01 \times x^5 = 5500 \times 2$ **[M1]**

$x = \sqrt[5]{\frac{11000}{6188.01}} = 1.1219...$ **[M1]**

12.2% **[A1]**

19 25   49   81   121   169 **[M1]**
    24   32   40   48
    8   8   8
$4n^2 = 4, 16, 36, 64, 100$ **[M1]**
$21, 33, 45, 57, 69 = 12n + 9$ **[M1]**
$4n^2 + 12 + 9 = (2n + 3)^2$ **[A1]**

20 $t = \frac{72.5\,\text{km}}{53.45\,\text{km/h}} = 1.356...\text{hours}$

[M1 M1 M1] [A1]

21 a) $(x + 3)^2 + (2x + 5)^2 = (3x + 2)^2$ **[M1]**
$x^2 + 6x + 9 + 4x^2 + 20x + 25$
$= 9x^2 + 12x + 4$ **[A1]**
$5x^2 + 26x + 34 = 9x^2 + 12x + 4$
$0 = 4x^2 - 14x - 30$ **[M1]**
$2x^2 - 7x + 15 = 0$ **[A1]**

b) $(2x + 3)(x - 5) = 0$ **[M1]**

$x = -\frac{3}{2}$ or $x = 5$ **[M1 A1]**

Lengths cannot be negative, so $x = 5$
[A1]
Perimeter $= 8 + 15 + 17 = 40$ cm   **[A1]**

22 a) i) $f(7) = 6(7) + 5 = 47$ **[1]**

ii) $gg(-2) = \frac{\left(\frac{(-2) - 2}{3}\right) - 2}{3} = -\frac{10}{9}$ **[1]**

b) $fg(x) = 6\left(\frac{x - 2}{3}\right) + 5 =$

$2(x - 2) + 5 = 2x + 1$ **[M1]**

$g^{-1}(x) = 3x + 2$ **[M1]**
$2x + 1 = 3x + 2$ **[A1]**

$x = -1$ **[A1]**

23 $y = x + 5$ **[M1]**
$(x + 5)^2 + x^2 = 15$ **[M1]**
$x^2 + 10x + 25 + x^2 = 15$
$2x^2 + 10x + 10 = 0$ **[M1]**

$x = \frac{-10 \pm \sqrt{10^2 - 4 \times 2 \times 10}}{2 \times 2}$

$= -1.381..., -3.618...$ **[M1]**
$y = 3.618..., 1.381...$ **[M1]**

$x = -1.38, -3.62$ and $y = 3.62, 1.38$ **[A1]**

24 $\frac{8}{n} \times \frac{7}{n - 1} = \frac{56}{n^2 - n}$ **[M1 A1]**

25 a)

Time, t (cm)	0 < t ≤ 0.5	
0.5 < t ≤ 1	1 < t ≤ 2	
2 < t ≤ 4	4 < t ≤ 7	
Frequency	2 3 9 5 3	

b) $\frac{5 + 3}{22} = \frac{8}{22} = \frac{4}{11}$ **[A1]**

c) Midpoint × frequency
0.5 2.25   13.5   15   16.5 **[M1]**

Mean $= \frac{0.5 + 2.25 + 13.5 + 15 + 16.5}{22}$

$= \frac{47.75}{22}$ **[M1]**

$= 2.17...$ **[A1]**
$= 2$ hours 10 minutes **[A1]**

A

Alternate angles are made when a line crosses a pair of parallel lines. The alternate angles are on alternate sides of the line

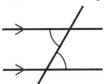

94

Angle of depression looking down this is the angle between the horizontal and the line of sight 123

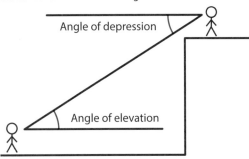

Angle of elevation looking up this is the angle between the horizontal and the line of sight 123

Arc part of the circumference of a circle

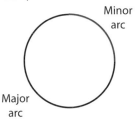

110

Asymptote a straight line that constantly approaches a given curve but does not meet at any infinite distance 63

Axis of symmetry a line through a shape so that one side is a reflection of the other 92

B

Bearing an angle measured clockwise from North to describe a direction 88

C

Circumference the distance around the outside (perimeter) of a circle 110

Co-interior angles are made when a line crosses a pair of parallel lines

94

Complement the complement of set A is everything outside of set A 8

Completed square form a way of simplifying or solving a quadratic equation by adding an expression to both sides to make one part of the equation a perfect square 45

Composite function a function that is made from two or more separate functions 66

Compound interest the overall interest earned on investment when the total interest earned in each period is added back to the original capital 25

Conditional probability situations where the probability of an event changes or is dependent on other events having already happened 143

Correlation the relationship between variables. It can be described as either strong or weak, and as either positive or negative 154

Corresponding angles angles which are in the same position and are equal 94

Cosine the ratio of the adjacent side to the hypotenuse 122

Cosine rule a rule connecting sides and an angle of any triangle usually used when the triangle is not right-angled. $a^2 = b^2 + c^2 - 2bc \cos A$ 126

Cube number the number you get when you multiply a number by itself and then again. For example 8 is a cube number as $2 \times 2 \times 2 = 8$. 8 is called the cube of 2 and can be written as 2^3, 2 cubed 6, 10

Cube root the opposite of cubing a number, so the cube root of 8 is 2 10

Cumulative frequency obtained by adding frequencies together to accumulate them 156

Cyclic quadrilateral a quadrilateral whose vertices lie on a circle 96

D

Density of something is its mass divided by its volume 22

Derivative the result of differentiation, the gradient function 64

Differentiation process used to find the gradient function 64

Direct proportion two quantities are in direct proportion if one increases as the other increases 56

Distance a measured length between two points 23

Domain for a function, the domain is the set of possible values of the variable 6

E

Element a member of a set 8

Empty set a set with no elements. Also called the null set 9

Enlargement a transformation in which the shape of an object remains the same but the size usually changes 134

Expand multiply all the terms inside the brackets by those outside the brackets. (opposite of **factorise**) 44

Expected frequency the number of times you would expect a particular outcome to occur when repeating a trial numerous times 141

Exponential growth an increase which follows a pattern predictable using an exponential function 28

Expression a series of terms connected by plus and minus signs 30, 42

Exterior angle the angles formed outside the triangle by extending the sides 95

F

Factorise take all common factors outside brackets. (opposite of **expand**) 45

Factor a whole number which divides exactly into another whole number 6

Formula a rule expressed in words or letters 42-43

Frequency density the ratio of the frequency to the class-width in a frequency distribution. Frequency density is used to draw histograms 158

Function a rule which takes one number and changes it into another 66

G

Gradient a measure of how steep a line is 64

H

Highest common factor the largest factor which is common to two or more other numbers 6

Histogram a chart drawn using rectangles that uses the area to represent frequencies 158

Hypotenuse the longest side of a right-angled triangle. It is always opposite the right angle. 122

I

Improper fraction a fraction in which the numerator is greater than the denominator 12

Integer a whole number 7

Interior angle angles inside a shape. Interior angles are the angles inside a polygon. The sum, S, of the interior angles of a polygon with n sides is given by the formula $S = 180(n - 2)°$ 95

Interquartile range the distance between the lower and upper quartiles 151

Intersection a set of elements that belong to both of two other sets 8

Inverse function functions which have the reverse effect to each other 66

Inverse proportion the relationship between two variables where one decreases as the other increases — 57

Irrational numbers a number that cannot be written as a fraction — 7

Irregular polygon any polygon which is not regular — 95

L

Like terms terms containing the same variable raised to the same power. These terms can then be added or subtracted to be combined. — 44

Line of best fit a single straight line which passes through a set of points and is as close as possible to as many of them as possible — 155

Lower bound the smallest possible value of a rounded quantity — 19

Lower quartile the value which 25% of the data are below or equal to — 151

Lowest common multiple the smallest number which is a multiple of two or more other numbers. For example the LCM of 6 and 10 is 30. — 6

M

Magnitude of a vector the size or length of a vector — 136

Major arc the longer arc connecting two endpoints on a circle — 111

Maximum point the largest possible point — 65

Mean a measure of average, found by adding all the values and dividing by how many there are — 108, 150

Median a measure of average, found by listing all the values in order and taking the value in the middle — 150

Minimum point the smallest possible point — 65

Minor arc less than half the circumference — 111

Mixed number a number containing a whole number part and a fraction — 12

Mode the value with the highest frequency — 150

Multiples a number which is obtained by multiplying two other numbers — 6

N

Natural numbers the counting numbers 1, 2, 3, … — 6

P

Percentile a number denoting the position of a data point within a numeric dataset by indicating the percentage of the dataset with a lesser value — 157

Perpendicular two lines are perpendicular if they are at right angles to each other — 83

Plane of symmetry a plane in a solid which divides the solid into two parts each of which is a reflection of the other — 92

Population density a compound measure that tells us how many people live in an area of a specified size — 23

Pressure is the force divided by the area over which it acts — 22

Prime number a number which has exactly 2 factors — 6

Probability how likely an individual outcome of an event is to occur. Probability is measured on a scale from 0 to 1 — 140, 142

Proper fraction a fraction in which the numerator is less than the denominator — 12

Proportional when two quantities are in proportion, when one is multiplied by a number, the other is multiplied by the same number. An example is the number of identical books and their total mass. — 21

Q

Quadratic expression an expression in which the highest power of x is x^2 — 54

R

Range
1) the distance between the largest and smallest value in a set of data
2) the set of y values for a function — 66

Ratio a way to compare two quantities with each other — 20

Rational numbers a number which can be written as a fraction where a and b are integers — 7

Reciprocal the reciprocal of a number is 1 divided by the number. For example, the reciprocal of 3 is $\frac{1}{3}$. — 7

Regular polygon A polygon is regular if all its interior angles are equal and all of its sides are the same length — 87

Relative frequency the ratio of the number of the successful outcomes to the total number of trials, which can then be used as an estimate of probability — 141

$$\text{relative frequency} = \frac{\text{number of successful outcomes}}{\text{number of trials}}$$

S

Scale drawing an accurate drawing in which the lengths are in proportion to the original — 88

Scale factor a number which tells you how many times larger an image is of an object — 90

Set a collection of items — 8

Semi-circle half a circle — 96

Similar two shapes are similar if they have the same shape but not the same size — 90

Simple interest a percentage of the original amount is added after each time interval — 25

Sine the ratio of the opposite side to the hypotenuse — 122

Sine rule a rule connecting the sides and angles of a triangle which is not right-angled — 126

$$\frac{a}{\sin A} = \frac{b}{\sin B} = \frac{c}{\sin C} \text{ or } \frac{\sin A}{a} = \frac{\sin B}{b} = \frac{\sin C}{c}$$

Speed the rate of change of distance with time — 23

Square number the result of squaring an integer — 6, 54

Square root the opposite of squaring a number. For example the square root of 36 is 6 — 10

Standard form a way to write very large and very small numbers using a number between 1 and 10 multiplied by a power of 10 — 16

Stationary point a point on the graph where the gradient is 0 — 65

Stem-and-leaf table shows data arranged by place value, for the purpose of comparing frequencies — 152

Subset if all the elements of a set C are in a set A then C is a subset of A — 9

Surds an expression involving a square root — 30

T

Tangent
1) a straight line that touches a circle or curve at one point only — 64, 96
2) the ratio of the opposite side to the adjacent side in a right-angled triangle — 122, 124

Term
1) an expression forming part of a larger expression — 11, 30-31, 44, 48
2) a single item in a sequence — 54

Term-to-term rule a rule which links one term in a sequence to the next term — 54

Time in speed distance and time, time is how long a journey takes, measured in hours minutes or seconds — 23

Translation a transformation which moves a shape from one position to another without changing the orientation or size of the shape — 135

Turning point a point on a graph where the gradient changes from being either positive to negative or from negative to positive — 62

U

Union the union of sets A and B is the set of all elements which are in either set A or in set B or in both — 8

Universal set the set containing all the things being considered — 8

Upper bound the largest possible value of a rounded quantity — 19

Upper quartile the value below which three-quarters of the data lie — 151

V

Variable a quantity that can take different values — 42

Vector a way of writing the position of a point or describing a movement from one position to another — 134

Venn diagram a way to show the elements of different sets — 8

Vertically opposite angles vertically opposite angles are the same as opposite angles — 94

William Collins' dream of knowledge for all began with the publication of his first book in 1819.
A self-educated mill worker, he not only enriched millions of lives, but also founded a flourishing publishing house. Today, staying true to this spirit, Collins books are packed with inspiration, innovation and practical expertise.
They place you at the centre of a world of possibility and give you exactly what you need to explore it.

Collins. Freedom to teach.

Published by Collins
An imprint of HarperCollins*Publishers*
The News Building, 1 London Bridge Street, London, SE1 9GF, UK

HarperCollins*Publishers*
Macken House, 39/40 Mayor Street Upper, Dublin 1, D01 C9W8, Ireland

Browse the complete Collins catalogue at
collins.co.uk

10 9 8 7 6 5 4 3 2 1

ISBN 978-0-00-867088-7

British Library Cataloguing-in-Publication Data
A catalogue record for this publication is available from the British Library.

Authors: **Chris Pearce, Andrew Milne**
Expert reviewers: **Mahesh Punjabi, Karl Warsi**
Publisher: **Elaine Higgleton**
Product manager: **Jennifer Hall**
Editors: **Laura Connell, Jim Newall**
Proofreaders and answer checkers: **Nick Hamar, Robert Connell, Ben Train**
Cover designer: **Gordon MacGilp**
Cover artwork: **Ann Paganuzzi**
Internal designer and illustrator: **PDQ Media**
Typesetter: **PDQ Media**
Production controller: **Lyndsey Rogers**
Printed in India by Multivista Global Pvt. Ltd.

This book contains FSC™ certified paper and other controlled sources to ensure responsible forest management.

For more information visit: www.harpercollins.co.uk/green

Cambridge International Education material in this publication is reproduced under licence and remains the intellectual property of Cambridge University Press & Assessment.

This text has not been through the endorsement process for the Cambridge Pathway. Any references or materials related to answers, grades, papers or examinations are based on the opinion of the author(s). The Cambridge International Education syllabus or curriculum framework associated assessment guidance material and specimen papers should always be referred to for definitive guidance.

The publishers gratefully acknowledge the permission granted to reproduce the copyright material in this book. Every effort has been made to trace copyright holders and to obtain their permission for the use of copyright material. The publishers will gladly receive any information enabling them to rectify any error or omission at the first opportunity.

Acknowledgements
With thanks to the following teachers who provided feedback during the development stages: Deepshikha Gupta, Global City International School; Sujatha Raghavan, Manthan International School; Mahesh Punjabi; SVKM JV Parekh International School; Pravin Yadav, SVKM JV Parekh International School.